Images of destruction

Images of destruction

David Wigoder

Routledge & Kegan Paul
London and New York

First published in 1987 by
Routledge & Kegan Paul Ltd
11 New Fetter Lane, London EC4P 4EE

Published in the USA by
Routledge & Kegan Paul Inc.
in association with Methuen Inc.
29 West 35th Street, New York, NY 10001

Set in Sabon 11 on 12pt
by Pentacor Ltd, High Wycombe, Bucks
and printed in Great Britain
by Cox & Wyman Ltd, Reading, Berks

Library of Congress Cataloging in Publication Data

Wigoder, David.
Images of destruction.

Bibliography: p.
Includes index.
1. Wigoder, David—Health. 2. Manic-depressive
psychoses—Patients—Great Britain—Biography.
I. Title.
RC516.W53   1987   616.89'5   86—31547

British Library CIP Data also available

ISBN 0–7102–1085–X (c)
     0–7102–1086–8 (p)

It is a common enough case, that of a man being suddenly captivated by a woman nearly the opposite of his ideal.

George Eliot

Contents

Foreword

by Anthony Storr FRCP, FRCPsych

'By the time I was forty I had destroyed two successful careers, served a prison sentence, been made legally bankrupt, lost a treasured professional qualification, attempted to kill two people, and isolated myself from most of my family and friends' (p.12).

Any psychiatrist reading these words would guess that the man who wrote them was suffering from manic-depressive illness, a major form of psychiatric disorder which afflicts at least one in a hundred individuals in our society. The causes of this illness are not fully understood, but are certainly multiple. A genetic factor is well-established; and it comes as no suprise to learn that Mr Wigoder's mother was herself unstable, and committed suicide when he was 35 years old.

Mr Wigoder's first medically diagnosed period of depression occurred when he was only 13, in 1955. He left school at 16, became a qualified accountant when he was 22, and a junior partner in a firm of accountants when he was 23. Like other manic-depressives, Mr Wigoder was 'hungry', never feeling that he could get enough to satisfy the gnawing sense of emptiness within. He worked compulsively, and although his hypomanic overactivity was intermittently interrupted by periods of depression, contributed a great deal to the expansion of his firm because of the fertility of his ideas. In 1968, a major period of depression put him off work for months. The story of his subsequent overspending, the thefts from his partners to repay his overdraft, his suicide attempts, his attempted murder of his wife, and his prison sentence are fascinating. How characteristic that, during the twenty-one months he spent in prison before he was paroled, he should note that he read 182 books, in addition to the complete works of Shakespeare! Prison seldom does any good to its inmates, but Mr Wigoder acknowledges two benefits from his sentence. He became fit physically, and he discovered that he could write.

After his second suicidal attempt in 1981, Mr Wigoder underwent a period of group psychotherapy as an in-patient in a psychiatric hospital. He has since embarked on individual psychotherapy as an out-patient, which continues to the present time. He gives a vivid account of his group therapy; of the problems faced by the other members of the group, and of the emotional interactions between them. He had to come to terms with violent feelings of hatred within himself, frightening in their intensity. More especially, he had to face painful memories of the appalling way in which his mother had treated him; her violent temper, her furious assaults on him. His account of his childhood vividly illustrates the complex interaction of the various factors at the root of mental illness. The genetic factor in manic-depressive illness has been amply demonstrated by research. But the effects of a child being reared by a mother who is subject to recurrent depression and grossly unstable is also devastating. This book very well illustrates the futility of the either/or approach to mental illness. Both inheritance and environment have to be taken into account if we are to understand our patients.

Over the past fifty years, a number of accounts of personal experience of suffering from mental illness have been published, but, considering how prevalent mental illness is, the number of worthwhile accounts is still small. *Images of Destruction* is a very welcome addition to the list. However accurately a psychiatrist may describe this well-known type of illness, he did not experience it from the inside, he was not there. This account will be found particularly valuable by psychiatrists in training, who need to learn how to enter in to the subjective experiences of their patients in addition to reading the standard, objective textbooks.

Mr Wigoder is unusually frank, unusually intelligent, and a gifted writer. I found his book compulsive reading. Both sufferers from manic-depressive illness and their relatives will learn much of value. Amongst other things, they will learn to recognize the illness at an earlier stage than happened in Mr Wigoder's case. If he had been properly treated from the beginning, much subsequent distress would have been avoided. Although we do not understand all the factors contributing to the prevalence of manic-depressive illness, it must be emphasized that it is a treatable disorder, in which both drugs and psychotherapy have an important place. It may not be possible entirely to abolish the patient's tendency to swings of mood, but the extremes can usually be controlled, and the patient can certainly be helped to understand himself better, and to run his life without running into the appalling problems which Mr Wigoder had to face.

Manic-depressive illness is a serious form of mental disorder which one would not wish on anybody. But it is worth recalling that there is another and more positive side which is sometimes overlooked. A surprising proportion of the world's most creative and original individuals have suffered from manic-depressive illness; and some would certainly have said that their sufferings were more than compensated by their creative gifts. Recent studies have shown that manic-depressive illness is particularly common amongst poets, including John Clare, William Cowper, Edgar Allan Poe, Robert Lowell, John Berryman, and many others. It may be that Mr Wigoder's new-found discovery that he can write will prove even more helpful to him than psychotherapy.

Acknowledgments

Over the years I have received help, often when I thought I least wanted or needed it, and always when I found it most difficult to ask. Now I can belatedly thank those who have been there at the right time – Lewis Johnman and Leonard Summer for their friendship; the staff at 'Shipley Grange', who infuriated and supported me; Gerry and Toni, whose door was never locked; Jo, who briefly but importantly gave me hope, and Simon, who knows he still does; but depression, like blood, is a family affair, and my concluding thoughts are of my sister and brother-in-law, who have sometimes been where they least expected to be, and of my father, who I hope understands what this is all about.

1 'Are you angry?'

My first memories are of blinding light and dark shadows and a dryness in my throat which made breathing difficult. I must have relapsed into intermittent sleep and restlessness. Later, when the blinding light disappeared, the shadows became people, and I could hear distant rattling noises and music. A cool hand touched my forehead and a female voice asked me if I was awake. I tried to move, but couldn't. Then I felt pain: burning, throbbing pain. An out-of-focus woman's face peered at me, and she asked me how I was feeling. Behind her I saw vast expanses of whiteness. I must have slept again, because, when I finally spoke through my parched throat, the face hovering above me belonged to a man who knew my name. I tried to move, but something made it impossible. I asked him where I was, and for a drink. I tried to move. Why couldn't I move? Another man, a black man, held a glass so close to my face that I could see nothing but weird, distorted shapes. Water dribbled down my chin. I wanted to tell someone about the pain.

When I eventually regained full consciousness, a young woman told me that I had been in the hospital for two days. By then my eyes were focusing properly. I looked clearly at her smiling face, and asked her if she had spoken to me earlier. 'Well, hi, I'm surprised you remember me,' she laughed. I told her that I needed to go to the lavatory. 'I'll undo the straps,' she said. Straps? What straps? I felt shocked and ashamed when I realized that I had been tied to a bed.

1

And when I saw bandages swathing my arms I wanted to scream that I was in pain. Then I saw the ridiculous, knee-length robe I was wearing. I asked where my clothes were, and was she a nurse. More smiles. 'We don't wear uniforms here,' she said. She supported me as I moved to the side of the bed, and called to another woman. They led me to the lavatory. Because I could not use my hands I had to ask them to help me urinate, and was surprised that I did not feel embarrassed. 'You'll be going down to the theatre as soon as the doctor says you're OK,' the nurse said, settling me back in the bed. I felt dizzy. 'Don't put those on,' I pleaded, as she began refastening the straps. 'I must,' she said, 'for your protection.'

That day, five years ago, remains a haze in my memory. My most vivid recollection is lying strapped to the hospital bed, next to the reception desk in the ward, feeling furious. People came to my bedside and asked me if I was English. I should be dead, I kept thinking: why wasn't I dead? A voice said: 'What's he doing here if he's English?' A motherly, garrulous woman held my hand and sat beside me. 'You'll like it here,' she said. 'When they let you up you can come and see my room.' I asked her why she was there. Someone behind reception looked down at me and told the woman to go away.

My next memory is of a pretty, young woman sitting on the bed. She wanted to know who should be contacted. 'How do you know my name?' I asked. 'And where are my clothes?' The hotel had sent a bag with the ambulance, she told me, before repeating her question. We battled with each other, politely. I told her that there was no one to contact. She asked about my family, but I refused to answer any questions until they unstrapped me. She set me free, and I sat up. For most of that day I resisted her continual requests for information. She remained friendly, brought me a tray of attractively set-out food, and wiped tears from my eyes. Finally, I told her about my wife, and provided a telephone number in England. When she told me that my wife wanted to speak to me, I refused. 'She wants me to tell you that she loves you. She's going to make arrangements to fly over and see you. Why don't you have a word with her?' I felt shamed by the nurse's friendly insistence, and agreed to speak to Helen. She said that she could be with me in a few days, and I told her to do what she wanted. Then I changed my mind, and said that I'd like to see her, too.

Two weeks later, on a Sunday, I returned with my wife from California to England. Pain-killing drugs made me permanently weary. I felt lethargic and withdrawn, and worried that everybody would look at my bandaged arms and know that I had tried to kill myself. When we arrived home I was surprised that a doctor, my local GP, whom I had never met, was waiting at the door of the house. He told me that he had spoken to a doctor from the San Francisco hospital[1], who had agreed to release me after being assured that I would receive immediate medical treatment in England. The GP explained that he thought I should enter a psychiatric hospital, and asked me if I was willing to go voluntarily. I was too drugged to understand the implication of the word 'voluntarily'. (Many months later my wife told me that, had I not agreed, I would have been detained under the Mental Health Act.[2]) I had not wanted to go home, and any chance of escape, even to a mental hospital, sounded attractive. My wife drove me there immediately. During the journey I pretended to sleep, trying to comprehend what was happening to me. I had to get away. I had to escape. Why wasn't I dead!

The following Tuesday, in June 1981, I sat anxiously on a shabby leather chair, in an old Victorian room, staring disconcertedly through a window at the distant scene of silent trees and summer skies. I desperately wanted to disentangle my confused thoughts, to create some order out of frightening chaos, to escape from the hospital. For a few bewildering moments I did not know what I was thinking – my mind felt as if it was blank, a totally empty space, yet at the same time crowded by contradictory thoughts. I could only survey the remote cotton-wool cloud-mountains, and hope that the banging in my chest would go away. Opposite me, behind his desk, sat a calm, neatly-dressed, grey-haired man in his early sixties. From time to time he glanced briefly at notes written down earlier that morning by his Sri Lankan female assistant, with whom I had spent almost an hour. He asked me questions, about my personal history, my family, my career and my feelings. I had had to wait two frustrating days to see him, so that I could persuade him that I should not be there. I tried to answer his questions clearly and confidently. I wanted him to understand that I shouldn't be there. 'I don't need drugs,' I said. 'I need to go home.' Like a host politely offering his guest a cup of tea, he ignored my words and asked, 'Are you angry?'

That was when my mind went blank.

When I heard that short, precise question, whatever reasoned explanations for my attempted suicide had been hovering in my mind immediately vanished. He had seemed so kind and helpful, but when I heard his question I felt shocked, as if a knife had been thrust unexpectedly into my chest by a friend. I had been betrayed. This kindly man didn't want to help me: he wanted to hurt me, to ridicule me, to keep me in hospital. I continued staring through the window, searching for a reply to his question, wishing that I was far away, floating on the billowing formations of summer clouds. I tried to concentrate. What did he mean when he asked 'Are you angry?'?

Inside the unattractive room I felt embarrassed by the silence. I wanted to say something, anything, to break the awful quietness. I must give him an answer, I thought. What should I say?

My left arm, firmly supported in an elegant, grey sling purchased a few days earlier in San Francisco, burned, itched and throbbed. The female surgeon had told me it wouldn't hurt. Another betrayal. Nerves had been separated, tendons cut; they had to operate quickly, she had said. There was no guarantee of success. My bandaged right wrist, less severely damaged, ached. I thought of the fear I had felt before the operations; of the long, tiring return flight to Heathrow; of the open ward at the mental hospital where I had been taken the day I came home to England, and of my wife and children, many miles away. I glanced at my arm, encased in plaster of Paris, a permanent reminder that my suicide attempt had failed. 'I'm not sure,' I replied, wanting to introduce sound – any sound – into the vast silence swelling across the desk. When I heard my answer, it belonged to a stranger, unreal and far away. I had uttered the words, but it wasn't me speaking. What had anger to do with the sadness and guilt I felt? A surge of self-pity overwhelmed me, and for a dreadful moment I thought that I might cry. 'I'm not angry,' I added reluctantly. 'I'm depressed and feel guilty.'

The elderly psychiatrist, speaking quietly and gently, twisted his verbal knife, offering opinions, making suggestions. 'How do you know you're not angry?' he asked. I sensed that he wanted me to agree with him. 'Perhaps I am,' I said. 'I don't know.' I was no longer fooled. He knew something about me that I didn't. I could interpret that, but no more. He reminded me of a friend, who once asked me 'who I was?' as though to prove that he, too, knew a secret which threatened me. I tried to appear calm, but felt as ignorant as a stupid child unable to answer simple questions in class. The psychiatrist continued speaking. He told me about a unit they had at the hospital. I forced myself to show interest. It seemed to be what he expected from me. 'It's a psychotherapy unit,' he explained, 'where people can talk through their problems. I think it could help you.' I agreed that he should make an appointment for me. He confirmed that I did not need drugs, that he could see no reason for me to remain at the hospital, and that I could therefore go home. Our meeting lasted less than thirty minutes. I left hospital that afternoon, determined to escape from them all.

When I tried to remember what had taken place at that meeting, I kept hearing his question – 'Are you angry?' I wrestled mentally with the puzzle for days. Throughout my life, until then, I had believed that I controlled what little anger I felt. Sadness? Now that, I knew, engulfed me from time to time. But anger? Surely I could not be angry? Surely I was strong enough not to give in to anger? If I was angry, I reasoned, it had to be with myself. For the second time in seven years I had deserted my family, destroyed a career and attempted to kill myself, I had no work, little money, and, I believed, no future. Stormy emotional waves from which I could not escape smashed inside my mind; instead of feeling that I was hopelessly submerged, I wished that I had already drowned. Before I managed to recover from one surging attack, another was already rushing towards me. One thought dominated my mind: unrelenting bitterness that I was alive. They don't understand, I kept repeating to myself, trying to eliminate the dreadful noise in my head, they don't understand. What right have I to be angry, when I'm the one who's wrong?

Emotional conflicts were not new. They had eroded my life for as long as I could remember. Unable to describe them, either to myself or others, I could admit only that I felt 'depressed'. And now, a new thought had entered my mind. Maybe I was depressed *and* angry. The more I tried grappling with the psychiatrist's question, the more I knew that I wanted to escape, to be alone, to vanish. But as these desires tossed inside me, another more calming one took over. I wanted someone to help me. Anyone. Perhaps the psychiatrist, perhaps the psychowhateveritwas. 'Are you angry?' had moved forward to 'Yes, I am angry', and I wanted to know what to do about it.

1985, London

Four years later, I sat in a cramped basement room in Bayswater, London. 'I'd say you were a mild manic depressive,' diagnosed a cheerful counsellor from MIND, that sunny July afternoon, as she pressed *Factsheet 4, Manic Depression*[3] into my outstretched hand. For a few hours I was shocked, but excited, to have an evil-sounding label to stick on my guilty shoulders. Oh well, I reasoned, I feel so terrible that it seems only right to be given a terrible name.

'The hazards of mania are plentiful, and sufferers may do

things they bitterly regret afterwards,' I read. That's me, I thought, bitterly regretting most of the things I had done in my life. I read on, remembering the counsellor's matter-of-fact question – 'Have you ever discussed lithium with your doctor?' I had thought lithium was a tranquilliser, but on page three of her organization's leaflet I learned that 'it is a mood normaliser'. That's what I need, I thought, something to keep my moods under control. The leaflet mentioned unpleasant side effects and blood tests. I imagined myself visiting a hospital once a month for my drug supervision and blood checks, and felt relieved: someone would be keeping an eye on me. Everything began to make sense. I had been wrong to tell the psychiatrist four years earlier that I would not take drugs. Drugs! That's what I've needed all these years. Why didn't somebody help me, years ago, when I was young? I felt elated that at last medical science had found something to resolve my problem. I decided that I was in a state of mania, because, in a neatly set-out table, it said that in a state of mania a manic depressive feels 'high, elated, euphoric'; and that was how I felt when I thought that lithium was a solution.

After the initial 'high', which lasted for less than an hour, I rapidly declined to a 'low'. I knew that I was unwell; but to discover that I was a manic depressive hurt. I knew that I was bad; but was I *that* bad? I worried about the diagnosis for four weeks, until an appointment was arranged with yet another psychiatrist, at St Mary's Hospital, in London. What would happen? What would he say to me when he heard my history of continual mental depression? Would he tell me that I really was crazy? Perhaps he would lock me up. Perhaps what I had was worse than manic depression. Perhaps I was a 'psychotic', as my wife had sworn in a legal affidavit, during stormy and vindictive divorce proceedings the year after we returned together from San Francisco. (I had been horrified to see that word on papers which would flow in and out of lawyers' offices and High Courts, drowning any expectation of a reasonable settlement.) I remembered that a therapist at the psychotherapy unit had said that if I was psychotic I would not be there. 'You're all neurotics,' he continued, 'the difference is that neurotics build castles in the air: psychotics live in them.' It sounded clever, but I was not sure that I understood what he meant.

I arrived at St Mary's, and was asked to fill in two psychological questionnaires, containing about one hundred statements, most of which had to be answered by ticking columns headed 'never, sometimes, often, always' or 'good, fair, bad, very bad'. I distrusted each line, worried that conclusions would be drawn from answers I found difficult to provide. If I ticked 'often' to the statement 'I feel suicidal', would they believe me? And was it true? Should I change it to 'sometimes', in case they decided to lock me up? Or was 'always' better, to let them know how bad I felt? As I waited for my appointment I thought about past medical consultations, arising from depressive illnesses. During a period of thirty-two years I had been seen by four GPs and six psychiatrists, who between them had plastered me with more labels than I had stuck on my travel-worn suitcases.

When I was thirteen years old, and had been unwell for a few weeks, the day came for me to return to school. My form master welcomed me back and wanted to know what had been wrong with me. I felt ashamed, and unwillingly handed him the doctor's certificate. 'What's this,' he said loudly in front of the class, 'nervous exhaustion?' I hated him for humiliating me in front of my classmates, particularly because I had told some of them that I'd had 'flu. A few weeks later he called me to his desk as I was leaving the classroom, and asked, 'How are your nerves these days?' He may have been taking a solicitous interest in me, but I had not forgiven him for what he had said on the day I returned to school, and I hated him more fiercely than I had previously. 'Fine,' I replied cheerfully, trying to hide my embarrassment.

In my early twenties, after regular periods of depression, a psychiatrist gave me the first practical help I had received. (Today it hardly seems like help.) I explained how I felt, omitting my greatest fear, that I was mad. He told me that depression was a common problem. I wanted to cry out in glee. I had never realized until then that there were other people who felt as I did. He affixed another label, 'anxiety neuroses', and prescribed anti-depressant drugs.

Fourteen years after I had felt humiliated by my form master, I experienced a year-long period of depression and withdrawal, the first time that I had been aware of feeling mad for more than three or four weeks at one time. Most people who knew me described it as 'a nervous breakdown': my GP diagnosed 'endogenous depression'. I quite liked that label, and enjoyed rolling it round my tongue. It sounded vastly more impressive than mere 'depression', and less degrading than 'anxiety neuroses' or 'nervous exhaustion'. That new label helped when explaining my problems to friends or business colleagues. 'From within,' I said with an air of superiority and confidence I never felt. 'It means that I suffer from a chemical deficiency which causes the depression.' They didn't understand what I was talking about: neither did I. To clarify the explanation, I often copied on a piece of paper an illustration of what it meant. I drew a horizontal line across the centre of the sheet and a large U-shaped curve starting at the top of the paper, dipping to the bottom and returning to the top. 'The straight line represents the normal level of activity,' I explained, 'the curve is my particular level. When I'm above the line, I use up too much chemical, and so, to make up for the excessive energy, my body dips below the norm. That's what it means.' I felt that even if I wasn't cured, I had a simple, respectable answer.

These labels have haunted me. On the one hand, I wanted to know what was wrong with me; on the other, I was frightened of what I might hear. Following each diagnosis I have felt ashamed, embarrassed, angered; the more so because I never felt 'cured'. Often, I have wished that, instead of depression, I could have been labelled with something more 'acceptable', like diabetes, although I doubt if that would make much sense to diabetics, particularly if they also experience depression.

All these thoughts, and many more, about my past periods of depression, rushed into my mind while I waited for my meeting with the latest psychiatrist, at St Mary's. I decided that I had had enough. I wanted to know precisely what was wrong with me. The time had come to stop messing about, fearful of what I might learn, and to face the awful truth. I wouldn't withdraw into confused silence, as I usually did when in the presence of doctors. I'd ask for – no, I'd demand – a full explanation. I wasn't an imbecile, or a coward. I could take what was coming. Couldn't I?

During the meeting I repeated my history of mental disturbance, and felt like an old record, playing a too-familiar tune. I waited for the final, the ultimate, verdict. Who, or what, was I? What would he say? Perhaps he'd merely confirm that I was an anxiety-prone-endogenous-manic-depressive-with-psychotic-interludes, and recommend that a stay in a locked ward might do me some good. But at the conclusion of the meeting he said: 'I wouldn't apply any name to your difficulties. They exist because of the person you are.' And he left it at that. Where did that leave me, I wondered? He confirmed previous opinions – no drugs, no straitjackets – and agreed that I needed help. I had wanted it from him, but he seemed unable or incapable of offering any solutions. What was so peculiar about me that it couldn't be given a name? I felt frustrated, and remembered the week at school, when I was fifteen, and my parents had refused to let me go on the annual camping holiday, because each time I had returned in previous years, I had had a bout of depression. Only one other boy in my year remained behind, and he walked through the corridors supported by crutches. If only *I* had a broken leg. . . .

After I left the psychiatrist, I felt relieved. He hadn't said anything which implied I was mad, had he? When my feelings settled, I decided that, as usual, nobody could help me, and I was pleased that I had not been labelled. Labels, I knew, were no answer. They stuck to me like emotional glue, each one leaving me in a stickier mess. I needed more than a label to define my confusion. Depression. What is depression, I wanted to know? One year it was sleeping for days on end; another it was hearing my voice, but not knowing what I was saying. At other periods I felt lost in a strange world which shrouded me for a few weeks and then cleared into exhilarating excitement. On several occasions I had been unable to work for months on end. Often, when I felt awful, I worked so hard that I could not understand how I kept going. I never knew, from one day to the next, how I would feel, or sleep. When I had severe headaches I wanted them to go, or for my head to be cut off; if I didn't have headaches, I wondered why.

After my appointment at St Mary's, one of England's best known hospitals, one which couldn't give me what I needed, from a space inside my head which I had difficulty in locating, I kept saying to myself 'Why can't I stop being angry?'

I had told the consultant about my course of psychotherapy treatment a few years earlier. 'Did it help?' he wanted to know. 'It was the best thing that ever happened to me,' I replied. 'Then perhaps you need some more,' he said. I had already decided that for myself.

After my attempted suicide in California in 1981, and my subsequent meeting with the psychiatrist who asked me 'Are you angry?', I voluntarily attended the psychotherapy unit he had referred me to. At the same time that one hospital was rubbing and manipulating my damaged arms, wrists and hands, another was tossing my mind and feelings in all directions. Physiotherapy worked effectively and speedily, and was soon forgotten: psychotherapy proved to be more stimulating, more exciting and more painful. And I dare not forget it, ever. I was almost forty years old then, and had to make a decision. Did I really want to know what troubled me, what had made me a depressive throughout my teens, my twenties and my thirties; or was the wish to be dead more inviting? It was a choice between discovery and destruction. I was exhausted from extended periods of chaos, when I could not live with people, concentrate on my work, or find satisfaction with any part of my life. For more than twenty-five years the best treat I could think of was to be dead.

Suddenly, after being asked 'Are you angry?', I wanted to give myself a chance to survive. Occasional psychiatric consultations offered no solutions; general practitioners wanted to solve my problems with prescriptions for pills in which I never had any faith; I didn't need to be locked up in an insane asylum: if none of these possibilities could help, perhaps more psychotherapy would.

My first period of psychotherapy had the impact upon me of divine revelation, but it had not given me sufficient faith in myself to survive recurring emotional agony. When it ended I had believed that I was getting to know *me*. Then, unexpectedly, a few years later, the new discoveries were buried under old destructive forces. I had hoped that Mr Field, at St Mary's, would resurrect me, and, in a way, he did, by telling me that he could do nothing except approve another period of psychotherapy. I recommended my self-exploration, but in a different environment. The first experience had been in a group; the second was more intensive, on a 'one-to-one' basis, and resulted in greater stimulation, greater excitement, and greater pain. This second intensive period of psychotherapy is continuing as I write these words.

As *Factsheet 4, Manic Depression* says, 'sufferers may do things they bitterly regret afterwards'. A graph of my suffering would show a consistent trend: inexorably, year by year, my bitterness has increased. New peaks of anxiety have been scaled by events and confrontations which I am still struggling to understand. By the time I was forty I had destroyed two successful careers, served a prison sentence, been made legally bankrupt, lost a treasured professional qualification, attempted to kill two people, and isolated myself from most of my family and friends. These bitter experiences, as well as a perplexing belief that I was mad, had to have some cause, particularly because I mentally plotted a second graph, one which depicted success. Why did I view my life in two separate parts, 'good and a success' or 'bad and a failure'? Why was it always either one or the other, and why was it mostly 'bad and a failure'? Psychotherapeutic treatment has provided the only opportunity for me to discover any answers.

The greatest consistency in my life has been that it has never settled down, and I wanted to discover why. When I began the risky voyage of discovery through psychotherapy, I found that I had to travel in several different directions at the same time: I had to visit my childhood, youth and adult years; I had to examine the present and think of the future; I had to explore a person I barely knew – me – and decide whether the journey was worthwhile. The journeys had one familiar route – they all marched through personal battles, which led to a major war. I have felt and thought of my life as a perpetual fight with the world. I wanted to convert the war into peace. Instead of filling my mind with images of destruction, and explaining my feelings through metaphors equally destructive, I wanted to negotiate a truce and eliminate confusion. Psychotherapy has proved to be a helpful negotiator, and without it I could not have written this book.

Why write a book? Because I had to. It became an obsession to put into words decades of personal frustrations, and a few, brief years of enlightenment. Some people, seeking relief, turn to drink, drugs, sports or sex – anything or anyone to help them survive – and I have sampled the choices; but my most enduring addiction is writing.

I first remember writing about feelings in 1972, eight years into my first marriage. I can recall several sheets of foolscap, frantically filled with flowing and almost illegible words. I recall more vividly the doubts those hastily scribbled words raised in my mind. Having believed my marriage to be successful, the feelings which tumbled out almost too quickly to understand, sounded ominous. I hid my jottings in a desk. Then I worried that my wife might discover them, so I threw them away, as if by that act what I had admitted privately had no meaning. It did not occur to me to ask myself why I should be worried if she did read what I'd written. I wrote nothing else for three years. Then, while in prison, I wrote short stories, essays, poems and a prolific stream of letters. Through devious channels I ensured that most of this writing survived. My prison writings astonished me when I re-read them during my earliest weeks of psychotherapy. They expressed feelings which, when written, I did not recognize. One example will serve to illustrate this point. I wrote a long poem about a castle I had visited in France, believing that I had written a poem about a castle in France. When I re-read it, six years later, I realized that what I had actually written about was myself, transformed into a grey, isolated hill-top fort, warding off invaders. After prison, I wrote nothing until I began participating in group psychotherapy. During that period I kept an irregular diary, which has proved helpful in recalling events as they happened, and ensuring an accurate chronological source of reference for many of the experiences described in this book.

I now know for certain two facts about my writing: whatever I wrote before I started psychotherapy reflected the person I thought I was, not the person I have since come to understand better; and, second, whatever I know about myself invites deeper and closer investigation. For me, writing is sometimes the only way I know to explain my feelings, and, because my feelings are often in turmoil, what I write one day may bear little relationship to what I write a day later. However, in the following chapters I have tried to write carefully about events and feelings as I remember them at the time they happened.

This is important, because most of the book deals with my experiences during group psychotherapy. Currently, during 'one-to-one' therapy, many new ideas and realizations have emerged. But as I am anxious to concentrate on my group therapy experiences, this later understanding does not form an important part of what follows, unless to omit it would make a nonsense of what I am writing about.

Nearly five years have passed since I ended my period of group psychotherapy. I could not have written what I now have during that experience: it took time for my awareness to develop, most of it after I left the group. Similarly, because I am currently experiencing intensive therapy, I consider it premature to set out precisely what additional understanding is growing from this second period of therapy. It is for this reason – the need for time to elapse so as to gain clearer understanding about feelings and behaviour – that most of this book concentrates on my experiences with the group and the effect they had on my understanding of depression.

Naturally, I have introduced many people who have entered, and often left, my life. Most names are fictitious, but the people are real. I have changed names, for obvious reasons, but not events – they are described subjectively, and I am aware of constant contradictions; but that is how my life has been, contradictory. The neurotics at Shipley Grange – the group – were the most 'real' people I have ever met. Most other groups – family, social and business – have usually been terrifyingly 'unreal'. Through the group, and later, through more intensive psychotherapy, the 'real' and 'unreal' have merged. This merging, which has enabled me to begin to understand myself, is the theme of the book. It is a personal case history[4], and makes no attempt to resolve other people's problems. I have written about what I have learned, not what I can teach.

I have learned many things about myself, but I remain unable to overcome that wide, chasmic isolation generally described as depression. This book attempts to describe what I, as a depressive, feel; some of the consequences of not understanding those feelings; and how I continue to seek greater understanding of myself and those people who come into my life. It emphasizes psychotherapy, not necessarily between patient (or client) and professional therapist, because I believe that many people are capable of giving others therapy, and are doing it most days of their life. Talking and sharing problems, feeling and understanding, kindness and cruelty, can all be therapy – good and bad. I have suffered more pain and enjoyed more pleasure since I began therapy than at any other time in my life. My process of self-discovery began with the psychiatrist's question 'Are you angry?', and I never expect it to end. Sometimes, I weep with fury when feelings which have disturbed and confused me from early childhood suddenly overwhelm me; at other times, I want to yell out exultantly as I gain a new insight into the person I am – and stop pretending that I am the person I thought I was.

My personal journey is powered by feelings, and to understand them I have had to examine words – words which I thought represented one thing, but often represented something else. Days when I realized that guilt, or sadness, were 'covers' for other feelings; days when I stopped pretending that I was perpetually 'confused'; the days I stopped trying to hide all my feelings under the verbal umbrella of 'depression': those were stops on my journey which became permanent personal landmarks, which I have to revisit regularly. The emotional scenery is rarely picturesque. Ugly, frightening, foggy feelings continue to darken my ability to face myself and other people clearly. Hate, anger and punishment are constant companions; love and forgiveness are often strangers.

The following chapters describe this self-discovery, moving hopefully forwards, and, in despair, disastrously backwards. Chapter 2, 'Neurotics at war', introduces my first psychotherapy encounters with the group at Shipley Grange. (As far as I know, there is no Shipley Grange: it is the fictional name of a real place. The friendly horse-chestnut tree is as tangible as the frightening encounters with the people who lived with me for six chaotic months.) It describes how we were expected to live together, and my early confrontations with talking, painting and drama therapy. In chapter 3, 'Inside the volcano', I move backwards, to the painful journey I had to make into my earliest years, and explain how memories and feelings, long forgotten or misunderstood, set me on so many paths of destruction. Chapter 4, 'Sinking not soaring', describes some of my relationships with non-family people, from schooldays to a period in my late twenties when I attempted to overcome the conflicts I had in childhood, rose like a new star, only to dim and fade into deep and terrifying periods of worsening depression. Chapter 5, 'Self-destruct', begins with my thirtieth birthday, when I believed that finally my past had met my present, and my present had no future — except death; and ends with the years leading up to my voluntary admission to Shipley Grange, a period of unexpected catastrophes and crushed dreams. Weaving in and out of these chapters are my experiences with the group — experiences which were usually an introduction to old memories and the worst of my bad feelings.

Chapter 6, 'Emotional equations', brings together much of what my various journeys into the past taught me. In a more detailed way, it highlights what I learned and felt during encounters with the group, and the relevance of those encounters to my difficulties in mixing with people; and how, after examining my past, the *me* I thought I was proved to be as 'unreal' as I had previously thought it 'real'. None of this was easy. Far from that, it was the most exhausting period in my life, when I had to face personal misconceptions, other people's onslaughts, and the fact that, for whatever reasons I may have acted in particular ways, I had to live with the consequences. Finally, chapter 7, 'Two of me', is a reflection of how I felt immediately after I ended my period of group therapy.

Forty years of living feels like a long time, long enough to have accepted reality as it is, not as I would wish it to be; but my oldest memories are often my most vivid, and the most recent are difficult to isolate from the past. One bad experience today can send me into a deep period of despair which recalls a thousand bad yesterdays. Struggling to free myself from my past usually seems like an impossible dream, and living with it is like an unending nightmare. If this sounds an unlikely route through which a liveable future may emerge, my only reason for continuing to explore it is that if I do not — there is nothing.

Many books — of which I have read a handful[5] — have been written on the subject of depression, by psychiatrists, psychologists, therapists and other -*ists*. Some are for 'the experts', others are aimed at depressives or the general public. I have read more than one whose author implies that their book will resolve 'everything', My opinion is that no book will do any such thing. At best, those books I have studied identify problems which may previously have festered away unrecognized: at worst, they may lead to dangerous self-analysis. I have read volumes, gasped with relief at newly-discovered explanations of why I am as I am. But when my space explodes those encouraging words are forgotten, ignored, resented. All I have done in this book is try to describe how I feel, how I behave, and why I feel slightly less fearful of the future.

2 Neurotics at war

Introduction

By the middle of September 1981, I had survived five of the most remarkable weeks in my life, as a resident member of a psychotherapy unit administered by a major psychiatric hospital in southern England. During that period I had lived with a group of people who amazed, horrified, infuriated and, occasionally, soothed me. Few, if any, of us understood the unrelenting distrust we felt towards most people: one of the unit's functions was to make us aware of this. Our lives had become intolerable weights of insecurity and fear, manacled by emotional disorders which scarred us with suspicions about ourselves and each other. Together, we attempted to share our experiences, and we tried to do this in ways which were new and confusing. We were introduced to several types of therapy, verbal and non-verbal. They were all frightening.

On Wednesday afternoons we assembled in the hospital's art room. (I had not painted, or even thought of painting, since leaving school, where I somehow or other scraped through Art at Ordinary Level GCE, achieving exactly the minimum pass mark.) Using ancient and damaged brushes, and an unlimited supply of poster paint, I began illustrating parts of myself which I had not imagined could be depicted so vividly. There were ten people during my fifth session; two members of the hospital staff, working full-time with the unit, and eight residents[1]. Art therapy began with us sitting on orange plastic seats, forming a circle, where we proposed,

19

and decided by a majority vote, which feeling or subject we wanted to express. Then we moved to separate, upright easels, and, in silence, created our work. An hour later we returned to the circle, to explain our paintings, discuss them — or ignore them.

Usually, the subjects proposed, whether by staff or residents, were predictable, often suggested as a direct result of recent confrontations in the group. Typical suggestions from residents related to people — *parents, family* or *children*, for example; and feelings, such as *love, hate, anger* or *rejection*. It made little difference to me what we agreed upon for the week's subject: whatever it was, my paintings were always abstract and violent, daubed with thick brush strokes in scarlet, purple, black and orange. Staff members sometimes supplied us with unexpected ammunition — *silence* proved lethal, I remember; but not as lethal as the dynamite which exploded during my fifth session.

Stuart, the senior staff member, a short, dark-haired, bearded Welshman, suggested something familiar to him, and novel to the residents. 'We could try a group mural,' he said casually, explaining, in response to our quizzical looks, precisely what a group mural was. Other subjects were proposed, but the mural sounded original, challenging, and, its most attractive feature, harmless fun. I willingly voted for it, having no conception of the catastrophe which lay ahead.

Attack!

The hospital's art room reminded me of school. I was surrounded by familiar, old and battered wooden stools, glass jars for water, unrinsed brushes stained with age, shelves stacked with paper, crayons, palettes, and sticks of charcoal; and the heady aroma of paint, turpentine and accumulated dust seeped into my nostrils.

To prepare for the mural, we selected a colour, our unique colour, for the duration of the session. I chose a vivid scarlet, and equipped myself with a large, new pot of the stuff. As soon as the subject had been agreed, I rushed to the paint shelves, determined that nobody should reach that glorious colour before me. I also selected two broad, heavy brushes and filled two jars with cold water. Then we organized the working surface. We were allocated our own 'territory', a sheet of white A2 cartridge paper. The ten sheets were spread on the floor and joined with Sellotape on the under-surface, five sheets in two rows, forming a great white rectangle at our feet. We hovered by our blank mural, while Stuart repeated the game-rules.

'We choose a personal symbol,' he said, 'and paint it on our own sheet of paper. When we've finished, we can do anything, and go anywhere, on the mural.' We agreed to paint for forty-five minutes. From that moment talking ceased.

Excited by this new venture, I wanted to participate in creating an original and unified picture, to prove that I was an important part of the group. My symbol was a large, six-pointed star, which I carefully centred on my sheet of paper. Other members chose geometric shapes, 'stick' figures and a house: someone wrote their name. When the symbols were completed, Stuart nodded for the second stage to begin.

Loading my brush, I painted free-style lines, moving clockwise from my star, linking it with the other symbols. I noted with satisfaction that my 'territory' was occupied by all the other colours. The mural grew into a colourful mass of bright, attractive, interweaving designs. I felt exhilarated and energetic, and decided that my next incursion round the mural should be different and inventive. Rapidly I added arcs, dots and circles to contrast with my original solid lines. My scarlet touched and merged with other colours. I no longer wanted to move in an orderly route, but darted between the other artists, dabbing paint where I could, filling in empty spaces, enjoying the image of my colour glistening brilliantly from the floor. It seemed unimportant that my fingers and clothes were spotted with paint, as I bent down or knelt on the floor, making quicker and larger scarlet patches. This is wonderful, I thought, proud of the fascinating designs flowing into each other as the mural developed.

Afterwards, I could not decide when friendship turned to enmity, but the later realization that such a spontaneous and unexpected change was possible left an awful and unforgettable memory which still haunts me. I began to resent the other colours. They took up too much space, and, even worse, abused my scarlet by covering it up. The empty white areas were disappearing, leaving me too little space to do what I wanted. I painted aggressively over other colours, splashing thicker and thicker layers of paint, so that scarlet, and not green, or blue, or yellow, could be seen as the dominant colour. I forced other brushes away with my own, gleefully stabbing the paper, delighted with the large scarlet mass which spread across the mural. In places, I saw, the scarlet no longer looked attractive, because other colours had watered it down or changed its tone; but I continued, withdrawing briefly to rush to a nearby shelf and grab another pot of paint.

Twenty minutes had passed when I looked at the clock. I became worried that I might not have enough time to do all that I wanted; but, at the same time, I was uncertain of what I was trying to achieve. The more effort I put into my painting, the less attractive the mural became. I noticed that some members had stopped painting and returned to their seats. Good! The prettiness and the colours of the mural ceased to be important. I was concerned now, not with colours, but with people. I had to show them all that I was in charge.

One male resident, Jim, had chosen yellow. I pursued him, determined to obliterate his colour, consciously intending to inflict pain, remembering how persistently he infuriated me in the group. I understood and enjoyed his fury when he realized what I was doing; but the harder he tried to regain his place on the mural, the more determined I became to eliminate him as a competitor. A few minutes later he walked away, defeated. Marvellous! I was winning.

The mural had become a liquid mass of disorderly colour, a

great expanse of mixed and unrecognizable tints, a vast, purplish quagmire. Undeterred, I continued my assault, rushing along each side of the rectangle, unstoppable. Part of me understood that what was happening was dangerous and wrong; but a wilder, uncontrollable force proved more powerful. A distant, inner voice was trying to say something to me. . . .

I knew that the rest of the group were incapable of understanding the purpose of the mural: where they had failed I would succeed. Reloading my brush with deadly paint, I stretched across to the centre of the paper and introduced a new symbol, a small red circle. That'll show them, I thought, that I want this group to be united. What better than a nice, red sun in the middle of this wasteland. But I could not stop. I enlarged the circle, from a diameter of six inches, to twelve, to twenty. Then I encountered a new problem; the others who were still painting appeared unwilling to help develop my new plan. Didn't they understand what I wanted to achieve? As my sun expanded they got in the way, them and their interfering paint. There was one exception: blue. Cathy had chosen blue, and I liked Cathy, so for a time we circled together, her blue bordering my red. We smiled at each other, both understanding our mutual feeling of power. But quickly the partnership dissolved; despite wanting her with me, she kept clouding over the advancing sun.

I looked at the picture and was upset to see that no matter how much scarlet I splashed on the drenched paper, it became inexorably uglier: from purple it had become a barren dirty-brown. I continued throwing paint wildly at the mural, desperate to eradicate the ghastly colour, my brush spearing the image in front of me. When Cathy stood up, and threw her remaining blue paint into my sun, I felt hurt, but strangely peaceful, too. I was alone. The mural was mine. Everyone had bowed to my scarlet power. Forty minutes had elapsed as quickly as forty seconds. Five more minutes remained; but having routed the enemy, there was no need to continue. My colour, bruised and fatigued, covered the whole, literally the whole, mural: there was not a cubic centimetre which I had not bludgeoned with my brush. I had won. Exhausted and elated, I rejoined the group.

Then, when I surveyed the monstrous, horrible mess on the floor, I realized that something had gone terribly wrong. 'How did it happen?' and 'What have I done!' I kept repeating silently to myself, as I understood the awfulness of my destruction. It was too late to change anything: the damage was complete and unalterable. What I most desperately wanted at that moment was to escape. Val, the female staff nurse, shattered the growing tension, and my hope of escape. 'Isn't it ugly,' she said, sounding bored. Her words were more powerful than bullets as they ripped into my feelings. I sweated with shame and humiliation. 'I didn't enjoy that. I felt threatened,' said Jim, not without some pleasure, I thought, as he quickly agreed with the woman who constantly terrified him. 'I couldn't continue,' he added. I thought that he must hate me more than ever, for we both knew that I had made him retreat.

My stomach churned. My mouth felt dry. My cheeks burned. My hands shook. Cathy, my friend Cathy, complained loudly, 'I thought we were supposed to work together,' and gave me a vicious stare. If anything else was said, I didn't hear it; my thoughts and feelings had retreated into history. I saw, through the mural, the repetition of numerous events in my life, when from hope had come disaster. I related the destruction on the floor to all that I had destroyed in other places and at other times. I did not know what to do with my shame and rage. Terrified of further recriminations, and the memories invading my mind, I rushed from the room, into the cool, damp afternoon. I did not want them; and I believed that they would want nothing to do with a power which could only destroy.

I walked hurriedly through the spacious hospital gardens, furious that I was in such a place, feeling guilty and ashamed. I had no alternative: I had to leave the unit, I decided. But it had become the only refuge where I could talk about, and share, some of my despair with others who were experiencing similar emotional chaos. Bitter tears streamed across my cheeks. A light drizzle cooled my face as I continued walking away from the unit, towards the nearby town. At the end of the hospital's main tree-lined roadway, I hesitated. Ahead of me was the fearful reality of a town, bustling with people among whom I felt hopeless. Behind, presumably happy at my departure, was another group, no less terrifying. I can't return, I thought bitterly, not after what I've done. I sat on rain-soaked benches or meandered through the chilly grounds for five hours, straining to make a decision. To leave the unit meant losing the only hope I had; to remain, I would have to humble myself before a group of people I despised and resented. Desperate to exhibit strength and power, I felt weak and useless. 'If only someone would come and help me,' my distant, inner voice pleaded. They didn't. I had to go to them.

Not knowing where else to go, I returned to the unit, expecting accusations, and intending to apologize. The battles which awaited me there felt less frightening than the false peace I had fantasized about when I thought of leaving.

War zone – Shipley Grange

The psychotherapy unit – part of the British National Health Service[2], and involving no financial cost to residents – was, and presumably remains, an elite and separate part of the hospital complex. Located in its own grounds, a quarter of a mile from the dismal, Victorian pile of bricks which housed closed wards and depressing corridors, where disturbed mental patients stumbled and muttered and shouted, Shipley Grange had originally been the residence of the senior hospital administrator. In more recent years it had been used as a staff training centre, before being assigned its present function during the 1970s. The ugly, gabled, red-brick house, shaded by horse-chestnut trees and flanked by unkempt grass, seemed as forbidding externally as many of the events were inside; but, architectural depression notwithstanding, it had become my weekday home, and throughout my time there, I entered its tiled porch with conflicting feelings of attraction and repulsion. Fortunately, one side of the unit's garden bordered open farmland. This closeness to striped fields of corn and throbbing tractors helped me believe that I was not really in a mental institution.

The senior hospital psychiatrist, the one who had asked me 'Are you angry?', was in charge of the unit. He attended one group meeting each week. His boisterous laugh and friendly smiles often deceived us into believing that his feelings towards the group were paternal and sympathetic. We were regularly disillusioned by his plain speaking and readiness to rip apart much of what he heard from the residents. I looked forward to his hours with the group with mixed feelings, because, although his thrusts could be devastating, his 'father' image gave them more meaning than similar attacks from most other members. 'He's no fool,' I'd say to myself. What disturbed me most was the additional time he spent with the unit staff, secreted away inside their office. What was he saying about me?

Normally, there were two experienced members of the hospital staff in daytime attendance, and one trainee. The nursing staff arrived at 9 o'clock each morning, and stayed with us until 5 p.m., except during their lunch break. Stuart, with whom I never felt at ease, remained with the unit throughout my stay; Val, a blunt and moody woman, with whom I started on terrible terms, but eventually felt very close to, left while I was there. She was replaced by Jo, who I could never accept, but who, ironically, was to play a crucial part in my life. I regarded the trainees as intruders. The staff participated in all formal and informal daytime activities, and on Tuesdays one of them worked overtime, joining the residents for the evening. Within practicable limits they acted and reacted as equally as they could with the residents. We like to think of ourselves as a democratic organization. This was a fallacy; but we preferred the pretence. Stuart, in particular, represented 'authority' from the day I started until the day I left.

There were rules, not many, all regarded by staff as essential if we were to live together and benefit from the unit. Residents received a typed copy before joining. We were expected to stay for not less than six months; to organize and administer the cooking, laundry, housekeeping and, to a limited extent, certain finances; not to drink alcohol or take drugs, prescribed or otherwise; to attend all formal meetings; to abide by majority decisions; not to indulge in sex with other residents, and not to 'act out'. I doubt whether any resident understood this last rule before joining, or that many understood it later. In various ways, these rules were flagrantly ignored when residents moved into an offensive position, which was most of the time.

Psychotherapy, being a talking therapy, requires verbal communication. Even its close relations, psychodrama and art therapy, non-verbal in part, included verbal discussions of what had taken place during a session. 'Acting out' includes behaviour which does not honestly express feelings. Thus, we were not expected to rush from meetings, as I did during the afternoon I destroyed the group mural; nor were we expected to attack each other physically, break chairs, attempt suicide, take to our beds, or refuse to eat, to mention a few of the examples of how this particular rule was broken by one or other of the residents most hours of most days. 'Acting out' included other, less easily recognized, behaviour: role trans-ference, being *nice* to each other, excessive zeal in performing housekeeping duties, and generally any devious act which conflicted with our feelings. It was hard work explaining to other residents that they kept acting out, but I tried to be patient!

However we were feeling, the rules which could not be broken were those relating to the organization of Shipley Grange itself. Each morning we collected a supply of food from the hospital kitchens, and, if we wanted to eat between Monday morning and Friday afternoon, we had to cook what was issued; and what was issued was generous to the point of waste. Similarly, clean linen was available, if we organized it, and so was a modest spending allowance for social activities, if someone remembered to claim it from the cashier's office on the allotted day. We could requisition light bulbs, Hoovers, heaters, soap and other necessities, provided that the responsible resident felt capable of filling in and signing the bureaucratically-inspired documentation.

There were no rules about entering or leaving the house during free time, although it was understood that if anybody intended returning after 11 p.m. they should tell another resident. Attendance at the unit was voluntary and so, therefore, was leaving. More than one resident stole away during the night, to avoid the otherwise inevitable confrontations with the group. Several ran away, as I did on more than one occasion, only to return sheepishly, often after another resident had hunted them out and comforted them. In the evenings, we could watch television in the living room, stroll to a local pub, play music on an exhausted record player, or entertain each other more dramatically by acting out.

During the day, routines were more rigid. Every morning, at 9.15, we commenced our first formal meeting, sitting in the obligatory circle, confined in a small room, and . . . well, the intention was that we talked, but, as I quickly discovered, talking was rarely easy. There were no agendas, no planned subjects, merely an opportunity for free-ranging discussion. At 10.30 we had a break, usually to everyone's relief, particularly the smokers – smoking, and drinking tea or coffee, was not allowed during formal meetings – reconvening half an hour later for a second formal session. Then, a long break, until 2 o'clock.

Each afternoon was different: Mondays were set aside for interviewing new applicants; Tuesdays for psychodrama, of which more later; Wednesdays, art therapy; Thursdays, a group social activity, such as swimming, gardening or a walk; and on Fridays we ended the week with an administrative meeting to elect those responsible for the various household chores.

This final weekly meeting was often bizarre and time-consuming. Fridays meant that, despite the relief most of us felt at escaping from the intense pressures of living together, we had to face the reality of returning to our homes, where pressures and fears were usually as poweful as at the unit. We had to cope with residents who suddenly announced that they 'had nowhere to go', or 'couldn't stand their family', or 'wanted to be locked up in a ward'. It was unusual, on Mondays, not to hear that one resident, at least, had contacted another during the weekend.

Staff attended all these meetings; but many of the more dramatic ones — crisis meetings — were called to deal with unexpected catastrophes which occurred when we were 'staffless'. Between 11 p.m. and 1 in the morning was a popular time for emotional traumas. When a resident faced, or more likely, refused to face, a personal crisis, sometimes by fainting or screaming or threatening to commit suicide, a 'crisis' was called. Everyone was expected to attend, even if it meant being woken from a deep sleep or letting supper go cold — and that could result in two meetings taking place at once. Written minutes were recorded in a bound book, left in the staff office the following morning.

Administratively, Shipley Grange was surprisingly efficient. Emotionally, it was chaotic.

Entry into the group was either by self-referral or, as in my case, at the suggestion of a medical practitioner or consultant who knew of the unit's existence. The unit could accommodate nine residents, but while I was there numbers averaged seven.

Having decided that I wanted to go to Shipley Grange, I had to attend two interviews. The first was with Stuart, an informal half-hour during which we gently probed each other. If he, or any other full-time staff member of the unit, considered an applicant likely to benefit from group psychotherapy, a second 'vetting' meeting was arranged, with all members of the unit present. I attended this meeting a week or two after seeing the 'Are you angry?' man, and found it a frightening and humiliating experience.

I was invited into the room set aside for formal meetings, a small annexe to the main house, and confronted the eight or nine strangers, most of whom asked me questions I would have preferred not to answer. 'You seem very arrogant,' said one resident, 'You won't get away with that here. How do you feel about that?' I did not feel able to admit that the way I felt about that was either to belt him, or rush from the room, so smiled politely and mumbled something about needing the opportunity. Another resident wanted to know about my recent suicide attempt, which I could not hide, because my arm was still in plaster, and succeeded in making me feel ridiculous, partly due to her age — she was nineteen, and I was almost forty.

Briefly, I explained why I wanted to join the unit, already convinced that they must all think me crazy and beyond help; convinced too, from several of the aggressive questions, that the charm with which I liked to think I could impress other people was proving, for some inexplicable reason, less than irresistible. Inwardly, I seethed at the degrading inquisition. Determined to avoid the humiliation of being refused admission, before the meeting was halfway through, I had decided not to join, even if invited. Just let one of them say no, I thought, and that's it.

After an hour, a vote was taken. Each person present had to say whether they thought I should or should not attend the unit, and why. I tried to hide my fear, waiting expectantly for a dissenter, but to my astonishment and delight, they all said yes. Six weeks later, early in August, terrified and uncertain about my future, I joined the group.

Enemy forces — the residents

Some of them were enemies from the moment we were introduced; others became enemies; a few were friends who became enemies when I felt betrayed or isolated. All of them, at different times and in different ways, reflected my own doubts and fears, although often I either could not or would not recognize what was being reflected. Very few stayed the agreed six months; and usually I was pleased to see the back of them. Pressures within the group were so intense that, for those who left prematurely, an insecure and frightening world away from Shipley Grange seemed immeasurably less severe than the unavoidable self-torment suffered in the confined environment at the unit, where every act could be questioned and every motive distrusted. I survived for six months, not because I was less affected by pressure, but because the fear of failing to grasp whatever opportunities were available to me was greater than the fear of doing nothing. As my anger and resentment towards residents and staff intensified, I realized that my feelings were with me all the time — whether inside or outside the group. I delighted in exercising what felt like power within the group; but inevitably, when my acts were criticized by other members, what had seemed like power crashed into pieces of degrading self-pity which appeared to be irreparable. But the unit remained the one hope in my life; and if, not to lose that hope, I had to suffer the others, I assumed that it was a pain I had to accept.

I had no idea what to expect from the group before I joined the unit. Six months later I felt even less certain what my expectations should be. During that period I benefited from one unchanging comfort: like myself, the residents were in severe emotional disarray, and that common denominator drew me to them, even those I despised and loathed. I felt bad and destructive, and their constant enmity towards me proved that the worst fears I had about myself were true.

Conflicts emerged within minutes of my arrival on the first Monday morning. I joined the group circle, feeling as isolated as a new boy starting school in the middle of an academic year. Because they all seemed to know so much about each other, I immediately resented the secrets which I felt were being withheld from me. But some things were not kept secret for long, and Bridget's home life was one of them.

A prerequisite of joining the group was that each resident had somewhere to live during weekends. Bridget, married for eight years with two young children, had joined the unit two weeks before me. On my first day, she arrived looking flushed, but sickly. She stormed into the room, slamming the door behind her, threw herself into a chair, and tightly clasped her arms across her chest like protective strapping. The meeting began. It was exactly 9.15. I waited. Silence. Bridget, obviously distressed, crossed and uncrossed her legs several times. Why doesn't someone say something, I wondered. I expected her to speak, or for Stuart, our leader, to lead. Long, painful seconds ticked by. Silence. Not a word. I felt embarrassed. Something was wrong with the woman. Why was nothing happening? I did not know what to do. The new boy had to learn the meaning of group therapy. For five minutes, nine of us, all adults, all there for a purpose, sat quietly, and said nothing. A few minutes earlier, in the living room, most of them had been chatting, discussing their weekend, even laughing. I felt so confused that I could not look directly at anybody, but cast surreptitious glances at Bridget, who seemed to have relapsed into a withdrawn stupor.

I felt relieved when, at last, one of the other women broke the horrific silence. 'How was your weekend, Bridget?' The group came to life. People coughed, chairs creaked, one or two spoke quietly to each other. Bridget began talking, vehemently and quickly, her words blurring into each other. The weekend she described sounded like a combination of horror stories from the Sunday tabloids. On Friday evening her husband had beaten her (she showed us the bruises on her arms and neck), pulled a large tuft of hair from her head, dragged her up a flight of stairs, raped her, and then vanished until Sunday afternoon, returning home drunk. She had taken her two children to her mother's house for protection, but had been refused admittance. Instead, the mother had called the police and her boyfriend to protect her from her daughter. On Saturday, a social worker had called and threatened to have the children taken into care, meanwhile providing overnight accommodation in a home for battered wives. Bridget had left early on Sunday morning, purchased two bottles of Cinzano, taken them home, and got drunk herself, apparently unable to explain to us what had happened to her children. On Sunday, when her husband returned home, he had taken the children to his mother, before returning to sexually attack his wife again. I listened with astonishment and disgust as her story unfolded. She had begun speaking loudly and violently, but gradually she became quieter, barely audible. What amazed me most were her continual assurances that her husband was not to blame, but her mother. 'He's a good husband and father,' she kept repeating. 'If it wasn't for that bitch [her mother], he'd never do the things he does.'

I waited, convinced that the group would help her, and that Stuart in particular would take some action on her behalf. I cannot recall all that happened at that first meeting; but I remember Stuart saying that it was about time she stopped blaming everyone else and participated in the group. His words shocked me. I had expected that she would be offered sympathy and help. Then, as though nothing had happened, he stood up and walked out of the room. It was precisely 10.30. The meeting had ended.

During the mid-morning break Bridget rushed to collect a glass of water, which from then on she clutched possessively in one hand, constantly looking at her watch. At 11 o'clock she swallowed a handful of pills. She told me later that she needed thirty-two pills a day, but that it was a condition of her joining the group that as soon as possible she stopped taking them.

I felt protective towards her, horrified at what I had heard, and furious with Stuart for what seemed like a callous disregard for her suffering. 'She's been like that every Monday, so far,' one of the residents told me. I began to wonder what I was doing there. At lunchtime I spoke to Bridget. She seemed frightened to talk of her problems after her initial outburst in the morning. 'It'll be all right, I know it will,' she assured me. 'It's the pills. He can't stand the pills, and they make me a useless wife and mother.' She looked at me and smiled. 'I go potty, sometimes,' she said. 'Didn't tell them in there,' she pointed to the meeting room, 'but I smashed up half the house on Sunday. He'd just spent hundreds on a new dining-room suite, and I smashed it all up.'

As that first day passed, I began to hear the 'in talk'. It was her third Monday with the group, and she had had almost identical weekends since joining. The previous Friday she had been advised, and had agreed, not to go home. I heard, or gathered, that most of the group, including one of the men, were terrified of her. They were frightened to speak to her, and more frightened of what she might do to them. On Thursday I understood their fear. We had finished our evening meal, most of us sprawled across chairs in the living room, when we heard a crash, then another, then, muffled through the closed doors, screams. Opening the door, the screams were more piercing, the crashes more thunderous. Upstairs, from the large bedroom where four of the women slept, Bridget was going berserk. We heard glass breaking, and thumping on the floor. Several of the group wanted to do nothing, others wanted to go to her, but were scared. Someone suggested calling the main hospital for help. Unable to understand why nobody would go and help her, I went upstairs. That'll show them, I thought. And I liked feeling that I was in charge – fearless, caring and responsible.

I knocked on the door. No response. I opened it, wondering what I would find, worried that something might be thrown at me. She sat on her bed, unmoving and silent. On the floor were scattered clothes, brushes, bits of glass and other odds and ends. She looked at me. 'You must think me terrible,' she said, 'but I had to, I'm cracking up. Tomorrow's Friday. Anyway,' she assured me, 'I only threw *my* things around.' I stayed with her for about half an hour, and we talked quietly. She was still affected by her massive drug doses, and her calmness was deceptive. So was mine. I decided that I'd be the one in the group to help her. I saw my role towards her as protector and guide. Where others had failed, I thought, I would succeed. 'They're no use, are they!' she said, lowering her head. She refused to go downstairs and attend a crisis meeting.

Two weeks later she left the group, only to be 'sectioned'

shortly afterwards, and confined for several weeks in a closed ward[3]. Then she was transferred to an open one, but detained involuntarily. After she was transferred I went to see her most weeks. The open wards were depressing, but separate from the main hospital, and I did not have to see the inmates who scared me.

We became very friendly as the weeks and months passed, and met each other several times in London after I left the unit. The last time I saw her, when she visited my wife and I, she carried a straw shopping bag. As soon as she entered our home she asked for a glass. From her bag she took a bottle of Cinzano, and poured herself several fingers of alcohol. 'So long as I've got this,' she said confidently, 'I'm OK.' She drank two bottles a day, and told us that she had reformed, that her children were marvellous, and her husband wonderful. After that last visit I knew that we were useless to each other. I have not seen her since then.

Meeting Bridget was not the only disturbing experience that first day. In the evening, several residents wanted to go to the pub. I agreed to join them, anxious to become part of the group as quickly as possible, although I dislike pubs and drink little alcohol. We clustered round two small tables, and I sensed that within the group were several smaller ones. I felt uncomfortable with them, unable to communicate, but desperate to belong. Next to me sat Alan, a skinny, balding man in his early thirties, who was coming to the end of his six-month stay. He looked tearful. I had decided already that I disliked him. His sad feelings, and pallid, unattractive face aroused no sympathy in me. I resented the attention he received from the others, who virtually ignored me, and became incensed at his conversation, most of which contained crude sexual innuendoes.

The following morning Alan began discussing his fears about his future, after he left Shipley Grange. I listened, interested in him because he had experienced what I had not: six months in a place which made me feel unwanted on my first day. He spoke about his ex-wife, who had left him, and another woman, with whom he had had a disastrous relationship. Much of what he said was unintelligible to me because he was continuing discussions which had developed during his months at the unit. He continued talking, interminably, it seemed to me, and then suddenly burst into tears. I resented his embarrassing display of weakness. Worried about voicing my thoughts, I said what I had been thinking for several minutes. 'If you treat women with the contempt you showed at the pub last night,' I said, 'it's not surprising that you have problems with them.' Through his tears he stared at me, and I knew that I had hurt him. The room fell ominously silent; not a word, not a murmur. I wanted to fade into the wallpaper, worried not so much by what I had said as by the disapproving looks from several of the residents. 'How could you say that!' one of them said angrily, 'Can't you see he's upset?' I could not explain that I felt upset too.

Alan probably never forgave me for what I said. During his remaining few weeks we smiled politely at each other, and unsuccessfully tried to talk. To me he was unwanted competition, and I looked forward to the day he was due to leave. What I could never forget or forgive was his continual tearfulness. I, too, often cried, but did so in the loneliness of my room, in the early hours of the morning, when nobody could know.

One of my greatest fears before I joined the unit was that I might have to share a bedroom. There were five in the house, only two of which were singles. I managed to move into one of these the day I arrived. It helped me survive those first days, and the weeks and months which followed. I felt comforted knowing that, however wretched I felt, I could always escape, eventually, to my private domain, where I could pretend that I was alone and untouchable. Untouchable was how I wanted to be. Seeing and hearing the other residents' daily turmoil made me determined never to break down in front of them. I wanted to prove what I was: strong.

I began looking after others, as I had looked after Bridget. I wanted to know all that went on at the unit. I wanted to be the one people would come to in their distress – and they came, even if I had to force them. I felt attracted to several residents, all women, and they confided in me many of their deepest fears and problems, often ones which they were too frightened to discuss at group meetings. I relished the secretiveness of those confidences, and the sense of power and control which grew within me. Once Alan left I believed that I had become the unopposed leader, which made me feel good and important. But it also made me feel bad when I had to face the consequences of 'being in charge'. Problems with individual residents began to emerge.

One of these had apparently begun during my early weeks at the unit. I say 'apparently', because I subsequently realized that it actually began when I attended the group vetting meeting, before I joined. The man who had accused me of being arrogant was Jim, whose yellow paint I eradicated from the group mural. Jim angered me more than Alan, and, while I was at Shipley Grange, I never properly understood why. In time I came to realize that we had both transferred childhood feelings to the other, but that knowledge was not enough to resolve our problem.

Ours was a complex relationship. I was drawn to him initially because he showed me most consideration on my first day, and seemed closest to me socially and intellectually. In his early thirties, he was tall and fair-haired, with a ginger-brown beard, and sad eyes which often glared furiously at his chosen foe. And for five months he glared at me. Initially, I felt like an innocent victim, unable to understand what I had done to upset him. After our early skirmishes he always apologized for his outbursts. When I understood that behind his raging violence cowered an impotent apologist, I learned how to get my revenge. Sometimes we called an uneasy truce and for a day or two pretended that we liked each other. Then he was gentle, kind and funny. But beneath that veneer lay a depth of hatred and terror which manifested itself in alarming and surprising ways.

Residents constantly broke the acting-out rule, usually adopting individual roles[4] which we thought would protect us from the threat of attack. Jim was as predictable as the rest of us; he offered sympathy to others, and expected it to be reciprocated. When I failed to meet his expectation, which meant almost every time I talked to him in group meetings, he visibly shrank from me, his body sinking into a hopeless bundle, his eyes blinking rapidly. Alan cried buckets; Jim serviced reservoirs. Great streams of tears poured down his cheeks into his beard, and he would burst out, 'Oh, God! I wish I was two years old and somebody would look after me!' Some of the women did; others, the ones I got on with more easily, understood his fears, but resented his weakness. I had never seen a man openly display such emotional incompetence. I despised him. The constant, tearful proof of his incapability made me feel more confident and secure. Jim was our 'baby'. I intentionally provoked him. I exercised an authority over him which, in our confusion, satisfied both our expectations. He needed me to threaten him, because that convinced him of his own vulnerability. I wanted him to be 'baby'. It made me feel stronger. Of the numerous conflicts which erupted between us, two come immediately to mind because they made me doubt profound beliefs I had about myself.

The first occurred in the early days, when, during a group meeting, he burst into another familiar, tearful, self-pitying rage, but not one directed at me at that moment. He had been talking in what seemed to me to be code language, and I was angry that something was being said which I didn't understand. 'If only I wasn't as I am,' he moaned between choking. 'How can I ever lead a normal life? I hate going to clubs to meet people.' Suddenly, I realized with a shock that I understood. I was furious that it had taken me more than a fortnight to make the discovery. Knowing that I had deciphered his code, and aware that most of the group except me knew already, I asked him if he was a homosexual, trying to sound casual and calm. 'Yes!' he snapped at me, his eyes reflecting hatred and fear. Unexpectedly, Stuart, who had a worrying ability to turn my comments about other people back upon myself, said 'Why did you ask him that?' 'I just wondered,' I replied weakly, sensing that I was now the centre of attention, but in a way I had not planned. 'Do you need to know everything?' he continued, and I knew that I could not escape. 'Instead of analysing everybody else,' he went on, 'why don't you start admitting your own needs?' His words had a familiar sound. He had said something similar to Bridget when she condemned her mother. My attack had backfired. I was being criticized and made to look a fool, and did not know what he meant.

Where that conversation might have led I could not then imagine, but Jim interrupted angrily, accusing me of despising him for being queer — the word he always used about himself. I denied the accusation. That morning Stuart obviously felt the time had come to make me more involved with myself. 'How do you feel about Jim's homosexuality?' he wanted to know. 'So long as he doesn't involve me, I don't care,' I retorted sarcastically. 'Then why are you so angry?' Val asked. Thankfully, it was 10.30 and the meeting ended. I told Jim, while we drank our coffee, that I had not meant to upset him. 'I know you didn't,' he replied, and we both felt better.

I went into the garden and stretched out on the grass. I knew that I did feel disturbed at what I had learned about Jim, and so, when we reassembled, I immediately raised the subject again, saying that I felt confused, and didn't understand why. Jim was furious at my renewed attack, although I could not have admitted then that that was what it was. 'How do you feel about homosexuals?' someone repeated. 'Well, rather like a father who says to his daughter, "I can't stop you going out with a black man, but don't ever bring one into my house."' Those words came out spontaneously. Some laughed, others sucked in their breath, as they had done when I made my accusation against Alan and his treatment of women. I knew from Jim's lowered head and shamed look that no matter what social or intellectual similarities we shared, our enmity had been cemented. My confusion became worse. I had reversed everything I had ever said about homosexuals. Since my teens I had met them through business connections in my work, and thought of them as different, but not unacceptable. Now I was aware that I resented 'them' deeply; and, what was worse, I had compounded my contradiction by using a racist analogy. It felt like another nail in a personal coffin of lost self-confidence. It did not occur to me then that I would have attacked anybody, given the opportunity. That morning it happened to be Jim.

The second example of conflicts between the two of us was a physical one, and occurred during a psychodrama session. I could never decide which I feared more, psychodrama or art therapy; both, being non-verbal, left me far more defenceless than when I could hide behind my words. Psychodrama was the physical acting out of feelings, the only approved and controlled acting out formally sanctioned. It took many forms, usually involving moving about within the meeting room, temporarily cleared of furniture. Like art therapy, we selected our games by majority vote. One of the games that afternoon was acting out feelings.

Each member chose his own feeling, and for ten minutes we were expected to behave as we felt when experiencing it. I cannot recall what my feeling was; it may have been anger or jealousy, or some equally destructive force; nor do I know Jim's. We had all been performing, and I found myself next to him. He glared at me. I'll sort you out, I thought. We grasped hold of each other, and a physical battle of strength began. He tried to move away, but I wanted the encounter. I pulled at his arm and he quickly responded, pushing me from him. I moved closer. Then he advanced, pushing me. He was strong enough to hurt me, and by then clearly wanted to. Our game had become vicious. We were not playing, but openly displaying our dislike of each other. I felt frightened and angry, but continued pushing, harder and harder. What he did to me seemed unimportant. All I was interested in was winning the battle. We hurt each other, neither of us prepared to retreat, each of us exerting increasing force. Abruptly, as quickly as our fight had begun, it ceased. He moved to another part of the room, and I was alone, convinced once more of his cowardice. I won, or thought I won, not because I was physically stronger, but because Jim gave in. It was what we both wanted. I think that had he emerged as the winner it would have destroyed his personal conviction that he could never be 'first'.

For me it was an empty victory. Of course, I was delighted to have once more established my power over him; but that brief reward quickly changed to punishment when I realized that I had enjoyed the violence. I resented his retreat. It stopped my outflow of feeling. The idea that I wanted to be violent came as one more shock; another contradiction. I had believed that violence disgusted me. Why, then, had I enjoyed it? The answer to that and other questions remained hidden.

At no time were there more than five men in the group. I detested them all, although for a brief period I thought that I liked the youngest one, Billy. As with so many of the group relationships, we demanded or were given roles which obscured our true emotions. When Billy arrived at Shipley Grange we promptly established our particular relationship. To me, Billy was a deprived kid; to him, I was 'authority'. I listened to him, advised him, angered him and supported him: I never discussed my problems with him. I thought that I had heard enough horror stories by then not to be shocked at personal revelations, but Billy managed to confound me. 'Can I talk to you?' he asked me one night when we were alone. 'There's something I must tell you.'

Billy wanted to stay in the group, but, more than any other resident, was in danger of being thrown out, because of his complete inability to begin the hard task of self-understanding. To prove his need, I suppose, he had decided to 'come clean', as he put it. 'Coming clean' to Billy meant telling stories, occasionally true, to gain group sympathy. That night Billy admitted shamefully a long list of lies, either of commision or omission, which he had told or not told the group. 'Don't just tell me,' I said angrily, furious at the deceptions, 'tell the group.' 'Oh, that's not what I wanted to talk about,' he replied. He was upset and had difficulty in continuing. Unlike my feelings for Jim, I felt sorry for Billy, and he knew it. He told me that I was the only one he could trust. So, like father and son, we sat on a sofa, and gave each other what we wanted.

The group knew that he had been in trouble with the law over a sexual offence — a relatively mild case of assault as far as he was concerned; and we knew that he was a glue sniffer. We knew, too, that he had stolen a motorbike, failed to comply with a Community Service Order, attempted to seduce one of the female residents, and wetted his bed most nights. Nothing else that he could tell me would come as a surprise, I thought. I was wrong. He described in detail how, at his mother's boyfriend's request, he had had sexual intercourse with her several months previously, the three of them sharing the experience. As an afterthought, he added that he had also done it with his three sisters. According to Billy, he had first 'pulled' his eldest sister when she was thirteen and he eleven. It seemed quite reasonable to him that he should progress methodically through the others. What disturbed him most about his sisters was that the eldest, now married, refused to see him. Apart from his anger at her, his main concern was whether he should tell the group.

I felt delighted that he had confided in me. Another first! It confirmed how necessary I was to the group. I needed that reassurance to compensate for the insecurity I felt when chinks in my armour made me feel vulnerable and weak, and got 'caught out' as Stuart explained. But Billy gave me something else which I did not understand at the time. Hearing his confidence fulfilled other needs. I liked the secrecy of talking together away from the other residents. His particular confidence added a sense of drama and excitement to my life. Reluctantly, I told him that he had to tell not only me but the rest of the group.

The following morning he repeated his confession, neither of us mentioning our talk the night before. Hearing it for the second time, I believed that, for once, he was telling the truth. I felt remote. Incest, like homosexuality, was an unknown experience, and there I was, unexpectedly involved. 'Why am I with these people?' I continually asked myself. Billy, meanwhile, received no direct response from anyone which seemed to offer him consolation, or a greater likelihood of remaining with us. He had launched his most powerful weapon. It gained him attention for a week or so, but we became immune to the personal horror stories which emerged from time to time. We had to give the group more than lurid entertainment.

Unwittingly, his confession acted as a catalyst. Suddenly, personal sexual feelings, until then seldom discussed, became important. Before he left – his was one of the midnight escapes – two of the five women residents described brutal rapes and assaults, none of which had been admitted previously. One of them had been attacked by her father when she was fourteen, and for seven years she had said nothing about it to anybody. In the group, she relived the experience, during psychodrama role reversal games, crisis meetings and prolonged and fearful nightmares. (She, too, spoke to me before confronting the group.) She received help because, unlike Billy, she wanted to be responsible for herself. He wanted the unit to become his surrogate home. When I finally understood that, my sympathy disappeared, and he ceased to be a 'son'. Briefly, we competed against each other. In that role he was as unwelcome as Alan, Jim or Stuart.

My relationships with all the men who attended the unit were hostile and disturbing. With the women, the days and nights were very different. Problems arose with them, but they provided opportunities for comfort and friendship which often helped me overcome periods of intense personal loneliness. This preference for female companionship was not a new experience: I had never found it easy to relax in male company, and had not yet begun to understand why.

The women in the group when I joined soon left; one was voted out for non-participation; another had completed her six months; and Bridget left after it became obvious that she was unable to exist without drugs. The first 'new' woman I met was Cathy, who came along to one of our vetting meetings as a prospective resident. She arrived with her parents, both of whom seemed anxious to talk to us before the meeting. They were worried about their daughter, they explained. She was so miserable, and becoming a disturbing influence on her brothers and sister. They spoke softly, the father cracking the odd joke or two; the mother, well-dressed and calm, apparently in charge. We were impressed. Not many parents took such an interest in their children. Their daughter sat on the other side of the living room, silent and ignored. Her parents wanted to join the meeting and were surprised when they were told that they could not. They waited in the living room.

Cathy was skinny rather than slim, colourfully dressed and heavily made-up with face powder, red lipstick and dark eye-shadow. She had short, auburn hair which emphasized her broad forehead and prominent cheek bones. Dark, round eyes threatened us angrily, like great cannon balls. Stuart explained how the unit was organized, before inviting her to tell us about herself. I felt anxious: it was my first vetting meeting as a resident, and I realized that her future could depend upon how I voted. We waited for her to speak.

She sat stiffly in her chair, her arms clenching its sides, her eyes aimed at the blank, cream wall opposite. She crossed her legs, and began incessantly tapping one foot on the carpet. We waited impatiently for her to start talking, but she remained silent, as though we did not exist. Stuart broke into the silence. 'Do you find it difficult to begin?' he asked. 'What d'you want to know?' she demanded aggressively. 'About you,' he replied calmly. 'There's nothing to tell,' she responded, her foot pummelling the floor. Eventually, after considerable prompting and encouragement from several of us, she began speaking. I had two instant reactions: she was poorly educated, and astonishingly articulate. When she spoke, she spoke clearly and passionately, and each word, including her grand vocabulary of foul language, sounded essential to what she was saying. There was no ambiguity, no uncertainty — and no stopping her.

She told us that she was nineteen, had left home recently after terrible family rows, but that, as a result of severe *anorexia nervosa,* had been forced to return. The eldest child, she had two brothers and a sister, all of whom she hated. But not as much, she said ferociously, as she hated her parents. I thought of the two caring people waiting anxiously a few yards from us, and said that I was surprised. 'They do that to be liked,' she said angrily, 'all they want is to get me out of the house. My GP said that I should come here, and the f......cow couldn't make the appointment quick enough.'

Cathy reminded me of Bridget, who sat beside me, and immediately supported the younger woman. Listening to Cathy's volley of personal crimes – violence, hatred of family, attempts at suicide, and others – I could imagine Bridget speaking as she might have, were it not for the drugs. After her initial outburst, Cathy spoke reluctantly, and had to be wheeled out of her angry silences. But her anger diminished slightly as time passed, and her voice quietened. Once or twice she smiled and her eyes shone brightly. When, in response to a particularly long silence, someone asked her if she had anything to say, she answered hesitantly for the first time. 'I'd like to come,' she admitted, 'but what's the point, 'cos I'm mad.' Further questioning elucidated that she was not quite sure what she meant by mad, except that she threw things and went wild. She looked unconvinced when Stuart explained that mad was just a word which by itself had little meaning. Unusually for him, he enlarged considerably on what he had said. 'I don't think you're quote mad quote,' he told her, 'but I agree that you have some problems to work through.' She was unanimously voted in. (Most applicants were accepted at vetting meetings, sometimes with a few no's. Provided we recognized some common problems, they seemed safe.)

Cathy joined a few weeks later. She was the first resident in whom I felt able to confide a few, a very few, of my own feelings; and, as well as the bad experiences, we enjoyed laughing and joking together. Unexpectedly, I had formed the nucleus of a sub-group, one which was to become a powerful and, at times, destructive force within the main group.

Barbara was in her mid-twenties and worked as a commercial artist. She had joined the group some months earlier, but after three days had left, storming out of an art session when another resident criticized her work. Now, suicidal and hopelessly insecure, she had asked to see Stuart privately, wanting to return. He explained this to us before she attended her second vetting meeting. What he had not explained was that she was gorgeous. Dark-haired, soft brown eyes, slim and shapely, and very demure; but not too demure, for she regularly flashed delightful smiles which set my mind racing in directions which would have broken at least one of the unit's rules. Whatever her problems, I knew, as I saw her swaying into the drive, many yards away, that my vote was cast already. I felt a surge of sexual excitement and expectation. Within two days of her joining the unit I ensured that my secret hopes would not be fulfilled.

Barbara told us, in her quiet, soft voice, that she knew that she had made a mistake when she left. She recounted years of emotional upheaval, including drug addiction, two abortions and what, for her, was the worst problem of all – her bingeing; an uncontrollable desire to stuff herself with food, any food, until she made herself sick and ill. Her relationships with men had been uncontrollable too. She was convinced that she would never find a man who would love her, or of whom she could be worthy.

I remembered that meeting, and her provocative smiles, on her second day at the unit. She had gone upstairs for a bath after the evening meal. At about 9 o'clock she came downstairs into the living room, wearing a short, sexy nightdress, her shapely legs bared to mid-thigh. Ostensibly, she had 'only popped in to collect a book'; but clearly, in my mind, she was saying something quite different. She popped out as quickly as she had popped in, leaving us all, in various ways, gasping. The other women in the room were shocked, and 'tut-tutted', a couple of them presumably jealous of the dazzling feminine vision which had floated in and out of the room. Billy whistled, and said loudly that he 'could fancy a bit of that', which didn't endear him to the other women, and Jim politely mentioned that 'probably there were no clean dressing gowns in the linen cupboard'. I said that if there were none, she had probably hidden them, and I started talking to Cathy. I was furious.

I could not hide my anger from myself, but took care that it was not apparent to the others. In some way I felt that Barbara had betrayed me; that she had understood desires which I believed I had kept secret; and that, by displaying herself so blatantly, she had damaged something of value to me. Alone in my room later, I could not forgive her for what she had done. The following morning my bad feelings towards her felt more vicious than when I had gone to bed.

Nine-fifteen. The meeting begins. As usual, an uncomfortable silence, while we hesitate to say what we feel. But that morning I wanted to be certain that nobody would start before I did. I took a deep breath. 'Barbara,' I began, 'why did you come into the living room last night wearing that sexy night-dress?' She gave me a surprised look, and Val, the nurse, smiled. I was pleased to see Stuart change position and study the floor, a sure sign that he was content. 'Sexy?' Barbara said ingenuously. 'Was it?' Conscious of my rising fury, I intended to launch a calm but accusatory attack. What I actually said was, 'No wonder you're always in trouble with men. If you ask me, you're a cock-teaser.' She stared at me in horror. At the same moment as she flushed and blurted, 'Oh, not again!' one of the other women asked me what a cock-teaser was, and Cathy roared with laughter.

I was once again accused of being brutal and unfeeling. In the meeting I remained unrepentant, but when I saw two women trying to comfort Barbara, crying hysterically during the morning break, I regretted what I had said, although I knew that it was true. I also felt upset, but my outward show of calm self-control fooled the other residents.

I expected that our relationship would develop into another disaster, but the reverse occurred. We often talked and confided in each other, but while on the surface we spoke of important events taking place in the unit, we never touched on our feelings, our true feelings towards each other. Often we were physically close, and once when she had a frenzied screaming fit I was the only resident who could calm her. Sometimes we went to a local pub for a drink. Not until a week or so before she left did she ever admit anything, and then to my embarrassment and surprise, she did it during a group meeting, saying quietly that for some time she had had sexual thoughts about me. I liked hearing that. Grudgingly, I admired her because she had the courage to say what I could not. The day she left she accused me and another resident, Linda, of having an affair.

Living with the women was frustrating, but I felt more at ease with them. I was married: they were mostly either single or separated. I needed female company. But encouraging it, I became deeply involved in their personal problems, always willingly to begin with, sometimes resentfully as the weeks passed and their problems, like mine, seemed unalterable and oppressive. I think about them a lot, and often miss them . . . some of them.

There were others in the group, with most of whom I had furious and bitter rows; but few left impressions as strong as those residents I have written about, except Linda, whose place belongs elsewhere in this book.

Earlier, I mentioned sub-groups. They were as changeable and unpredictable as the weather. I discovered that each sub-group had precise, and sometimes subtle, functions. There were short-term sub-groups, sharing a particular common experience, such as drug addiction or bed-wetting; but these were less influential than those which had as their fundamental relationship experiences rooted deep in early childhood and home life.

Jim, Barbara and Julie, a divorced woman with two estranged children, formed one of these sub-groups. The three of them believed that they had come from stable homes, where their parents never quarrelled, and gave them constant love and protection. As children, they explained, in remarkably similar accounts, animosity and violence did not exist. Barbara attempted to prove her point one day. She told us that the worst thing she could remember was the 'bath-cleaning problem'. Her mother insisted that Vim was best, and always left it in the bathroom, but her father disagreed, and, as often as her mother brought the Vim, so he went out and replaced it with Ajax. 'But they never argued about it,' she said. Barbara, like Jim, was determined to refute any suggestion that home life had not been beautiful and idyllic, at least until her teens. When the rest of us doubted this, those in that particular sub-group accused us of trying to destroy their lives, or add to their problems. One woman gave us an ultimatum: 'If you don't stop criticizing my home life, I'll leave.' She did, after three weeks.

The other main sub-group which evolved during my months at Shipley Grange was the one which began with Cathy and myself, and subsequently included Linda. We shared a different experience. Chaos reigned in our child-hoods; that is, identifiable chaos. To us, the story of the bath-cleaner, and the accounts of peaceful domesticity, sounded suspicious. 'If your Mum and Dad was so bloody marvel-lous,' Cathy asked one day, 'what are you doing here?' As usual, when she spoke, she fired a deadly missile.

A memorable example of acting out the differences between these two warring parties took place one evening in November, and during the following morning.

Cathy, Linda and myself used to stay up late, long after most of the others had gone to bed. An unspoken, but understood, routine developed over a period of several weeks. Those not in our group were made to feel unwelcome when we shared our social time together. That evening the three of us were chatting and unsettled, discussing the meanings of our latest paintings. Suddenly, Linda threw a cushion at me. I threw it back. Cathy joined in. More cushions flew through the air, followed by books, pencils, fruit and anything else that came to hand. It was 1 o'clock in the morning and we were laughing loudly and chasing each other noisily around the room.

We became more adventurous, and began moving the furniture around, saying how fed up we were with the old arrangement. Chairs were stacked on sofas, rugs on the table, lamps on the rugs. We turned on the record player and Neil

Diamond joined the group. Soon the room was in turmoil, and we were adding to the noise and chaos with loud, uncontrolled peals of delight. Nothing but the fitted carpets and curtains remained in their original place. In the centre of the room was a massive heap of furniture. We were sprinkling pieces of a jig-saw puzzle over the mess when the door opened slightly and Jim peered anxiously through the narrow gap.

'What on earth's going on down here?' he asked. 'The noise woke me up. What's happening?' His worried frown added to our amusement, and I stared at him seriously, trying not to laugh. 'Don't worry, Jim, it's only Linda having a fit.' He looked balefully at her and said, 'This can't go on, Linda, you'll have to do something about it. Look! Look what you've done to this room. I can't take any more, I'm going!' And he rushed out of the room, hearing our roars behind him.

Jim's intervention brought us back to reality, and we tidied up, made hot chocolate drinks, and went to bed, still laughing.

The following morning. Nine-fifteen. Silence, briefly. Jim glared furiously at everyone before staring at Stuart. 'I'm leaving the group,' he announced, 'but before I go I want to know what was going on downstairs last night.' He described to the rest of the group the chaos, noise and explanations which he had encountered the night before. Some of the other residents complained that they had woken up, but had been frightened to go downstairs. 'That sounds like an angry act,' Stuart commented. Looking at the three accused, he asked us why we were angry. We pleaded not guilty, explaining that we had not been angry, we had had some fun, that was all. We said very little because the more we tried to speak, the more we were convulsed by laughter. 'They're all crazy,' yelled Jim; and the others in his group, those who had not shared the fun, listened, nodding their heads in disapproval, not understanding that an act of such blatant physical enormity had been enjoyable. After the meeting, Cathy, Linda and I were furious. 'Bet they wished they'd done it,' said Cathy, and we curled up in sympathetic sub-group laughter.

Jim did not leave that day. He, like the rest of us, needed to belong to a group – any group which would have him.

Enemy forces – secret agents

In this chapter I have tried to describe the scene, as I saw and felt it, when, for the first time, I had an opportunity to meet and confront other people who, like myself, did not know how to accept their family, work colleagues and other groups who had come into, and often passed out of, their lives. We knew that most of our personal relationships were chaotic. What we did not understand was that we each had a stranger to confront – a shrouded figure whom we suspected, but could not identify, as the creator of this chaos.

The strangers were with us constantly; in organized, formal unit meetings, during free time in the week, and in our individual outside lives. In the group we were given the choice – did we want to become acquainted with our personal stranger, or not? I had made my choice before I joined the unit – or thought I had. But my stranger had not yet decided whether or not he wanted to be part of the group – perhaps, yes, no, sometimes, or never? Therapy seemed to highlight many things – I tried to remember to call them feelings and behaviour – especially distrust; and the most distrusted among us were the strangers. Through organized therapies we suffered and began to recognize emotional turmoil which, on most days, had several of us convinced that we could take no more. During my six months, fifteen residents were at one time or another members of the group; of those, only four stayed for the full period. One or two survived less than a month, most left within three. (We were nursed by five staff, only one of whom, Stuart, was with the group throughout my stay.)

Despite being hurt in our war-games, we needed each other: the confrontations were between our strangers, our secret agents, and most of us thought that we were willing to find out what we could about them. There were other, more comforting bonds, which I began to feel after a few weeks. As each resident's personal history emerged, I recognized that the most potent force we shared was the disruptive experiences in our teenage years. But I was mistaken. Slowly, as we delved more deeply into our behaviour and feelings, I discovered that what brought us together may have seemed one thing, but was really something else.

Residents arrived at the unit at a time in their lives when momentous and destructive behaviour made some form of help inevitable. What none of us realized in our first days and weeks was that our latest crisis was a mere scratch compared with the deep scars which had been inflicted at a time when we were too young to understand, but old enough to be affected by what had happened to us. Jim, the unit's 'baby', verbally expressed our real bond most accurately: 'Oh, God!' he said when feeling helpless, 'I wish I was two years old and somebody would look after me!' Whether or not we could admit it, his cry was for us all.

Intellectually, I grasped the significance of this quite quickly. I tried to inject this knowledge into my mind, believing that the fix would enable me to control my emotions, my stranger. The Wednesday afternoon when I destroyed our group mural created no new major problem within the group, except to the extent that I permitted it to. But that act of destruction was, for me, a turning point at the unit, and from then on I kept an irregular diary, in which I tried to record what I was learning, slowly and painfully, about myself. I thought that this diary was a clever idea: I could not understand that it was an effective way of isolating my stranger from the group, from any group, from anyone, even from myself.

I shied away from discussing many of my emotions and confused feelings. It was too painful and too hard to bare myself continually in front of others. Invariably, before I could begin to understand what I was doing, and why, I had to be attacked, more often by the staff members of the unit than by the residents. Staff were there to make everything better, I reasoned. Residents had their own problems, so how could they possibly help me overcome mine? When my secrets were revealed, I discovered to my horror that preconceived ideas I had of myself were at best distorted, and at worst, completely false. These public trials hurt, badly; but they were also exciting and rewarding. Afterwards, when alone and frightened by what I had experienced, I could make more sense of what had happened; but I felt that I needed to be protected from the group before I could assess my new-found understanding. My diary was controllable. If I wrote it all down, I thought, it will be there for ever, like a personal Bible, providing me with emotional Guidance and Faith.

That was another mistake. The secrets I committed to paper were true, I believed, and must be what I had to change in my personality if I was to survive the outside world. I wanted to let my stranger in: what I was doing was keeping people out. I did not realize that understanding aspects of my behaviour was one thing; living with feelings was something very different. Nevertheless, what I wrote then has proved helpful in later years, in the way that a French phrase book is useful to glance through before holidaying in France, after an absence of a few years. I had not recognized that intellectual understanding was a false peace. That realization came much later, long after I left the unit, when I began my current 'one-to-one' intensive therapy.

The most difficult secret I had to share at Shipley Grange was the admission that I was closer to the 'baby' than I wanted to believe. How could I, a mature man, a husband and father, an ambitious careerist, be a baby? How could my stranger still be in short pants? I worked hard, as hard as when pursuing my career, to grasp this reality. I discussed it with the group, convinced that if I discussed it intelligently, I would grow up. Secretly, I believed that I had solved my problems. If I armed myself with my newly-acquired intelligence, and wrote it down neatly, I would be better equipped to fight on. Not for one day at the unit did I believe that my war had ended. I just needed to strengthen my defences from invaders, I reasoned.

In my mind, I translated the war into an academic exercise. Determined to come top of the class, as I had regularly at school, I struggled to learn each new lesson perfectly. I had to understand why I despised Jim, feared Stuart, missed Val when she left, spent hours trying to protect Bridget, had to be the leader. There were new lessons to learn each day, and through the privacy of my diary I thought that I had become an excellent student.

My secret intelligence was so secret that I succeeded in deceiving not only members of the group, but myself. Unaware of what was happening, I created an armoury of disinformation, and most of it misled its author more than its intended victims. It was not that what I wrote was inaccurate. Most of it was impressively *right*. It simply did not alter the way I felt.

However, there was one fundamental lesson I could not learn. It led me into tortuous emotional battles during those months; the same battles which all residents had to fight, and which so many refused to. It never occurred to me that I was one of the refuseniks. We all came to recognize our stranger, whatever we called him, and showered him with descriptive feelings – hate, fear, sadness, and many more; but, because we were constantly under attack, we became battle-weary. We needed time to recover. When our feelings were at their most raw, and our memories most vivid, we collapsed, not from today's or yesterday's battle, but from the earliest childhood battles we could remember. When Jim's plaintive plea to be a two-year-old made me exasperated, I was denying what I later admitted; that my emotions, the ones which have proved and continue to prove most destructive, are those of a helpless child, wounded and isolated, screaming for attention. Was that another mistake? Either I was or I was not a child or a man. Which? The screams were still there; but I was forty years old. I had to be one or the other, I decided.

My stranger and I, attacked in the group by day, and comforted at night by my diary, joined forces, and invaded my past.

3 Inside the volcano

Introduction

The early years of my life were seldom out of my mind before or after I joined the psychotherapy unit. Most days I recalled bitter memories and miserable, confused feelings. Occasionally, I glowed, mentally and emotionally, when a happy childhood memory warmed me, like a sudden ray of brilliant sunshine. At Shipley Grange I examined my bad feelings with savage intensity, wanting to understand how they affected my behaviour. This concentration on bitterness and misery was so wearying and upsetting that I, and the others, craved for moments of easy relief. We wanted to forget the badness; but it refused to go away. Sometimes, when I could not cope with my unhappiness, I persuaded myself that I was exaggerating how miserable I felt; and for an hour, or perhaps a day, I believed that my life was not the awful failure I normally thought it to be. I walked jauntily through the hospital gardens, laughed a lot and felt elated that my days with the group were proving successful. Then, unable to escape from the realities which emerged through the group, I felt tormented by our talking, painting, drama and social experiences. My bad feelings exploded, and my self-deceptive cheerfulness crumbled into a small heap of suspicious memories.

Time bomb

Another Wednesday, another shock – art therapy once again opened up my feelings with the precision, if not the delicacy, of a surgeon's knife. I painted *parents*.

The difference between the unmistakable images in other members' paintings, and my own, intrigued and disturbed me. Their *parents* identified two recognizable people, a mum and a dad, usually with the group member appearing prominently in the picture. Cathy's crayon drawing, for example, depicted a high brick wall, slanted across the centre of her sheet of paper. She stood belligerently behind one side of the wall, unseen by her parents, wielding a vicious knife which pierced the protective bricks; on the other side the knife had changed into a deadly, two-pronged fork, thrust into the stomachs of Mum and Dad. Jim painted an idyllic family: his parents and their two children held hands in front of a modern, detached suburban house; a neat lawn edged by pretty flowers, and a car parked on the drive completed the picture. A thick, black cross daubed angrily on the loving group obliterated his fantasy. Cathy's and Jim's predictable fury comforted me: they felt as enraged as I did. In contrast, I resented Val's picture. Hers was a happy, humorous, gaily-coloured scene of washing swaying on a line, and smiling faces, unthreatened by murderous knives or black destruction. Damn her! I thought, cursing well-adjusted therapists, and wishing that I, too, could paint and speak cheerfully about my parents. Visually, all the paintings except mine had one similarity: nobody had to ask what they meant. I wondered why, the day we painted *parents*, mine was different, showing no clearly identifiable people.

For a few seconds after we agreed to paint *parents* I could not decide how to portray them. In my hand I tightly clenched several brushes, each dripping with one of my favourite, vivid-coloured paints. I thought of my mother, and drew a big, black circle, with a small opening at the top, and then began stabbing quickly inside the circle. As my thoughts merged with my feelings, and the paints merged on the paper,

I extended the small blotches of paint into long, curling, coloured fingers. Twisting brush strokes swept upwards, like flames from a fire, mingling at the top, where they escaped and licked the circle's outer rim. When I had filled the circle with my scarlet, orange, purple and red, I thought of my father, and overpainted a small area at the bottom with a dab or two of pale blue. I secretly named my painting *time bomb*, and rejoined the group.

As often happened during art therapy, I felt that I had lost control of myself, like the day I destroyed the group mural. I tried to act calmly when I stared at my *time bomb*, but felt angry and upset. Initially, I directed my silent anger at the group. Why had they drawn such simple pictures, which required no explanations; and why were they so unfeeling that they asked me what mine meant? 'My black circle is my parents,' I said reluctantly, 'the large fiery part inside is my mother; the little bit of blue at the bottom is my father; and the flame escaping at the top is me.'

Despite feeling frustrated that I had to explain my abstract pictures, I flattered myself that mine were the most imaginative; and, if I understood what I had painted, I enjoyed being able to decide how much, or how little, I was prepared to divulge. But when I intentionally withheld part of the meaning and nobody probed me further, I felt rejected, angry – and very lonely.

The shock I felt after completing my painting was not that it illustrated the turmoil I associated with my parents – I had known that for too long; what terrified me was that, conscious of my anger, not only towards my mother and father, but towards all members of the group, I wanted to punish everybody, to hurt them as badly as I was hurting. I wanted to explode as surely as my time bomb had exploded; but I continued acting calmly, hoping that nobody would suspect how enraged I felt. At the same time I wanted someone to tell me that they liked my painting. The colliding and intertwining colours looked as attractive and dramatic as an exciting firework display. It isn't *all* bad, I thought.

By the time I decided that I wanted to tell the group about

these feelings it was too late; the meeting had ended. I walked hurriedly from the room, feeling angry because I needed more time to explain, but there was nobody to listen; and nobody to punish, except myself.

I wanted to overcome my difficulty of talking about my feelings, but I did not trust my words, or my listeners. I knew that I frequently spouted gobbledegook during talking meetings. My words sounded false and unreal when I heard them, as if somebody else was speaking. Often, I felt bored and remote, and spoke in a tedious monotone. I wanted to escape from this withdrawn verbal barrier, but needed help. When it was offered I resented the intrusion into my private world. Once, after I completed what I thought to be an intelligent analysis of a resident's problem, Stuart thanked me sarcastically for my lecture. I felt humiliated, and angry, that my own distrust of what I had said had been perceived and criticized. When I felt the unreal, distant *me* speaking I wanted to shout at my listeners that it wasn't me they were hearing, and why the hell didn't they understand! When the real *me* exploded through my paintings, and members of the group asked for explanations of what they meant, I wanted to yell out that they should leave me alone – it was none of their business what *my* paintings meant. I felt that I slid perpetually along an uncomfortable see-saw, from one contradictory *me* to another, isolated when I withdrew behind my controlled words, and threatened when my uncontrolled paintings could not be hidden. 'Getting in touch with your feelings' – the unit's official anthem – sounded like a suspicious rule in a game devised by therapists to keep themselves employed.

Time bomb increased my contradictory suspicions. It should have been a painting of my parents, but I stared at it and saw myself. They are me, and I am them, I thought. The riotous colour occupying most of the space and flaring out from the top is myself out of control; the unmoving, pale blue dot is myself in a state of withdrawal. What a crazy jumble of agitated chaos! What is real, and what is unreal, and why do I think of myself as two people? Suddenly, I was thirteen: that was when real and unreal became separate and distinct conscious entities; when I thought that I was mad, after returning home from an enjoyable week at school camp.

When the secondary school which I attended in central London was incorporated within the state education system as a boys-only establishment, it retained several unusual facilities, legacies from appreciative, and wealthy, past scholars. One inheritance was land in Berkshire, on gentle slopes lapping the river Thames, where a school camp was organized every summer term. Each school year spent one week there, and in June 1955 I went enthusiastically on my second trip.

During study periods we mapped out land surveys, described field explorations of wildlife, measured rainfall and temperatures, and generally did as many things as possible to contrast with the cement-based environment of central London. In our leisure time we rambled across undulating and scented countryside, and sang round night-time fires, clasping steaming mugs of watery cocoa. We tried energetically to erect, and then re-erect, tents which collapsed; and tried even more energetically to escape from latrine-digging squads. Masters, spiky and aloof at school, exchanged scholastic gowns for coloured shirts and short trousers, and were transformed into kids not much older than ourselves. It was an exciting week in the school calendar; a holiday treat during term-time.

When I returned home from the second year's camp I felt unwell, and missed what remained of the summer term. On the day school broke up for the holidays, two friends came to see me. They hovered at the front door, wanting to know what had been wrong with me. 'I've had 'flu,' I lied, disturbed by their visit. 'Got some bad news for you,' one of them said sorrowfully, 'you're not going into Arts.' I tried to hide my shame.

Because of the school's high entry standards only one-third of each new year's applicants were accepted. The ninety boys were divided into three forms, where, for the first two years, we all studied the same curriculum. In year three, my next school year, we were streamed, into General, Sciences or Arts. Academically, I performed reasonably well during my first four terms at the school, placed usually between fifth and tenth in the form order. In my fifth and sixth terms, critical to the following year's streaming, I plummeted to seventeenth, and then twenty-second position, in a class of twenty-eight. My friends had been streamed as I had hoped to be, in Arts; I was going into General, which I thought of as the school's educational rubbish tip. How could I have failed? What would people think of me?

From the day after I returned from school camp – a month before my humiliating academic catastrophe – I slept for unusually long periods, sometimes for most of each day and night. During the first week I rarely got out of bed, and never dressed. Strange, disturbing sensations confused me when I was awake: my bedroom looked unfamiliar; people's voices echoed when they spoke; the sound of my own voice seemed to come from several inches behind my head. Something I could not recognize separated me from my surroundings. I was frightened to leave my bedroom. My sister lingered at my bedside like an unwelcome stranger whom I did not want to know. Noises – traffic from the streets below or milk bottles rattling outside the nearby dairy – worried me. When our family doctor visited me he asked me to remove my pyjama top. I refused. When he tried to undo the buttons I pushed him away. My mother told me not to be silly.

We lived in an old and large Victorian house near Marble Arch. The ground floor and basement had been converted into a women's fashion boutique, run by my mother. My bedroom was three floors above. I lay in bed, wanting her to stop working far below, and come upstairs, so that I could tell her how strange I felt; but when she popped in to see me I pretended that I was asleep. In the evenings, when my father returned from his tailoring business, he came into my room, and, if I spoke, I heard my remote voice saying things which were not true. One evening he asked me what I'd been doing all day. 'Reading', I lied. I hadn't read a word: my books seemed as inaccessible as the people who kept troubling my rest, or the distant sounds from nearby streets.

At the end of the first week I stopped sleeping during the day and, feeling restless, needed to get up. Everything looked blurred. I felt that I was moving extraordinarily slowly, like an intruder lost in the darkness of my own home. Opening the wardrobe doors in my bedroom scared me, and I did not know why. Unable to decide what to wear, I walked round the house in pyjamas, spending most of my time in the living room, incessantly playing old seventy-eight records on a clockwork gramophone. I listened to Danny Kaye and Frankie Lane, hummed their cheerful songs, and kept bursting unexpectedly into tears. When I heard footsteps on the stairway I returned hurriedly to my bedroom, where I cried continually, hoping that nobody would hear me, but wanting somebody to understand that I felt peculiarly unhappy.

My favourite aunt came to see me. 'Why don't you get dressed,' she said, 'and we'll go to see a film?' I told her that I had seen every film in London, and she smiled at me. I heard my words, spoken by a voice I hardly recognized, but could not believe that I had uttered them. I had not been to the cinema for weeks, possibly months. And I never lied to my aunt. She asked me if I wanted to go out for tea: instead of replying I ran into her arms and cried. Later, my mother came upstairs from the shop, and I heard the two sisters whispering behind the door. I felt upset and frightened that I had lied, and expected to be told off by my mother, and shamed in front of my aunt.

By the end of the second week, I wanted to leave the house and walk to a nearby park, but after I started dressing I regretted my decision. Then I didn't. Then I did. I did not know what I wanted to do. Everything I did or thought of doing exhausted me. When I was dressed I worried that my clothes looked odd. Combing my hair, and looking at the bathroom mirror, I saw my face, but it belonged to a stranger.

My mother asked me to buy some meat, and gave me a £1 note. I felt happy to be walking into the sounds which had come from so far away when I had stayed in my room; but as soon as I left the house I was convinced that there was something unusual about the way I walked, and looked. People passed me on the pavement, and I believed that they knew that something was wrong with me. I felt pleased when I recognized the familiar zebra crossing and the local Underground station; and worried, because people seemed to rush past, trying to avoid banging into me. I strolled into the sunshine, half closing my eyes, thinking, 'Everybody's staring at me.'

I walked and thought in a foggy world which appeared to surround my body, and felt relieved when I returned home. My mother opened her hand for the change from the £1 note, and asked where I had put the meat. Her question confused me. What meat? She sounded angry when I told her that I hadn't been to the butcher's. She asked for the money. What money? I remembered that she had given me some money, but could not remember where it was. I searched through my pockets. So did my mother. She started shouting and accused me of stealing it, of buying sweets. I shouted that I had not stolen her money, or bought sweets. She told me that I would have to stand in front of her until I admitted the truth, but I kept repeating that I could not remember what I had done with her £1 note. She made me recount many times exactly where I had walked, who I had seen, which shops I had been into. I began crying, insisting that I hadn't been into any shops, and didn't know what had happened to the money. Then she told me to go to my room and 'wait till your father comes home'. When he did, I had to explain everything to him. Why wouldn't anybody believe that I had lost the money? They reminded me that years earlier I had stolen from them. Speaking softly, they told me that if I admitted the truth I would not be punished. I remained adamant. I had not stolen the money. I must have lost it. I wanted to be left alone, to escape to my bedroom and climb into bed.

Throughout their interminable inquisition I felt that part of me was standing in front of my mother and father, hearing, but not listening to, what they were saying, while another part of me was lost in a misty, empty place where I was completely alone. I knew that I had not stolen the money: why wouldn't they believe me? They must believe me, I kept telling myself, because I cannot let them know that during my strange walk, when everybody was staring at me, and I felt so odd, I reached the nearby canal, and tore the £1 note into shreds, and threw them on to the water. At times, facing them, I imagined that perhaps I *had* spent their money on sweets – surely I would not destroy a £1 note and throw it away?

Then, one morning, I woke up feeling refreshed and full of excitable energy. I wanted to dress quickly, and return immediately to school, to see my friends. Everything seemed normal. The frightening mist had disappeared.

My bedroom was untidy. I made my bed, examined and tidied cupboards, rearranged my books, and fingered my clothes, remembering how they had worried me. When I looked at the mirror, the stranger had vanished. I saw myself clearly, and wanted to cry out with pleasure. I asked my sister how I had been. She said that I had slept a lot and not spoken much. I felt relieved. Thank goodness she did not know. I felt happy – having a bath, washing my hair, choosing clothes – knowing that my sister did not realize that I had been mad. I stayed in my bedroom most of each day, counting and sorting through my stamp collection, and reading voraciously. I could not believe that I had been unwell for almost a month. What had been wrong with me? What would people think? I felt relieved when my parents told me that there was no point in returning to school that term, because, irregularly, for a few hours, my unwanted, foggy stranger returned to bewilder me.

Then my two friends arrived with the terrible news that I had failed to get streamed into Arts. I dreaded the beginning of the next term, when I would have to live daily with my disgrace. I wanted to ask my mother to speak to the headmaster, but felt too ashamed to admit or discuss my failure.

At the end of July my father put me on a train at King's Cross and I travelled to Cumberland, in the north of England, to spend the summer holidays with my aunt. I could not understand why there were tears in his eyes, and was shocked when he cuddled me. During the first few days with my aunt I moved uncomfortably between my misty, confused world and excited anticipation of a long, enjoyable holiday. She gave me the love and attention which I wanted, and within a week the fog finally cleared. From then on I had a marvellous time, making friends with local children, exploring the Lake District, and visiting Scotland; and, financed by my aunt, I took a girl out on my first date. Each day brought some new pleasure, and I waited expectantly for the next, until the end of August, when I wished that I did not have to return home. I wanted to remain with my aunt. I wanted to confess that I had lied to her; that I had not seen all the films in London: but I was frightened to talk about my illness, and worried that she might be angry at my deceit.

On my return to school, in the despised General stream, the form-master asked for my medical certificate and embarrassed me when he said loudly 'Nervous exhaustion'. I needed to prove to everybody – my family, my schoolmasters and my friends – that there was nothing wrong with me. After a few weeks my summer illness lapsed into an old memory; by Christmas it had become little more than a half-forgotten dream.

The following year, when I returned from school camp, I had another bout of depression, and again believed that I was mad. The foggy unreality which surrounded my actions and words terrified me. I wanted to understand what was happening. I had the same symptoms: days of continual sleep, feeling isolated inside my secret mist, and always hearing my voice from behind my head. My parents insisted 'that something bad must have happened at camp', and infuriated me when they would not believe that I had had an enjoyable and trouble-free week. If I did not tell them what was wrong, they threatened, they would speak to my headmaster. They never did, but their threat worried me. I wanted them to help me; not to spoil a treat.

On weekdays my father left the house early for work, and returned late in the evenings, so that during the week I did not see much of him. On Saturdays he helped my mother in her business. One Saturday morning during this second period he stormed into my bedroom, and shouted that I had lazed around for long enough. He rarely shouted, but that day he yelled that there was nothing wrong with me that some work would not put right, and insisted that I get dressed and tidy my room. As soon as he left me alone I threw myself onto my bed, and, between tears, thought of his furious eyes and swelling cheeks. He doesn't understand, I cried, banging my head on the pillows. I remembered my mother crying 'I wish I was dead'. I understood what she meant. If I was dead, I thought, he'd be sorry that he had shouted at me.

I needed to confide in my mother, to tell her how I felt. After tormenting myself for a day or two, I eventually snuggled up to her one afternoon in our living room, and tried to explain my strange feelings and behaviour. I was amazed and relieved when she said that she understood exactly how I felt. (I had not mentioned that I felt mad.) She told me that she had always known how similar we were. I told her about my father's fury the previous weekend, and she explained soothingly that he had no feelings, and I must not expect him to understand. For a few hours I thought that I had the best mother in the world.

That evening my parents rowed violently, and I knew that it was because of me. I expected trouble. Why had I told my mother what my father had said, I thought? I should have known it would lead to this. I waited anxiously in my bedroom, expecting to be summoned downstairs, but I was left in disturbed peace.

The time bomb exploded after I had gone to bed. Suddenly, in the darkness, the bedroom door flew open, crashing loudly against the wall, and, silhouetted by the hallway light, my mother appeared in her night-dress. She looked and sounded like a nightmarish witch. 'How dare you be ill?' she screamed. 'How dare you pretend to be ill, when I'm the one who suffers in this house!' It isn't *him* I hate, I thought, as I banged my head on the pillow, it's *her*. Why doesn't she kill herself, as she keeps saying she will!

I spent another summer in Cumberland. I enjoyed my holiday, but not as much as I had the previous year, because my sister came with me. What I wanted was to be on my own, far away from my parents, and protected by my aunt. I didn't want to share her.

When I was fifteen I suffered from my third consecutive annual bout of depression, at exactly the same time of year. School camp, according to my parents, lay at the root of my illness, and I was not permitted to go again. Eliminating that enjoyable school activity from my life made no difference; my periods of depression returned more frequently, and with them my growing conviction that I was mad.

But there was another *me*, and reconciling the two was difficult. Apart from the days when frightening memories of my depression disturbed me, my obsession with madness was replaced by an obsession to succeed at school. The year I first suffered from depression I missed eighteen days' schooling during the summer term, was placed twenty-second out of twenty-eight boys, and failed to achieve my Arts streaming. The following year I lost twenty days, advanced to second place in a class of twenty-nine, and received the Middle School prize for history. In the next year I lost another eighteen days, and came first, out of twenty-five boys. In eight examinations that term, I was placed first, second or third in all but one subject – and was awarded the form, and, for the second year, the history, prize.

That'll show them, I thought. But nothing made any sense. How could I be mad if I worked well at school? Why didn't anybody know about my dreadful secret?

Those were the years when I consciously divided my life into separate compartments. One of me lived at home, the mad one; the other, the normal one, went to school. Whatever happened, I used to tell myself guiltily, no one must know about the mad me. To ensure that my secret remained hidden, throughout my years at school I never took a friend home, unless my parents were out of the house, or I was enjoying a brief period of reconciliation with my mother. I never told any of my friends about my home life; and I rarely told my parents anything about school which I did not have to.

At school, where I thought that I lived the *me* I wanted to be, I felt relatively secure. At home, where nothing was predictable, I wanted to look after my mother and sister, to prove that my mother was right when she had said, years earlier, when I was ten, that I was 'the man of the house'. When my parents could no longer live together, and my father left home, I felt elated, and, encouraged by my mother, I told him that I didn't care if I never saw him again. Influenced by my mother's persistent indoctrination, I blamed him for all the misery at home. My mother is ill now, I thought, because of his unfeeling and unmanly treatment of her. I thought that his leaving would enable my mother, sister and I to live in peace. But, after he left, my mother's, and my, disturbed emotions, far from bringing us together, resulted in feelings erupting between us which had previously been hurled at my father.

Within a few weeks of his leaving, I felt two different kinds of hatred. Towards my father I felt emotionally distant and bitter, although I felt guilty and ashamed at what I had said to him. On the rare occasions when we spoke to each other my voice had the impersonal intonation I sometimes used in group meetings at the unit. I tried to persuade myself that he did not exist. My hatred towards my mother was fearful and violent. We shouted at and attacked each other with vicious, inflammatory verbal threats; slammed and bruised innocent doors, and threw unsuspecting, harmless little bits and pieces at convenient walls. I hated her more than I hated him; but she gave me enough of herself for the hate suddenly to turn to love or admiration. Often I wanted to protect her, to make her well and happy, and I tried – we both tried. But the emotional truce never lasted for more than a day or two, and our ongoing war became more exhausting and frightening as each new battle took place. When we fought she shrieked at me, 'Go and live with your father, see how he'll look after you!' It was a terrifying threat. I thought that I had disowned my father: I knew that I could not disown my mother.

My mother's mental health led her into a world which was either subdued by barbiturates, or hopelessly disordered by irrational behaviour which alienated almost everybody who knew her. She enlisted a company of telephones, strategically located in the bedroom, living room, kitchen and shop, and commenced a tactical, telephonic advance into other people's lives, invading their privacy, day or night. She smilingly invited local shopkeepers into the house for a cup of tea, and drowned them in her sorrow. If the nearby grocer or chemist asked me 'How is your mother?' I assumed that he had seen a hot-water bottle or suit of clothes flying through the air, thrown from one of our windows on to the public pavement. It amazed me that nothing she threw into the street ever hit anybody. Sometimes, I laughed at these wild acts, but my shame and anger festered. She became incapable of managing her business, spending days in bed sleeping, or, when awake, telling friends, relations, customers or strangers what a terrible husband and son she had. Her erratic behaviour disturbed everyone, from close family to inquisitive neighbours, but as quickly as she lost one supporter, she recruited another. The anxieties and fears expressed by other victims she chose to attack provided some comfort. I was not her sole adversary.

When I was twelve years old I would not have dared to express any intentional, visible sign of resentment towards my mother; two years later I did not know how to stop my provocative attacks. I realized that we were incapable of preserving our occasional reconciliations, and, despite the inevitable counter-attacks, I enjoyed displaying what I thought of as independence, and she called arrogance. She understood that I was rejecting her, and accused me of being worse than my father. 'I hope you feel guilty for what you're doing to me' became one of her most accusatory catch phrases. Occasionally, anxious for some pretence at domestic peace, I apologized; but the apologies were insincere, and she knew it. I did feel guilty; but I also felt victimized and angry, and ashamed that I should come from such a despicable family.

Each member of my family – mother, father and sister – seemed to me to be separate and unrelated. In different ways, my mother and father appeared as grotesque misrepresentations of what parents should be. That left my sister, and we forged a strong bond which I believed was brotherly and sisterly love. She made me feel needed. I wanted her to be my responsibility.

With my mother's increasing loss of health and supporters went reduced profits from her shop. When I was fifteen, after an absence of a year and a half, my father returned to live with us, in an attempt to resolve the financial mess which had developed. My feelings of hatred and anger worsened. I felt trapped. I wanted to leave home, but treasured my school career, and hoped to go to university. To do that I needed my parents' support. My GCE examinations were coming nearer, and I felt an awful terror, convinced that another bout of depression would descend, and deprive me of the success and freedom I wanted. I regarded both parents as threats to my future, but needed them for the same future I believed they threatened. I reminded myself that without their support I could not complete my schooling; that, if nothing else, they provided me with a bed and food. It didn't make me feel any better.

I began suffering from prolonged and painful headaches, which the doctor diagnosed as mild migraine, and for which he prescribed tiny Migril tablets which never helped relieve the pain. I could not sleep easily. Often, after a long night's homework, I worried that I would not wake up in time to go to school, as I lay restlessly in bed listening to the quarter-hour chimes from the nearby church until 2 or 3 o'clock in the morning. I could not then know that these symptoms –

headaches and insomnia – would influence much of my future life.

All these, and many more, memories of my teenage years burst into my mind when I looked at my time-bomb depiction of *parents*. The hatred I felt towards them became so overpowering during my first months at Shipley Grange that I knew that it would be impossible for me to live with myself until I discovered a way of discarding my terrible feelings. I had lived with these bad feelings for years, but had thought that I had them controlled and defused. The paintings and talking and dramatic acting-out sessions were forcing me to accept that I had fooled myself. My feelings, expressed through behaviour and words at the unit, had never been under control. They must be to blame for all this, I thought bitterly. If only my teens hadn't been so bad, I wouldn't be here, in a mental hospital. If only my teens hadn't been so bad, I wouldn't have suffered from almost thirty years of debilitating headaches, restless insomnia – and depression. If only. . . .

I related my feelings to those of other residents. We all suffered, and wished that our teens had been less emotionally traumatic. Jim became aware of his homosexuality when he was fourteen; Barbara had started taking drugs at the same age, and had an abortion a year later; Cathy had been raped at fifteen. Everyone had unforgettable experiences which had terrified them. In the early days at the unit I believed that the mistake I had made was to have pretended, as I grew older, that my teenage years had not affected me.

For many years I believed that my childhood experiences had been good for me. Because of them, I reasoned, I had thrown myself energetically into my school work, and become ambitious. If I had not had such misery at home, I told myself, I may not have had the motivation to work hard and succeed, so that I could leave home. Had I not felt the need to get out of the house as often as I could, perhaps I would not have met so many interesting people, and learned how to mix socially.

But those old beliefs were fading rapidly. My childhood

had been bad for me. Somehow, I had to come to terms with the past, so that I could face the present. I tried to rationalize my depression: 'Due to disturbed childhood.' If I could put my bad feelings into something uncertain called 'the past', where they belonged, then I would be on the road forward. During my early days at Shipley Grange, I was convinced that, if I could learn how not to hate my parents for what they did to me during my teens, my depression would vanish; I would stop being incapacitated by tension headaches, and start sleeping properly. If I did all that, then I would kill off the part of me that was mad. 'Do you want to hate your parents all your life?' Stuart asked me once. 'No', I replied, wanting to forgive them, not for their sake, but for mine.

Forgiveness was a word which worried me. When people cliché'd to each other 'forgive and forget', I did not understand what they meant. How do I forget? And, if I cannot forget, how do I forgive? If I cannot forget, why *should* I forgive? Forgiveness, like love, was high on my list of uncertainties. To try forgiving, I decided, I had to stop blaming my parents for the emotional mess which had become my existence. Remember the good things, I told myself: remember that I never went hungry, that I received a decent education, and learned which knife and fork to use. But psychotherapy did not seem to be an experience which encouraged forgiveness or love: it frequently felt like a corrupt and insidious torture designed to lower my spirits and heighten my hate.

Flirting with forgiveness made me feel that my time bomb, far from being defused, was likely to explode into catastrophic self-destruction.

Family eruptions

'Forgive and forget?' I knew that I could never forget; could I, perhaps, forgive? Before I could contemplate forgiveness I had to decide who I wanted to forgive; and, before I could decide, I had to learn that, instead of forgetting, I had to remember. Remembering my teenage experiences was painful, but not difficult; they rose like engulfing flames whenever I felt bad, sad or mad. Other memories lay waiting to be stoked into activity.

As we struggled at the unit to ward off the threats we each posed to the others, I gradually became aware that we had more than teenage experiences to share. Jim's plea to be two years old began to seem less contemptible when I heard 'baby-talk' from other residents, or watched their behaviour. The night Cathy painted *parents*, she wetted her bed. It took her several days of frantic foot-tapping before she shamefully told us; but she felt pleased, when, after her brave admission, two other members made similar confessions, and the group discussed, among other things, how to deal with their soiled linen. Barbara, one evening when distraught, ran into the kitchen and forced food into her mouth, crying, 'I want to be sick.' She sounded like a baby screaming for her mother's milk. Another resident curled into a foetus shape and refused to move from his chair when accused of wanting to attack the group. Bridget threw things, knowing that one of us would ask her what was wrong. I did not wet my bed, or cry out that I wanted to be two years old. Often, when under stress, I came close to Barbara's need to be sick, buying several bars of chocolate and gobbling them as quickly as possible; and when I felt helpless, a distant inner voice shouted 'help me'; I knew that I withdrew from people when I felt destructive; and I remembered my grandmother's tales of my throwing toys from my pram. But I could not admit these personal peculiarities, or recognize the feelings which accompanied them, until I released my energy through more talking and painting therapy.

I painted two *self-portraits*. The first was not very different to my time bomb, except that then I had been thinking of my parents, and related the fuse to my teenage years. How do I paint myself? How do I feel? Like exploding! My self-portrait had the same violent colours, but a new image of destruction. I painted an angry, active volcano; a rough, destructive triangle inside which oranges and reds fought with each other, and molten, purple rock spewed upwards, breaking into great chunks of black, gaseous débris which tumbled down the sides. It reminded me of the excitement I felt when seeing pictures of erupting volcanoes in full spate, particularly one in Iceland in the mid 1970s. Volcanoes, like earthquakes, hurricanes, tornadoes, tidal waves and thunderstorms, had always excited me.

That painting, and accumulated talking and acting out, began another journey at the unit, the journey which was to provide me with more self-knowledge about my emotional stranger than I had ever known. I began to understand that I felt that I existed in two extreme emotional states: when something dramatic was happening I felt dynamic and hyperactive; when I felt dormant and useless I fantasized about death. Both were potentially fatal.

The second *self-portrait*, a half-profile, painted several weeks later, illustrated another part of me which I needed to understand. I started with my nose, and drew a triangle; then I added another, for an ear; then two more, for eyes, and a fifth, for my mouth. A profusion of triangles fought their way into my painting, cutting sharply into each other, until they combined into one large, asymmetrical, triangular head. The completed picture was a confusion of multi-coloured three-pointed shapes, distorted where they joined and overlapped. 'I wouldn't want to be in there,' someone said, 'it looks treacherous.' I felt that I had cut myself into jagged pieces, like broken shards of glass. Looking at the picture after I had pinned it with the others, on my bedroom wall at the unit, the triangles became the numerous compartments into which I had divided my life.

Erupting volcanoes, treacherous triangles, exploding bombs – how could I stop painting destructive images and start recognizing myself? When and why did *I* feel the need to destroy?

In a group meeting we discussed deceit. A resident said he had stolen money from his parents whenever he had been able to. Suddenly, I was seven years old. I had stolen money, I confessed. 'Why did you need to take?' Stuart asked. 'Because I wasn't getting what I wanted,' I replied.

But when I thought about my early childhood theft, other memories, memories I had either forgotten or dismissed as unimportant, petty incidents, came into my mind. Recalling those memories I could *feel* the memories – and they were painful. The unit was helping me by making me examine myself. When I felt angry or ashamed or guilty after talking or painting or acting, for the first time in my life I journeyed backwards while the feelings were with me. I had always done that when I felt seriously depressed, but until then my memories had stopped at the time when the depression had started – when I was a teenager. Unexpectedly, I began re-living – and feeling – an earlier age, and, again for the first time, I could share what I felt with other people, if I wanted to. I was beginning to 'get in touch with my feelings'.

I remembered that, when I was seven years old, three years before we moved to central London, my mother was usually in bed when I left for school. I didn't understand why she left me alone when I wanted her to be with me. To escape from the loneliness I used to leave early, often before 8 o'clock, although the local school was less than a ten-minute walk away; but arriving too early at school was as lonely as being at home. When I remembered that she was in bed, I realized that the belief that she began her years of 'bed-life' when I was in my teens was false. And so, too, was her explanation that she was exhausting herself running her business to support her family.

One morning I called up to her, telling her that I needed a clean shirt. She flew half-way down the stairway. 'How dare you shout at your mother!' she screamed. After that I tried ironing my own shirts. If it was winter-time, I only ironed the collar, hiding the rest under a sweater; but I felt ashamed and angry because I knew that I was not dressed properly.

Another morning I saw five £1 notes sticking out of a jar on the kitchen table. When the memory came back to me at the unit I felt as I did that morning, a third of a century earlier; angry that I was alone and either had to make my own breakfast or wait until lunchtime to eat at school; ashamed when I opened the linen cupboard and saw no freshly ironed shirt; and thrilled, gaping at the money, and holding the crisp notes, counting them several times. I knew that they had been left there by my father – the week's housekeeping. Five pounds! A fortune to a seven-year-old in 1949. I was frightened to keep the one note I stole, but unable to replace it after I held it in my hand. I wanted to buy jam doughnuts for breakfast. I folded the note into a thin tube-shape, and inserted it inside my school tie. The possibility of detection terrified me, but the temptation to take a whole pound note was irresistible. I knew that I would be accused of the theft, but *she* was in bed, and was not there to see what I was doing; all I had to do was to say that I knew nothing about it.

When I left the house I felt terrified, guilty – and exhilarated. A pound note! How could I spend it? I wanted my doughnuts, but was frightened that the shopkeeper would ask me where I had got the money. I wanted sweets, but felt the same fear. The tube of money hung guiltily round my neck, and I wanted to remove it so that I could fondle it lovingly. At the same time I wanted to go home, and replace it. I felt brave and frightened and astonished at my audacity. I worried that my mother might come to the school, but persuaded myself that she would not notice that any money was missing. I was so full of fear that the excitement vanished; I felt sick, and then proud; I wanted my school-friends to know what I had done, and decided to buy everyone in the class chocolates. But what about the teacher? What would she say? I became desperate, not knowing what to do with the awful pound note. For the rest of the day I dreaded returning home.

When these memories and feelings returned I could not recall what I had done with the money. Then, suddenly, I remembered. I saw myself walking along a narrow pathway between houses. I undid my tie and removed the pound note, tearing it into tiny paper scraps, which I hid behind some bushes next to a garden fence.

I destroyed a £1 note, just as I did five years later, when I had my first bout of diagnosed depression. Occasionally, I had remembered the theft, and felt ashamed; but not what I had done with the money. I never linked the two acts until my memory began functioning at Shipley Grange. And when I tried to understand other thefts, I connected the similarities of each act; I had stolen when I felt angry and rejected; I had destroyed what I had stolen; and I had wanted to punish an enemy.

What else had I forgotten?

My parents kept asking me if I had seen the lost pound note, or taken it. I said that I knew nothing about it. For several weeks I felt guilty and afraid. One Sunday afternoon, while my father was painting the outside of the house, I confessed to my mother. She asked me why I had done it, but I had no explanation. She wanted to know what I had spent the money on, but I was too frightened to admit that I'd thrown it away, and lied that I had bought doughnuts and sweets and comics. She cuddled me and said that I was a good boy to have told her the truth. I had shed my unbearable weight and hadn't been told off. Better still, I had been told that I was good. She agreed not to tell my father.

An hour or two later I was in the garden, when my father called me into the house. He told me to go to my room, and followed. He made me undress, produced two suitcase straps, and tied me to the bed; then he removed his belt and started beating me. I screamed, and kept screaming. 'I'm not stopping this until you stop that noise,' he said. The strapping was painful, but my tearful fury was directed at my mother. She had promised not to tell him. After I stopped crying, my father unstrapped me, and went to the bathroom to get a bandage to cover my bleeding backside. I couldn't believe that I was actually bleeding from a beating by my father. Nothing like that had ever happened before. I heard my mother sobbing, and assumed that she felt sorry for breaking her promise.

I thought that I had fully recalled that episode when another memory returned. For months after I admitted that I had stolen the money, every time I was in trouble with my mother, she terrified me with the worst punishment I could imagine. 'I'm going to tell your aunt,' she threatened many times, 'I'm going to write today, and tell her, unless you promise never to (do whatever I'd done) again.' I begged her *never* to do that. My aunt, the one I stayed with after my early bouts of depression, was my mother's sister, and I idolized her.

More memories. Many months after I confessed my guilty secret my parents were invited to a wedding. My mother looked glamorous in her evening gown; my father's black suit and bow-tie looked smart and impressive. I was proud of them, and of myself, because, for the first time, I was being left on my own in the house. I waved goodbye to them from the front door. Half an hour later they unexpectedly returned. My mother slammed the front door behind her and screamed at me: 'You've ruined my evening. How can I ever trust you on your own in this house?' She dashed upstairs, returning moments later to the living room holding a white £5 note, which she kept for emergencies and about which I knew nothing. 'Well,' she said nastily, 'at least you didn't steal this from your mother.' I sat uncomfortably on the shame she saddled me with, and felt guilty that I had ruined her special evening.

When those memories, and feelings, returned, I knew that I had distrusted my parents many years before my teens. It was a startling discovery. Uncountable, fearful memories flashed through my mind and magnified my feelings: the day I fell into a river and was scared to go home because my mother would scream at me for dirtying my clothes; the afternoon I ate some grapes which she had bought for my father, and she made me stand up on a chair for what seemed like hours; a Sunday, when my father was wallpapering our dining room, and my mother had shrieked at him and then collapsed on the floor, prostrate and unmoving, drenched in water spilled from the bucket he was using; a bowl of cereal tipped over my head after I shouted that I could not hear *Dick Barton* on the radio because my mother would not stop talking.

These seemed tiny memories to be recalling, but the fear and guilt I felt had been immense. I realized that I had been terrified of my mother for as long as I could remember. Destruction acquired a new meaning.

The weekend after those memories returned, I read some old school reports. One of them, dated November 1948, when I was six years old, reads 'a few times has been rough with some children'; in the next report I had 'been a little kinder to others this term . . . since this remark was written he has been very unkind to several children.' Then I remembered that when I was three, and at my first nursery school, I told my mother that my mouth had been washed out with soap at school, because I had bitten another child. So, I thought, I have always had a violent streak in me. Why? And a dishonest one. Why? What was happening when I was three that made my violence at school so serious that it had to be dealt with by mouthwashing and written reports? And why were most memories of my mother? I felt like a detective hot on my own trail.

Four years old, possibly younger. My mother had taken me out for afternoon tea in Bournemouth, where I was born, and where we lived until 1947. I knew that I had to be on my best behaviour, but must have misbehaved at the table, because she reached under the red-and-white squared tablecloth and viciously pinched my thigh. I cried. She pinched me again, telling me that only babies cried, and that I was disgracing her. When I continued crying she told me to leave the table and wait for her outside the restaurant. Waiting for her to finish her tea was more agonizing than the painful pinches. Painful pinches . . . painful pinch . . . pinching money . . . deceit and destruction. Eat your heart out, Sherlock Poirot.

Reliving these experiences, I understood that my adolescent depression was not the beginning of my emotional confusion and aggressive behaviour. The memories of so many bad childhood feelings felt like attacks far worse than any made upon me by members of the group. After ten weeks' psychotherapy I entered a world I had not known existed inside me . . . and there was much more to come. Each tarnished memory of my early childhood altered previous conceptions of my self-understanding.

Piecing together the clues to my identity demanded a close, and at times, brutal investigation into my feelings and behaviour at the unit; but examining myself was not enough to resolve the confusion which surrounded me. My personal acts were not always as self-induced as I thought. Often, I reacted impulsively to what other people did. This 'knock on' effect disturbed me, because, while my intended acts seemed reasonable, my actual reactions to other members of the group invariably contradicted what I had expected to do. Unless they did what I expected, I felt threatened; and when I felt threatened I spontaneously defended myself, without considering possible repercussions. I wanted to warn them, to say, 'Watch out, I'm dangerous!'

But at other times I believed that I was acting reasonably, and not expecting the impossible. I thought, be careful, they're dangerous. Sometimes they were.

Days, weeks and months passed, and I knew that I was beginning to understand more about why I reacted as I did. This incipient awareness frightened me. Knowing why I reacted in particuar ways was one thing: unravelling my feelings in time to control my behaviour was another. I had progressed – by moving backwards through my life – and realized that teenage and early childhood behaviour was closely related to almost every reaction I displayed in the group. The most powerful link between my childhood and adult years was the fear of destruction. Although I felt destructive towards others, I felt that I was the one being destroyed. When I destroyed the group mural I hurt myself more than any other group member. When, as a boy of seven, I destroyed my parents' £1 note, I believed that I suffered more than they did. Rising high above any one specific act of destruction, my feelings towards my mother overpowered me. Knowing that she exerted such power made me want to understand why she had needed to terrify me.

From my early childhood I had known that my mother had been unhappy as a child. She told me that her mother had ill-treated her, and that I did not know how lucky I was to have one who loved me. In my teens she described her bitter childhood memories more emphatically, demanding my sympathy; but I listened with bored indifference, because by then I was too engrossed in my own suffering to have much sympathy for anybody else. However, at the unit, her past became important to me. She was dead, so I had to complete her personal puzzle from uncertain shapes created from my own memories, from what I had heard other people say about her, and from what I knew of her behaviour as a wife, mother, daughter and sister.

I asked my father why he married her. She was an exciting person to be with, he said, energetic and ambitious, and mixed well with people. He had never met anybody like her. He felt sorry for her, he added, because she seemed miserable at home, and told him stories which at first he could not believe, until they were corroborated by other members of the family. He married her because it was wartime, and people did things then which they might not have done in less ominous times. He told me that while they were engaged she threatened to commit suicide − when she was eighteen − unless he married her, and helped her escape from her parents. So! she had felt as bad as I had at the same age, I thought. Had her parents destroyed her childhood as I felt she had destroyed mine?

Rene and Jack − my maternal grandparents − were both non-practising Jews. Rene was the eldest of seven children in a poor family. Her parents emigrated from Poland and settled in London's East End slums in the 1880s. Jack's history, rooted in Russia, remains shrouded in a mystery which he buried with his death. He rarely spoke of his mother, and never about his father. When he recalled his past, he began in the year 1914, when he was sixteen years old and joined the army. He had two brothers, one of whom worked for an agricultural investment corporation in South Africa, an unusual career for a Jew in the 1920s. The other brother emigrated to New Zealand. Also, he had a sister and a non-Jewish step-sister, both of whom he detested. The dark lady in the mystery is his mother, an American citizen, who at some period in his childhood crossed and re-crossed the

Atlantic Ocean, probably exchanging husbands at the same time. He never said so, but I think that she deserted her children.

My grandparents married in 1920, when Jack was a handsome man of twenty-two, with twinkling eyes and a waxed moustache, and Rene an unattractive woman eleven years older. (Perhaps he wanted a mother?) They ran small businesses — a wet fish shop, a general store, and tobacconist and confectionery shops — and, financially, must have been relatively successful, because in 1935 they moved from the grim environment in east London to Bournemouth, more elegant then than it is today, where they bought a seaside guest-house.

My grandfather served in France during the First World War, and in the Second spent some time managing a cinema in Coventry: part of his 'war effort', he told me; 'to get away from her,' according to my mother. During his absence his wife supervised the business, which was used by American GIs on leave. After the war, more prosperous, they travelled to Italy or the South of France most summers, and in their later years, during my teens, regularly spent two months wintering in Majorca.

My grandmother was a tough, rough, stocky woman, uncultured and uneducated, with a loud, harsh voice and a keen, protective desire for financial security — if she had been mean to others, she never was to me. I remember her as firm but gentle, accusing me of 'having eyes bigger than my belly'. She was always kind to me, and, in her way, generous; happy for me to spend weeks holidaying with her, shaking her head at my greediness one minute and loading my plate with thick, sweet pancakes or delicious home-made cheesecake the next. She loved recounting tales of my escapades as a little boy, which both embarrassed and delighted me. After I was married, when my wife and I took her for an afternoon drive in our car, her hardest struggle was to accept our invitation to go out for tea. 'Ja...ack, tell them to take us home and save their money.' But she enjoyed being spoilt almost as much as examining the menu and whispering, 'When I was your age you got all this for fourpence.' Towards the end of her life, suffering like the rest of my family from my mother's terrorism, she used to cry, 'I blame myself. I was a wicked mother.' I preferred her cheesecake to her tears. She died in 1972, a bitter, disappointed, senile old woman.

Jack died ten years later. He had a charming, old-fashioned courtesy, mainly towards women, and especially towards pretty ones. When I was a young boy out walking with him, he insisted that I wear my school cap, so that when we passed 'ladies' we could raise our hats together and say, 'Good morning, Mrs Whateveryournameis, how are you? Isn't it a beautiful day!' He loved people who adored him, was generous to the point of foolishness, gambled away most of his hard-earned profits on women, dogs, horses or the stock exchange, and remained until his death a big kid.

We shared many secrets. When my birthday arrived, there were always two envelopes: one, from them both, addressed by my grandmother, enclosing a sentimental card, a ten-shilling postal order, and a wobbly-written note – 'Don't spend it all at once, love . . .'; another, from him, enclosing at least £1, and a scribbled warning – 'Don't tell Nana, love Grandpop.' He confided in me when he lost a large sum of money on the stock market, terrified that my grandmother would find out; I confided in him when I met the first girl I wanted to marry, terrified that my mother would find out. He spent hours with me, talking and walking, brushing my hair, and warning me not to damage his precious home-grown strawberries. He paid for my study fees ('Don't tell', etc.), and had an unending interest in my career. He let me serve customers in his shops, when I was five years old, and took me with him to his wholesalers and suppliers. I showed him the wonders of the international telex system when he was eighty-two, as great a thrill for him as my weighing out a quarter pound of Quality Street chocolates had been for me.

In his last years we enjoyed sunbathing in my garden and sharing our experiences. Attended by my wife and I and our two children, he reminisced about his years in the army, helping to run a hospital in France; or acting as a bookies' runner in the 1930s; or offering lay medical advice to his poor female customers, before the Welfare State arrived. I told him of my latest business trip, to America or Saudi Arabia, and his eyes sparkled with vicarious pleasure as he remembered his own travels. When I lobbed an occasional question about his family he batted his eyelids, mumbling, 'Oh, that's all a long time ago,' and changed the subject.

At times he was gloomy and resentful, and these changes of mood upset and confused me when I was young. He became withdrawn, and unexpectedly snapped at me, or told me to leave him alone. Sometimes he grumbled to himself, and, if his words were audible, they invariably directed suppressed fury at my grandmother. I quickly discovered that a well-planted kiss on his forehead was enough to welcome me back into his world. The greatest loves of his life were himself and women. Not far behind, I liked to believe, was myself. He is the only man I have trusted.

Rene and Jack shared two things throughout the years I knew them: they loved travelling; and they were terrified of my mother, their eldest daughter. The marriage was not happy: it was bonded together by Rene's stern authority and Jack's childishness. When she yelled at him, frightened that he was jeopardizing their security, he sulked. If he was happy, she sulked, knowing that whoever gave him pleasure, it was not her. After she died, he said, 'She was a hard woman, but I miss her.'

My mother was born in 1922 when her parents were struggling to earn their living. According to my grandmother, my mother was a difficult and 'nervy' child, who cried incessantly. My father told me that, as a baby, she was left alone for hours in dark corridors behind the fish shop, and regularly walloped — by my grandmother — if she refused to stop bawling. By the time my mother was five, and competing with a younger sister, Rene had nicknamed her the 'ugly duckling'. The second child, my aunt, was 'a beautiful baby, not like your mother,' my grandmother used to tell me. My mother blamed her parents for her miserable childhood; and never forgave her sister for being beautiful.

This was desperately confusing for me as a boy, because my grandparents and aunt seemed to represent everything good in my life. I could not believe that such loving people had made my mother miserable; and, because I knew how miserable my mother made other people, including myself, I equated *good* with three of them and *bad* with her.

My father's parents were practically unknown to me. The only memories I have, shocking ones, are of monthly visits I made with him to see his mother in her last years, when she was senile and helpless in hospital. When I was nine years old, I discovered that she was in a mental hospital, for mad people, and told my father what I knew. He was furious. 'She's not mad,' he shouted; but I thought of the strange behaviour and peculiar faces that stared at me each month, and did not believe him. She terrified me, and I hated him for making me go to see her. I did not think of her as a grandparent: she was 'his mother'.

His family was poor and deprived. One of seven children, he grew up in the wretched, cluttered streets in the East End, where his own Jewish grandparents had immigrated from Poland. He was forced to leave school at fourteen, bitter at not being allowed to continue his education, to work in the family sweat shop – euphemistically referred to as a tailoring business.

When, as a boy listening to her continual complaints, I asked my mother why she married my father, she laughed bitterly, and said, 'He was kind and I was young enough to be impressed because he spoke about politics and listened to Beethoven.' They married in 1941, while my father was attached to the Pioneer Corps. I was born thirteen months later. For the first three years of my life I lived with my mother, in Bournemouth, near my grandparents and aunt. My father could have seen me only on rare occasions, until 1945, when he was demobbed.

For a brief period, during the Second World War, my mother may have been content, although I doubt it. When she was nineteen, and married, she left home, settled into a small flat, and managed a clothing shop in Bournemouth;

and, for the first time in her life, she had a possession wholly her own – me.

She used me to reflect her own fantasies – a walking, talking, two-legged, human Rolls Royce. She told me hundreds, perhaps thousands, of times, that she had worked long, arduous hours so that she could afford to buy me the *best* food. My manners as a child were *perfect*. I could be taken anywhere, she enthused proudly, ignoring her violent attack on my thighs. When I had my mouth soaped for biting a child, she insisted that the headmaster provide her with a written apology and promised never to hurt me again. (I doubt if she examined why I had the need to cannibalize my schoolmates.) If her later behaviour is a reliable guide, I expect that she did all this for her own gratification – to prove to her parents, and particularly her mother, that she could be not merely a better parent, but the *best* parent.

As soon as my father returned from one war he became a combatant in another. My mother presumably feared him as a dangerous threat, invading her maternal territory. Conversely, she probably welcomed him as a competitor, convinced of her own superiority. Among my earliest memories of her are earnest explanations of how *she* was the one who brought me up, who cared for me, who slaved for me, who made herself ill for me. When I was older, and less controllable, she added that if I did not repay her for her love, she would kill herself for me.

She succeeded in alienating me from my father, partly because he was unable to match her emotional force, but mainly because, on the few occasions when I tried to defy her obsessive power over me, her punishment proved horrific. She translated any act of mine which disturbed her into a combined attack from my father and herself. 'How dare you treat me like your father does, when I'm the one. . . .' I realized, as my father and my grandparents must have, that I could never win. Her conviction that we all threatened her had devastating effects. My father probably gave up on his marriage within a year or two of living with her; and if he retreated from her, he must have retreated from me.

My mother's destructive powers isolated her from the care and love she wanted. My grandparents saw her as seldom as possible; my father faded into a grey, submissive shadow; her friends may have considered disconnecting their telephones. I had thought that my teenage rebelliousness had been the beginning of my attacks on her. Recalling my theft as a seven-year-old made me realize that our war had begun much earlier.

Thinking about and discussing these clues to my identity, another truth emerged. I realized that for many years before my conscious teenage rejection of my mother and father, I fantasized that my 'real' parents were not my true parents. My grandfather was the nearest I had to a father, I believed; and my 'real' mother should have been my aunt.

The memory of my mother viciously pinching my thigh when I was four contrasted with happier memories and feelings, at the same age, when I spent time with my aunt. She never pinched me; not physically, anyway. I shared wonderful days with her, sitting on the soft sands at Bournemouth licking ice cream, being fussed by her boyfriends; or the two of us walking for miles along the beautiful cliff-edged chines to Sandbanks, laughing and holding hands, or chasing each other to the seashore. When I felt lonely or frightened my secret wish was to be sheltered by her motherly love.

But she made me miserable, too. In 1949 I ran into my mother's arms, crying hysterically, when the sounds of an aeroplane's engines droned overhead. My aunt was in that 'plane, off to California, and I felt that my happiness was flying away with her. I wanted to know when, if ever, I would see her again. My mother cried with me, but I suspect that her tears were not for her departing sister. Then, when I heard that she was returning to England, I dreaded seeing her, because my mother kept threatening to tell her about the £1 which I had stolen.

My aunt's life thrilled me. After two years in California, she worked as an air hostess for BOAC, travelling around the world. I studied atlases with devotion and regret. One week she was in Hong Kong, another in Beirut, or Rome, or New

York. She was on the flight, in 1953, which brought Edmund Hillary home to England, after his conquest of Mount Everest. Exotic postcards and exciting presents arrived unexpectedly, and from time to time, she came in person. She described strange countries, and imitated stranger people, whom I recognized from my stamp collection, maps and picture postcards; she suddenly appeared through a door-way, laughing, dressed in a kimono, bowing at my feet, and waving a folded fan in front of my face; or placed a hand-carved seat from Egypt in the middle of her living room, and told me to sway on it while she explained how uncomfortable it was to sit on a camel and look at the Pyramids.

I did not hear her arguing with my grandparents, or issuing threats. She gave them presents and went on holiday with them. When in England she lived with them; when she was away travelling, they missed her. I was hopelessly mistaken in my childhood interpretations of my aunt's relationships with her parents; but I did not know that then.

And then, when I was twelve, she married an officer in the Royal Navy, and I walked along the beach at Bournemouth crying bitter tears. How could she continue being my fantastical mother? As though reading my thoughts, before her wedding day she told me that she did not want children. 'I've got you,' she said. 'I'd be too frightened to have children of my own. I'm not sure that I could love them as much as I love you.' I felt relieved, but deeply suspicious of her new husband, whom I regarded as a thief, stealing from me the person I most adored.

My private fantasies about my grandfather and aunt were not as private as I thought. Once, after a particularly bitter family row, my parents explained that, whatever difficulties existed at home, they, and nobody else, looked after me, protected me and encouraged my education. I understood what they were saying, and knew that my grandfather would not welcome full-time responsibility for me; and that my aunt was moving frequently from one home to another with her smartly-uniformed husband; but I rejected what my parents said, and resented them for disturbing my dreams.

Smouldering dreams

'Forgive and forget?' I felt bewildered. I forgot nothing; instead of forgetting, memories painfully reappeared, like untreated and undiagnosed injuries. I felt sad and angry when daily experiences at the unit inflamed past feelings; but, because I thought that I had cured many complex problems in the group, I hoped that old, smouldering wounds could be healed. I wanted to cry out, 'Why has it taken so long to receive help?' After the early pangs of self-pity became less hurtful I confronted each newly-assessed memory, examining it suspiciously, as though it were an unknown disease for which I had to discover a remedy. When I succeeded in persuading myself that I understood my feelings I felt optimistic and excited. Perhaps, at last, I was ready to experiment with forgiveness.

I thought of my mother. She did not know what she was doing. She never meant to hurt me. It wasn't her fault. She wasn't to blame. She was ill. She suffered. So did I, I thought ruefully.

'The ugly duckling' had grown up with ugly feelings, desperate not to remain emotionally hideous. She wanted to transform herself into a sophisticated and admired conceit — and God help anyone who tried to stop her! But her substance was fear, and when her family and friends offered help she turned on them and they became frightened. I suffered for her when I remembered her most devoted companions, green barbiturate tablets on her bedside table, waiting to take her from a threatening world, like unsigned death warrants. I searched for reasons to forgive her, and mentally filed them under 'Must Forgive Mother'; and wrote lists in my secret diary, worried that I might forget that I had to forgive.

She trained me to be an expert in social graces, so that in my teens I felt confident when I escorted her to dinner; and she taught me to dance, the two of us tripping lightly across our living room carpet to a Victor Sylvester fox-trot, or whisking energetically to a cha-cha. With her support I felt at ease when introduced to people many years older than myself. I enjoyed believing that I was a man before I wore long trousers. As a teenager I felt proud to be by her side when she laughed and chatted intelligently with her friends and business acquaintances. In a room full of people she was never alone: and when she attracted attention I shared it with her.

She acted impulsively, which could result in her throwing a saucepan full of hot soup at me; but I remembered other, more pleasurable flings. Occasionally, while my father was a 'non-resident', when she finished a busy week's work on a Saturday, she ran excitedly upstairs, laughing and happy, calling to my sister and I, 'Pack some things, quickly, we're going away for the night'; and I, her man, made the necessary bookings at an expensive hotel, where we indulged in a brief, hedonistic, financial orgy. 'You pay the bill, darling,' she'd say, handing me a bundle of notes; and I looked forward to the day when I really could.

Memories of the two of us, talking for hours about our future, reminded me of the ambition she willed into me. Hopes which might have been fantasies felt real and attainable when we shared our dreams. Listening to, and influenced by, her insatiable desires, she made me hungry for success. I can do it, I believed, encouraged by my frenzied need to do what she wanted.

At other times, when she was drugged into semi-consciousness, and looked pitiful and helpless, I wanted to soothe her, to help her find peace and comfort through me. Until my concern for her changed to deep resentment, I promised that I would protect her. My promises were given sincerely, and, just as she knew when my words were dishonest, so, knowing that I wanted her to get well, and cared for her, she briefly regained her lost energy and returned to the world which I needed to share with her.

Frequently, when family friends or relatives condemned her for her irrational behaviour, I felt angry, and defended her, insisting that it wasn't her fault, she was sick and needed help. I suffered from her violent temper and her furious assaults, but, even when I suffered most, I could not forget what she was like in her happier days.

The youthful compassion for my mother which I had thought could never return, re-emerged as I struggled to balance our emotional books. Compassion and forgiveness felt like true friends.

I thought about my father. I had not experienced the poverty he had known; nor had I been forced to abandon my education. He worked hard to support us, rarely missing a day's work, and, when necessary, had been prepared to learn a new trade and take over my mother's ailing business, to avoid financial ruin. Sandwiched between our worst days were memories of long talks, into the early hours of the morning, discussing politics and current affairs. He introduced me to one of my greatest loves – classical music – and helped me appreciate sounds and emotions which remain with me today. When I spent my pocket money on old seventy-eight record sets of a Beethoven symphony, he was the one I wanted to approve of my purchase, not my mother, who preferred Lena Horne.

He also made me vaguely aware of something promising which, as a child, I could not understand. My mother's relationships with her parents and sister were in constant turmoil; from one week to the next it was impossible to know whether she would croon lovingly to her father on the telephone, or menacingly demand money to pay for her latest medical bills, threatening, if he refused, to tell her mother of other financial blackmail she had extracted deviously from him. My grandfather's terror that his wife would discover his illicit payments produced prompt financial dividends. 'I'll make them pay for what they did to me,' she said to me many times. In her family there were always fraudulent accounts to settle.

But my father's family – brothers and sisters – were friendly towards each other, and, what most confused me, calm and unchanging. I did not hear them shouting, or viciously issuing threatening demands; they behaved as though they actually liked one another. Sometimes, when my father was in partnership with his elder brother, Steve, making waistcoats in the 1950s, I went to their garret workshop near Carnaby Street in Soho. One Friday Steve was counting the cash they had collected for their week's work. 'Here you are,' he said cheerfully to my father, 'take a bit extra, you've got two kids, I've just one.' I knew that the difference between my grandfather secretly sending a £100 cheque and Steve giving my father an extra two crumpled bits of paper was more than £98. Why aren't we like his family, I wondered? And why does my mother hate them all?

I mentally handled the few good memories with delicacy, trying to forgive. They were fragile and full of flaws; but they were all that I had. I wanted to keep them intact, to set them side by side with the ones which made me feel perpetually bad. Despite the dangerous implications of my mother's reasons for instilling into me her desires, I had nothing else to cling to: they were my hopes for eventual peace. I hoped that those fractured memories would overcome hatred. Gnawing inside me was one serious doubt: the person I most wanted to forgive seemed to be the least likely to benefit from my efforts. I may be able to forgive my parents, I thought, but how can I forgive myself for the destruction and misery I had caused?

When I painted my volcano I had seen three people in its writhing images of violence and fury: my parents and myself. But when I examined my childhood more carefully I realized that somewhere, erupting with the three of us, were other members of the family, of whom my grandfather and aunt seemed to be the most elusive. Occasionally, when we exhausted ourselves with our badness, residents struggled unsuccessfully to introduce some good. On those days I mentioned my grandparents and aunt; but they were too good to want to share with anyone, and my references to them were oblique. I thought that if I admitted how good they were, then my problems would seem less serious. I was there to eliminate my bad feelings; if I revealed that there had been love and kindness in my childhood, the group might wonder why I was there.

I wanted to concentrate on my parents, but other thoughts interrupted my attempts at reconciliation. Often, I wanted to escape from the unit. I fantasized that I could create a new, secret world, where nobody knew me. Then, when I forced myself to remain, I felt desperate. How can I forgive! My desperation worsened when I realized that inside my volcano was another layer of surging fury which I had to contain – my sister, Ruth.

During the worst years at home I believed that it was my responsibility to shield her from my mother. When Ruth was nine, I heard a scream from my mother's bedroom. My mother, lying in bed, had asked my sister if she loved her more than her father; Ruth had said 'No'. My mother had risen angrily from the bed and slapped her, leaving a hand-sized swathe of maternal appreciation on her cheek. I went berserk, calling my mother every name I could think of, and upending several pieces of furniture, before running out of the house, dragging my sister behind me. After that, when I started going out with girls, I often insisted that Ruth came with me, frightened of what might happen to her if she was left alone with my mother. I liked to think of myself as a good, protective brother.

I was twenty-two when I married my first wife. Ruth, then seventeen, refused to come to the wedding, saying that she was frightened to disobey my parents, who had made it clear that they disapproved of my marriage and would have nothing to do with it. 'It's all right for you,' she said, 'you're not going to have to live with them.' I didn't understand: she had been disobeying them for years; and by then my mother had moved out of the house, leaving my sister with my father, with whom she got on well.

The sister I had protected had turned from me, and, nearly twenty years later, I had not forgiven her. I could not think of her, or see her, without feeling overwhelmed by her act of betrayal on my wedding day.

Before starting psychotherapy treatment I had most of the family data in my mind, but I had not processed it into any meaningful whole. Stuart's words – 'Do you want to hate your parents all your life?' – hung inside my mind like a newly-unfurled flag of potential independence. I tried to program myself into a state of forgiveness. I must stop hating. I want to be free. To stop hating, I must forgive. Where do I begin? I updated my diary, and included a note about the difference between *must* and *want*.

My behaviour in the group seemed to indicate that I acted out a role which I had inherited from my mother. Like her, I wanted to powerfully control other people. I wanted to dominate them. I insisted on being the centre of attention. If they refused to satisfy my demands, then I wanted to hurt them. I wanted to be the *best* resident, best able to understand my past, best able to communicate, best able to begin a new life, best able to forgive – best able to control.

I felt bitter towards my mother when I realized how much of my behaviour reflected the power which she had exerted over me; but tinged with the bitterness was a suppressed pride and pleasure. I believed that, even though my behaviour had proved destructive, somewhere mixed with my badness was some goodness. I wanted to eliminate the parts of my mother which damaged me; then I would be left with a positive and rewarding *me*. I liked my creativity, my competitive ambition, my willingness to accept responsibility. All I had to do, I reasoned, was to learn where to draw the line between reasonableness and unreasonableness.

I wished that my mother was alive; but she had committed suicide four years before I joined the group, leaving a legacy of lifeless skin on her bedroom carpet. I had a desperate need to tell her that I understood her; that she was right, the two of us were close, and always would be. I wanted to explain that my hatred towards her, and my fear, could change to love and trust if she would stop attacking, and listen to me. I felt furious that she was not there to listen. She had never been there to listen. . . .

Three weeks before my GCE examinations I recognized the dreadful symptoms; one of my mad periods was descending, and I felt terrified, convinced that I would fail every subject. On a Sunday morning I wanted to study, but could not concentrate. Downstairs I heard my parents snapping at each other. I rushed from my room and shouted at them, 'Shut up! I'm trying to study, and you're making it impossible.' My mother repositioned her anger: I was in the firing line. 'How dare you speak to me like that! If it wasn't for me, you'd never have got this far. Leave this house! Leave!' I did. I raced to the front door and started walking, humming familiar tunes, lost in my frightening, gloomy, lonely world. I wanted to escape, from her, and from the terror of failing my examinations. That'll show her, I thought, as I marched away from her in time to my music.

I had no idea where to go; anywhere seemed preferable to returning home. By the following morning I had hitch-hiked 200 miles, without a penny in my pocket, and arrived in Warrington, in the north of England. A policeman saw me walking alone, at 5.30 in the morning, and told me to accompany him to the police station. The police were kind, providing me with food – I was starving, having left home before lunchtime the previous day – and settling me comfortably on a mattress inside an unlocked cell. My dreamy world surrounded me, and I was worried that, because I believed that what I said to them made no sense, they would think me mad. I tried to imagine what was happening in London. When I awoke my father was standing by the cell door, holding a bag containing fresh clothes.

I slept for most of the time on the return journey, but as we came closer to London, and I felt rested, I thought about my mother. I'll have to apologize, I decided, but I'll explain how much more work I have to do, to pass the exams. When my father and I arrived home, she was at the front door. She looked coldly at me: 'I hope you know what you've done to me,' she said, and walked away, holding the arm of a man I had come to detest.

Her affair with Mr Schole – she begged, cajoled and threatened me with ghastly punishments if I did not call him 'Uncle Harvey', but I never did – began when she decided to start her business, and bought storage equipment from his company. Throughout my teens he was a quasi-member of the family. 'Just a very dear friend,' she assured me. He was someone else to hate, because when my mother felt well, he was the person she was most likely to be with. He further disrupted an already disrupted household.

On the other hand, he had his uses; frequently, he had to face my mother's fury, when it could have been me. I enjoyed the pain and humiliation he suffered from her harsh and unreasonable attacks. Why is it, I wondered, that the men in her life put up with her? Schole was old enough to be her father, and she treated him as she presumably would like to have treated my grandfather, who wisely lived in Bourne-mouth, too far away to be attacked by anything other than threatening telephone calls. . . .

However many bad memories disturbed me, I continued drumming forgiveness into my mind; but instead of advanc-ing, I retreated. While I forced myself to balance the good and bad, I suspected that my wish for peace was a fantasy. Peace to my mother was as alien as it was to me: we would not have known what to do with it. In an attempt to succeed, I wrote to my father, trying to explain what was happening to me. He was surprised by the contents of my letter.

People who have not felt the need for, or experienced, psychotherapy or similar self-analysis, seem to be unable, or unwilling, to understand the depth to which one probes personal feelings. In my letter to my father I set out the bitterness I had felt as a child, and referred to quantities of bad memories which neither of us had previously discussed. I expected him to understand what I was saying, and felt frightened when, a week or so later, he arranged to come and see me. I regretted that I had written. Writing to him was within my control. How he might react was not. Had I angered him by what I had said?

No, he assured me, he was not angry, but dismayed. He had not realized how profoundly I had been affected by events which he thought were in a distant past that he remembered, but from which he had recovered. We wandered haphazardly through my mother's life: her numer-ous consultations with psychiatrists, her suicide attempts and financial excesses; her unpredictable mood changes. 'Nobody knew what was wrong with her,' he said, adding, 'She used to analyse them.' In death, I could feel my mother's heat. My hatred turned to pity, but then the pity became pity for myself, and the hatred returned. When I thought of her suffering I thought of my own, and doubted if I had any idea what forgiveness was.

My mother was dead: my father alive. He and I had talked tentatively about feelings and events which had created years of impassable barriers. Hopefully, if I remembered not to forget the good memories I had retrieved from the past, and meticulously listed in my diary, our attempts at mutual understanding would bring us closer together.

I remembered Friday nights when I was seven or eight years old, and he returned home and magically produced Mars bars from empty walls; alternate Saturday mornings, at the same period, when he travelled with me from Middlesex to Marylebone, where I had to receive ophthalmic treatment for my eyes; the weeks he had tried to help before I went to prison: but accompanying each good memory was something bad. He had ruined a birthday surprise for me by letting slip that I was going to receive a Meccano set sent from California by my aunt, and then frightened me that I would not receive it because there was customs duty to pay before it could be collected from the post office. On one of my Saturday. morning trips to the hospital I left a bar of chocolate on the station seat, and had wanted him to buy me a replacement, but he had said that I should have been more careful.

I felt angry that so many apparently minor bad memories kept getting in the way of wanting to forgive my parents. When I remembered one bad memory others returned. I was surprised that so many of them involved money: my parents had promised me a bicycle if I passed my Eleven-Plus examination, and made me wait for nearly two months before buying it, because they were short of money; my father had told me that my success at school was less important to him than my getting a job and earning some money; he had told me that he couldn't afford to buy me a twenty-first birthday present.

I tried to believe that individual memories were not, in themselves, important. What was important was living in the present, not the past. Forget the past, I repeated continually, it's destructive. But, however hard I tried, I could not change how I felt. Forgiveness? Study the list!

When I wrote to my father from the unit, I also wrote to my sister. I wrote of other memories which I had begun to understand. I told her how, while my father was rejecting me, he was embracing her. The week he had told me that he could not afford a present on my twenty-first birthday, he had bought her a new coat. When he left home he saw her every Sunday. I told him that I did not want to see him, but waited anxiously to be invited to one of their afternoon meetings. Until these, and other, memories, and the feelings which accompanied them, returned to me at the unit I had not realized how bitter I felt towards her. My letter set it all out. I wanted to stop resenting her, to forgive her for her act of betrayal on my wedding day.

I played on her the same emotional balancing trick which I had been practising on my parents. Yes, I thought, she had my father; but I had memories of my mother, grandparents and aunt telling me that they never felt towards her the way they felt towards me. Those were secrets which I kept to myself, in the same way that I withheld secrets from the group. To admit my good fortune might dilute the bitter medicine I doled out in my letter.

Had I been honest with myself I would have admitted that when I posted my letters I did not know how to forgive. They were not truly attempts at reconciliation, but muddled accusations, wrapped in soiled feelings. I wanted them to tell me that they were sorry for what they had done to me. I wanted them to hurt as I did. My feelings were bad and powerful. Exploding bombs, erupting volcanoes and treacherous triangles hung on my bedroom wall and filled my waking time – and proved more potent than Stuart's seductive proposal of independence.

I believed that I had tried hard to forgive, and, occasionally, I think that I succeeded, but only during brief moments when I felt at peace with myself. My destructive feelings always returned, and then forgiveness felt less important than revenge. Revenge may have satisfied my fantasies, but it worsened the real injuries I hoped to recover from at the unit.

Many people have told me 'don't be so hard on yourself'. Like most of the other help I have been offered, I ignored what I heard because I grew up believing that I had to do everything for myself by myself. I gave up expecting or receiving help from an early age. But when residents or staff at the unit repeated what I had heard, and previously ignored, I tried to pay a little more attention.

I played my intellectual games trying not 'to be hard' on others, in order to forgive them, and lost. Worse than that, many of my self-imposed rules prevented me from understanding what I was doing. Instead of being honest with the group, I often hid from them many of my thoughts and feelings, and because of that I failed to understand some feelings that took several more years to unravel.

For example, I did not tell the group something which worried and disturbed me throughout my period of treatment: that my mother and aunt both died on the same day, 14 March, but in different years, when they were fifty-five. Their identical deathday is merely a coincidence; but when, recently, I mentioned it to another therapist, he helped me solve a riddle which had disturbed me for years. Why, after my mother died, did I feel less close to my aunt; and why, after they were both dead, did I feel more close to my mother?

Part of the answer, briefly, is that they were both very similar people, but I had created such a perfect fantasy of my aunt, that I refused to acknowledge any of her bad characteristics. She was selfish, bitter, jealous and dishonest; and she never trusted men. After my mother died, and I stopped colouring my two mothers in unalterable shades of black and white, the fantasy changed to reality, and my aunt became what she really was: an aunt whom I loved, not a mother. She no longer had to *pinch* me, and within a year of my mother's death was confronting me with many of the problems I had previously thought my mother's preserve. The three of us formed one of my most treacherous triangles, one which I knew had different angles after their deaths.

Trying to rush into quixotic attempts at reconciliation with my family used up energy which I slowly came to realize would be better devoted to understanding myself. When I was able to recognize that, I slowed down, stopped exhausting myself on others, and began to scrutinize myself more closely. I continually tried to control myself. Don't blame others, I told myself, the past will not change.

Meandering through my childhood memories and feelings was at times as relaxing as a casual stroll across familiar springtime countryside, which, despite its familiarity, offers fresh and wondrous vistas of new life. Then, delighted and curious at each discovery, past behaviour which had previously been accompanied by bitter feelings was transformed into an understanding about myself which felt like a rebirth. Instead of wanting to shout out uncontrollably that I needed help or wanted to destroy, I acquired a strength which I trusted, a profound self-acceptance that I could grow out of the pretence behind which I had been hiding, into someone with whom I could truly survive.

I was surprised that, once I accepted feelings rooted in my childhood as unavoidable reality, I felt more natural and mature. Before I joined the unit, had anybody told me that there was a child screaming inside me, I would have felt brutally assaulted, as though my manhood was being threatened. After I had examined my early years, and acknowledged that I had tried to bury them as I grew older, I wanted to hold on to them. I knew how difficult this would be, but I also knew that not to do so could only lead to more pretence.

At other times, instead of strolling calmly through my childhood, I felt hopelessly and frighteningly lost in a bewildering maze from which there seemed no escape. I detested the labyrinthine paths I had to explore, convinced that I was always moving in the wrong direction. Every thought and feeling I had ended in a blank, impenetrable bitterness. I doubted if I would ever be freed from all that I loathed about myself.

But the most important hours I devoted to self-exploration were those trying to accept that these conflicts − the pleasure of new understanding and the pain of old confusions − would not merge into a neat, orderly whole. The more I wanted to tidy myself up, to pigeon-hole good and bad, right and wrong, madness and sanity, the more I panicked each time I felt disorganized. Although I felt more of a mess as my self-understanding increased, it was a comprehensible mess, like an untidy room which has been long neglected. I could not stop myself doing what I had always done − trying to place each messy part of me into a self-contained compartment − but I did have some reasonable idea of what it was that I was sorting out. Whereas I had previously been throwing scrambled feelings into hidden heaps, I was at last sorting out feelings which I could identify, and emotionally stacking them where they could be seen.

The most rewarding result of this personal reorganization was that I kept colliding with myself. The collisions hurt, but not as painfully as the hidden punishments I had not understood. Thinking of myself as mad, for example, had been an awful self-imposed beating: interpreting mad into several recognizable feelings may sound like playing word-games, but for me it was a transition from a meaningless abstraction into a meaningful reality. Instead of shrouding my fears in a foggy emptiness I explored confrontable, though unwelcome, truths − like anger, shame and violence.

Anger emerged most dramatically from my excursions into childhood. I had always thought of anger as a yelling, throwing, door-slamming, knife-wielding, hysterical expression of hatred. If I expressed my anger as a child I was severely punished. It was safer not to be angry, or rather, not to be seen to be angry. I gradually realized that anger, the anger which lay growling behind my pleasant facade of self-confidence when I was with people, did not have to erupt into explosive fury, as it always had in my childhood. My mother's anger had made me fearful of exhibiting mine. I thought that it was wrong – naughty – to be angry. When I understood, several weeks after joining the unit, that anger was neither right nor wrong, but normal, I felt that I had off-loaded an enormous burden. Suddenly, one day – and it was sudden – I knew that bound closely with my periods of depression and my painful headaches and wearying insomnia, anger had hurt and throbbed inside me because I believed that it was wrong to release it. That was my greatest discovery, when I explored my childhood, that it was reasonable and normal to feel angry; and not only was anger normal, it could be expressed without pinching thighs, or making threats, or throwing things. I wanted to shout with joy, 'Yippee! I've found a new emotional world where I can be angry and normal!' But the discovery created another problem: how do I recognize anger, having spent a lifetime trying to pretend that it didn't exist?

It wasn't – and isn't – easy. And it required more, much more, than an examination of my past.

At Shipley Grange we did not say, 'Today's Tuesday, let's discuss our childhood.' We weaved in and out of all periods of our lives when we wanted to, depending upon how we felt and what was happening. Without the re-examination of my early years I could not have made sense of what took place later. I felt that my detective work was proving productive. There was more of me that I understood. And, although I could not believe it at the time, my attempts to forgive were not wasted.

It became obvious to me that my behaviour and feelings in the adult world were no different to those I had grown up with from the earliest days of my life. I wanted to satisfy myself that I understood what my childhood had created for me, and how I could benefit from what I understood. I wanted to quell the destructive emotions which disrupted my life, and dismantle the multitudinous triangles which separated it into exclusive compartments. To do that I had to stumble past my family and peer beyond my childhood horizons.

The stranger hovering by my side when I started my journey had appeared, briefly, as guilt and an urgent desire to forgive. But the stranger was no longer a stranger. It was not forgiveness or guilt which forced me anxiously forward: it was furious anger.

4 *Sinking not soaring*

Introduction

When I was sixteen I charged aggressively into my future
armed with two obsessive ambitions: I wanted a family in
which I was the benevolent, responsible, loving and loved
husband and father; and I wanted material prosperity — a
home, a smart car, holidays and money in the bank —
financed by a successful business of my own. They were
ambitions powered by a desperate need for revenge. I wanted
to humiliate my parents with my success.

Six years later, a few weeks after I knew that my hopeful
ambitions would become reality, I cleared my bedroom of
personal possessions, removed my books from the living
room, and, while the house was empty, left home. I had not
told my family that I was going, partly because until the night
before I didn't know myself, but mainly because I wanted to
surprise and hurt them with my rear-guard attack. It was the
weekend that I knew my parents and sister would not be
coming to my wedding.

Leaving home felt like conquering an old enemy who had
imprisoned me and indulged in unrelenting torture. I wanted
to escape to untormented territory, and had already staked
out my claim. I was engaged to be married, had qualified as a
chartered accountant, and, fifteen miles away, a kind
gentleman named George Wimpey laid brick upon brick of
what was shortly to be my new home. Included in my luggage
was a ream or two of headed notepaper which named me as
the sole practitioner of my small but expanding accountancy

practice, and my future wife had a file of documents which proved that between us we had saved enough money to buy our first few marital possessions. I had a book full of names and addresses of friends, acquaintances and business contacts, and a head full of ideas.

I hoped that I had escaped from my childhood enemies and that they would subside into a graveyard of buried memories. If I had read *Jonathan Livingston Seagull*[1], which was not published until many years later, I would have imagined myself looking down at my past with soaring contempt as I contemplated my newly-discovered freedom. My *high* was uplifted optimistically by future expectations; when unpleasant feelings disturbed me I persuaded myself that they were parts of my armoury designed to protect me from danger. I had survived the past and, protected by what I had experienced, I could overcome any future adversary.

But, despite what I thought of as my successes, I knew that I remained threatened. Some threats I overcame: I had already passed my professional examinations and crushed the threat of academic failure; I bluffed my way through days of depression, and avoided having to admit how odd I felt, and I staved off financial poverty by working at part-time jobs as well as having a full-time one and time-consuming studies. Other threats were so confusing that I refused to admit their existence.

I exuded self-confidence when with other people, but seldom felt relaxed with them. Like my mother, I was never physically alone in a room full of people, yet I felt strangely disassociated from them. They worried me. What did they think of me? Were they really interested in what I was saying? What did they say about me when I was not there? Why was my head always buzzing with thoughts unrelated to what they were saying? I forced these doubts into a space inside me which I left unexplored for twenty years. At Shipley Grange the hidden threats became reality.

Yes-No and Alter ego

Many of my inner doubts emerged through art therapy. That does not mean that it necessarily clarified my confused thoughts and feelings; more often than not my paintings hung round me like a dreadful private show on permanent display. Psychodrama was less accessible because, once a game had ended, there was usually nothing as indelibly frightening as the pictures hanging ominously on my bedroom wall to remind me how I had felt. Also, unlike art therapy sessions, when we only painted one subject each week, during the hour or so devoted to permitted acting out on Tuesday afternoons, we played three, and occasionally four, games. Too much happened too quickly. Sometimes I enjoyed painting: I never enjoyed psychodrama[2].

However, I remember vividly the first game of my first psychodrama session, two days after I joined the unit. I had no idea what to expect, except that several residents said encouraging things like 'Whew, wait till you've seen this!', and 'Christ, I wish it wasn't Tuesday'. It was, and we played *Yes-No*.

The meeting room was emptied of furniture. 'For those of you who haven't played this before,' Stuart began, 'imagine that there's an invisible line stretching across the centre of the room. We'll split into two teams. For the first half of the game one team is *Yes* and the other *No*. We must not cross the line, or say any words other than yes and no, depending upon which team we're in. Any questions?'

I had several, but said nothing. I wanted to say, 'That sounds like the most stupid game I've ever heard of,' and, 'What's the point of it?' and, 'What are we supposed to do?' and, 'What d'you think I am, barmy?' but I said nothing because I felt confused and withdrawn among my unfamiliar companions. I wondered whether I should be a *Yes* or a *No* – but couldn't decide. As it happened, it made no difference.

The game began. Everyone kept to the rules. No one crossed the imaginary line or used forbidden words. The *Yes*

team mouthed 'yes' and the *No* team mouthed 'no'. Some of
the yesses and noes were uttered quietly, some noisily. Mostly
they kept changing, as members moved to and from other
members. One resident went up to another and spat out a
verbal phlegmful of 'no' across the barrier, receiving a
thunderous 'yes' and an intimidatory raised fist in reply.
Another sing-songed a pretty little 'yes' tune to a nearby *No*,
and either received a lyrical negative or a contemptuous
denial, I can't recall which. The noise inside the small meeting
room increased. Members moved along their side of the
barrier which wasn't there, selected team opponents, and
attempted to ensnare them into a yes chat or a no argument
or a no show of sympathy or a yes shout of fury. An
unpleasant ganging-up occurred when a few *Yesses* verbally
assaulted an isolated *No*, but she was quickly joined by some
protective team-mates. The noise became deafening.

'OK, let's change over.' And it all began again, with violent
or tempting *Noes* becoming equally violent or tempting
Yesses. Some members yelled furiously and loudly, others
withdrew into quieter responses, and a few, to my amazement, seemed to enjoy themselves.

The game ended and we sat on the carpeted floor to
discuss how we had felt. 'Did you find that difficult?' Stuart
asked me. 'Yes,' I replied, feeling angry and humiliated.
While the rest of the group participated in their verbal plate-
throwing, I had stood as unmoving as the wall next to me,
unwilling to join in what seemed to me to be the most
unbelievable nonsense I had ever seen. He asked me why I
hadn't taken part and I remembered that once or twice he
had come over to me and said 'yes' or 'no', while I stood
silently by the wall, and I had looked at him spitefully. 'I
couldn't see any point in it,' I replied. 'Do you always have to
have a reason to do something?' he wanted to know. 'Yes,' I
said, wondering if he expected me to say 'no'.

My behaviour during that game upset me. I felt ashamed
and frightened that I had found it impossible to mingle with
the group, particularly when I realized that that was how I
often reacted when I was with most groups of people. The

apparent silliness of *Yes-No* seemed much less disturbing than the unanswered question in my mind – why couldn't I join in?

Four months later we played the same game. I had a marvellous time, shouting at, cajoling and teasing other members. By then I felt more in charge. I wanted to show the newer residents what to do. Come on, I wanted to say, it's only a game. But I felt upset and guilty when a newly-arrived female resident covered her face with her hands and ran crying from the room because she, too, couldn't join in. The game ended in a subdued silence: we all knew what she was suffering.

Another game we played was *alter ego*. ('Alter 'oo?' someone asked.) Its deceptive, intellectual-sounding name quickly became less important than the crude feelings it generated. The game required four participants: two who sat opposite each other; and two more, one of whom stood behind each sitter. The rules were more complicated than those of *Yes-No*. The two sitters could say what they wanted only to each other. The two who stood, the sitters' *alter egos*, could say what they wanted, but only to their opposite *alter ego*.

Ho, hum, I thought, what's this all about? At first there were no volunteers. Cowards! I thought to myself, moving to one of the chairs. 'Come on Larry,' I said cheerfully to one of the male residents. Val and Stuart, who had played the game with other groups, acted respectively as my and Larry's *alter ego*. We started speaking.

'Why didn't you deal with the laundry yesterday?' I said calmly to Larry. ('You lousy, good-for-nothing layabout,' Val said noisily above my head, to Stuart.)

'I forgot,' Larry replied quietly. ('What the hell's it got to do with you?' Stuart shouted at Val, pushing his shoulders forward.)

'You didn't forget, you just didn't want to do it,' I continued. ('You lying, lazy, useless heap of refuse,' Val sneered at Stuart a second later.)

'I'll get it done, don't worry,' Larry said truculently. ('You

fat, pompous, bossy git, mind your own bloody business,'
Stuart shouted more loudly at Val.)

'But we're short of sheets,' I said angrily. ('If you raise your
voice at me, you snivelling little runt, you'll regret it.')

'You think we've all got to do what you say,' Larry said,
speaking as angrily and as noisily as myself. ('It's . . . like
you who've ruined my life,' Stuart yelled at Val, wildly
gesticulating his arms.)

'No I don't, but you never do anything here, and we're all
fed up with it.' ('Yes I do, and you'd better learn that pretty
damn quickly or I'll get rid of you, you whining, miserable
apology for a man.') I was fast losing my temper, conscious
of our *alter egos*, pleased at what Val was saying on my
behalf, and angry at Stuart's counter-attacks.

That is an abbreviated version of an encounter which
lasted for ten minutes, but it illustrates the effect of the game.
Within a few minutes, Larry, whom I detested, and with
whom I had wanted to have a row for weeks, and I, were
yelling, swearing and hurling vicious verbal attacks at each
other. Val's and Stuart's noise was submerged by ours. Or, to
put it another way, what Larry and I were feeling, and
initially hiding, came out furiously into the open. Our *alter
egos* were in command and we were out of control.

The bout exhausted me. I felt frightened that my anger had
erupted so viciously and unexpectedly, and pleased that I had
attacked an enemy. Shocked by the game's ferocity, nobody
volunteered for a second round. *Alter ego* was not played
again while I was at the unit.

These two party-games helped explain what happened to
me when I confronted other people. Unlike my self-exclusion
during *Yes-No*, I seldom physically wallflowered myself in
the presence of other people; and, unlike *alter ego*, I seldom
allowed my true thoughts and feelings to show: but I realized
that, whatever physical pretences I normally exhibited, most
of my contact with people was the *me* I wanted them to see,
not the *me* I actually was. Both games highlighted the extent
to which I tried to hide myself. And after my barriers had
been psychodramatically removed I was once again surprised

that I felt better, not worse, when what I had attempted to hide was brought out for public trial. Feeling better was a relative verdict, as if I had been accused of murder and had my charge reduced to manslaughter — or, in the case of *alter ego*, Larryslaughter. For brief periods, after each trial, I sometimes felt more comfortable with the group, but I invariably withdrew into angry, sullen, self-imposed isolation.

I realized that this isolation had developed from childhood. I thought of my inability to play *Yes-No* as one of my triangles. My parents were the participants at either end of one side, and I was sharply angled at a distance from them both. *Alter ego* reminded me of hours spent listening to my mother talk, while my angry thoughts swelled up inside me. Both games made me think of other groups I had lived with, in my social life, in my business, at home, with my wife and children, and at school.

'A boy of excellent character'

I left school — after taking my Ordinary Level GCE examinations — with a satchelful of mixed memories and a conviction that nobody had detected my guilty secrets, especially the one about being mad. I had wanted to go to university, but my need to become financially independent, so that I could leave home, was greater than my academic one. The hand-written testimonial, given to me by the headmaster when I turned my back on school, states: 'a boy of excellent character and good academic ability, who has worked extremely hard and thoroughly deserved his success in the General Certificate of Education. He has wide interests, including music and rambling. His work has been throughout so painstaking and methodical that I predict success in any career upon which he embarks.'

In the group we discussed success, specifically my desperate need for it. I described my fear of failure before I took my examinations. That was one of the days when Stuart told me that I demanded too much of myself. 'But my exams were important to me,' I said. 'You've probably always been like that,' he replied, 'because that's what you knew your mother demanded from you.' I set my memory in reverse gear, and recalled past academic and business challenges. I had enjoyed success: but why had I felt that once I had achieved what I wanted it was inadequate? Racing backwards into my school years, I mentally crashed into Dr Dory. If I had not demanded too much of myself, how could I have satisfied his expectations?

Most masters at school wore their university gowns like veils of concealed authority, but, provided we did not disrupt their lessons, they rarely exposed their powers. One of the swaying, black shrouds feared by many boys belonged to the awe-inspiring, diminutive Doctor. Three incontrovertible facts were known about him: he did not have a nickname; he wrote books, one of which was an official history textbook; and he gave the longest detention line we had ever heard – 'Manners maketh man is the motto of Winchester College; but good manners need not be confined to Winchester College.' Rumours circulated that he never smiled, never joked, never played games – sporting ones, anyway – and seldom spoke individually to a boy, except to answer a question or invoke a punishment. In our first two years we were alarmed by his ominous reputation for demanding rigid discipline and unyielding excellence: in the third year he became a reality.

My consternation at having failed to achieve Arts streaming was compounded when I learned that the infamous Dr Dory was to teach me history – for the next three years. He loomed ahead of me like a threat as punishing as his line, and as forbidding as his scholastic gown. I believed that the remainder of my school career lay in tatters, tucked under his shrouded folds.

His first words to us, approximately, were: 'By your next lesson you will have acquired a hard-bound, foolscap-size book, which will be required for your corrected notes. During my lessons you may use a school exercise book to take rough notes, which will be written up and expanded as part of your weekend homework. Any boy . . . I repeat, any boy who fails to present his corrected notes during the first lesson of the week will receive a detention and one hundred lines. Is that clearly understood?' Before anyone replied he continued: 'This year's syllabus commences with the reign of George the Third, but I consider that an inadequate start, and so for one month we will examine the years from 1714 to 1760, an important period in our country's history. We shall therefore work particularly conscientiously during that month. When Queen Anne died. . . .'

Dr Dory made a profound and unforgettable impression on me, but, until I thought about him at the unit, I had not connected my efforts to win his approval with similar ones to please my parents or impress my business colleagues. I wanted to satisfy him so that I could feel satisfied. He rewarded my efforts with more merit awards than he gave any other pupil while I was at the school. When he first marked my work *good* I felt delighted. But after he wrote *excellent* I mentally whipped myself if all I received was a *good*, wondering what I had done wrong.

Three years later he told me that I had gained the highest pass mark in Ordinary Level GCE of any boy whom he had ever taught, and the highest awarded that year by the University of London – 92 per cent. He also told me that it had been a pleasure to have me as a pupil, and invited me to join him at the local library so that he could show me how he was preparing research documentation for a newly-commissioned book. I could not understand why, when I expected to be glowing with pride at my success, the first thing I did after leaving him was to rush to the lavatory and cry. For years after that final meeting I felt angry that my success had only been at Ordinary Level – why not Advanced Level?

'A boy of excellent character' the headmaster had written. I was pleased to have such a commendation, although nobody ever asked to see it, but what about the *me* who was omitted from my glowing report?

In the previous chapter I wrote that I felt 'relatively secure' at school. It was a very relative security, related to the chaos at home. I scorned and feared authority at school: I was the first boy in my first year to be caned, which gained me a few hours of admiration and a sore backside; I loathed the prefects' strutting confidence; I was a regular in the detention room, and had two immutable classroom enemies — whoever happened to be the form prefect and, from my third year, the one boy who occasionally ousted me from my place at the top of the form.

But my worst fear at school was a physical one: games. When we played rugby I protectively cushioned myself in the second row of the scrum and what I lacked in bravery I made up for with frantic exhortations. 'Come on! Push! Push! Get the ball!' I shouted as loudly as I could, hoping that nobody would notice that I kept my feet as far away from it as possible. On the cricket field I was convinced that the hard, red-leather ball was about to be fired from a cannon and bloody my face or mangle my crotch, and shielded myself by standing as close as I could to the boundary. When I faced a threatening bowler at the wicket I fervently clasped my hands round the bat and pleaded to a God in whom I desperately wanted to believe to save me from imminent destruction. But I enjoyed cross-country running, a controllable, teamless pursuit where I was responsible to no one but myself, and where there was nobody to tell me what to do.

I nervously collected school clubs and societies as though they were glittering social trophies, but they often dulled into gloomy memories of failure. I quickly disposed of those which did: the chess club faded because I could not plan sparkling moves and was consistently beaten; the music master welcomed me into the orchestra and made me raise high the trombone, which I could not hold on to, literally or metaphorically, so I blew it away as soon as I decently could, and I discarded the drama society when I felt frightened that I would forget my lines and not glisten brilliantly on stage. I prized other activities, polishing and shining them until they reflected what I expected to see of myself. At different times I was chairman of the music and history societies; and in my last year I was president of our dance committee, mainly because, thanks to my mother, I was one of the few boys who not only knew what the fox-trot was, and could confidently dance its steps, but was also prepared to teach my classmates what I knew of the terpsichorean art.

At separate periods during my five years at secondary school I had three close friends, in a one-to-one relationship. The first was the only boy who had come with me from my junior school, and we remained friends for a year; the second shared my enthusiasm for classical music, and the third was a chum from my form who had the decency not to beat me in examinations.

Friends invited me to their homes. I dared not invite them to mine. Ashamed that I could not explain why, I felt uneasy with them. The *alter ego* which escaped at Shipley Grange constantly hovered behind me when I was with them.

At the end of it all I left school feeling inadequate. I had wanted to pass at least nine GCE subjects, and resented failing two of them. I felt ashamed of the tricks I had played to evade the rigours of games. Most important of all, I thought that leaving school at sixteen, when I had expected to progress into the sixth form, and then on to university, would make me seem, in the opinions of my peers, an academic weakling. After I had smiled and said goodbye to masters and friends I decided not to join the old boys' club. I locked my schoolfriends into a disused compartment, and, within six months of leaving school, did not see or hear from any of them.

'A boy of excellent character'? I enjoyed reading the words, but never believed them.

High-flyer

The word *workaholic* was not part of the language in the 1960s. I first heard its nasty sound when I visited New York in 1972. Men in short sleeves, overdosing on their careers during hectic, humid weekdays, told me proudly: 'Don't have time for it (theatre, reading, listening to music, spending time with their family, etc). Not me. I'm a workaholic.' On another visit a few years ago I met several female *workos*. It's a peculiar irony that those who make their boast – in England the translation is usually 'don't get home before eight very often' – never appear to understand what they're saying. They wouldn't admit so cheerfully to being a *wino* or a member of Gamblers Anonymous. Most of the *workos* I know remind me of myself, drugged into over-activity by obsessions they cannot control and may not understand.

I used to laugh scornfully at a client friend of mine who refused to work outlandish hours, strangely preferring to be at home to put his young children to bed. No ambition, I'd say to myself, feeling sorry for him. He did other things which I found difficult to accept, like planning in advance when to change his car, and going regularly to the same resort each year for his summer holiday. How tedious and unimaginative, I thought. When he heard of the long hours I worked he said 'don't know why you do it'. Nor did I until we discussed it at the group. We used a different bit of jargon: instead of overworking I was told that I was *escaping*.

At school I escaped hard, but not as hard as I escaped after I left. I stopped dreaming of becoming a professor of history at Oxford when a family friend suggested accountancy. 'Who's ever heard of a poor accountant?' people said approvingly. Yes, I liked the idea of not being a poor accountant. 'Hard, though, getting the exams,' said others. No, I did not like the idea of failing. I investigated this newly-proposed career and discovered two important facts: only one trainee in thirty who signed articles at sixteen passed his examinations, all of them, first time; but, if he did, at the age of twenty-one he could acquire a respectable and valuable professional qualification.

I spent five years terrified that I would not be the one in thirty. Yes, I had to succeed. No, I must not fail.

Between the formal lines of the letter from the Institute of Chartered Accountants in England and Wales, which congratulated me on passing my final examination, I read: 'You are real. You are successful. You have all that you wanted.' I walked through the streets singing aloud, feeling taller than the lamp-posts, wanting to shout out with glee to every passer-by that I was a success. For the first time in my life I felt secure and financially independent.

And then, a day or two later, I felt frightened. It can't last, I thought, all this success. Something is going to go horribly wrong. Something is bad. I could not understand why, whenever I felt good, I convinced myself that it was too good to be true. Feeling good felt as unsettling as feeling bad. Dr Dory's approval felt good – until I remembered that, despite my 92 per cent at Ordinary Level, I had failed him by not continuing my history studies. Qualifying as an accountant, having passed all my examinations first time, felt good – until I remembered that I did not have my own business.

Whatever I achieved was not enough. 'You could never satisfy your mother, could you?' Stuart said one day at the unit. On another occasion, after insisting that I wanted to control the group – which I denied, knowing that it was true – he commented, 'Even if you did, it wouldn't meet your needs.' I wanted to ask him what my needs were, but knew that he would not give me an answer. *Not enough* and *wanting to control* worried me. My parents had not given me enough and my mother had wanted to control me.

My career advanced rapidly. When I was twenty-three I became the junior partner in a firm of accountants, with two other partners and twelve staff, and introduced to it the small private practice I had built up. My partners and I shared a vision of our future: a large, profitable, reputable and respected practice, developing expertise beyond the mundane routine of ordinary accountants' work. Five years later we had eight partners and about eighty employees, and the turnover had increased by more than 1500 per cent. Credit for this achievement was shared by all the partners, but I knew, as did the others, that much of the development was due to my creative ideas and unabated desire to get bigger, to get enough.

Often, my ideas were novel, and I fought hard to have them accepted, quickly feeling angry and rejected if they were not implemented immediately. I enthusiastically worked long hours, but when I left my office the business travelled home with me. In the evenings, even if I wanted to, I could not forget about my latest scheme or problem. Many nights, when I felt exhausted but unable to sleep, I sat at my dining-room table writing lists of what I wanted to do the following day, or preparing a summary of my newest idea.

I looked forward to weekends as a time to make up lost sleep and refuel myself, but on Saturdays, after a tiring week's work, I usually had a headache. Each day felt like a threat because I dreaded that my plans might be thwarted by an unexpected and uncontrollable bout of depression.

Once or twice a year this dread became reality, ruining my self-esteem. Then I felt hopelessly inadequate, totally incapable of working to a regular routine. Sometimes, during the working day, having forced myself out of bed in a state of mental exhaustion, I left the office on the pretext of an appointment and drove to a nearby park. There, hidden behind clumps of trees, I slept for an hour or two, before returning grudgingly to my desk. I tried to convince myself that I was just tired, and that in a day or so I'd feel better. My guilty escapes from the office, and the bad feelings which overwhelmed me, felt like shameful secrets to be hidden: to admit them meant admitting failure, and I did not know how to do that. For a few days I survived by shuffling papers meaninglessly across my desk, trying to avoid contact with staff and clients – and recouping in parks. Inevitably the day arrived when the foggy, nightmarish world which had haunted me from my teens returned, and I withdrew from my family and business. I tormented myself: what would my partners think of me?

When I first became a partner there were two of them. Charles West was approaching sixty, and planning his retirement within five years. Malcolm Saunders was seven years older than me. Within a year or so we were joined by a fourth, younger, partner, Gary Norton. Our business family, in which Charles was the father, acquired several more sons as we expanded.

Charles was a short, grey-haired, bow-tied, pipe-smoking man, who loved his wife, business, garden, Freemasonry and London club, probably in that order. He was as reliable and exact as a calendar. 'He's at his club,' the rest of would joke, 'so it must be Tuesday'; or, 'Mr West is off to Torquay next week, so it must be the third week in May.' His feelings would have been deeply ruffled had he suspected that his sons mocked the punctiliousness he preened with studied care, but we were careful to keep our amused thoughts to ourselves. We had good reason to. His finicky insistence on orderliness included a plan as precise as a perpetual almanac for the continuance of the business he had established in the 1930s. He expected us to keep it revised and up to date, and in return was prepared to relinquish control.

As his retirement drew near, working with him became more difficult. He had not imagined that the one-man firm he founded could have expanded so rapidly. He disliked having to concede that most of the dynamism came from his younger partners, and tried, but failed, to fit neatly into the larger group. Despite his carefully-timed withdrawal he resented the idea of leaving *his* business to the rest of us and often said, with a forced smile, 'I envy you young chaps.' Determined to prove that what he had lost in years he retained in dash, while the rest of us accelerated forward in comfortable family saloons, he screeched to a noisy halt with the burning enthusiasm of a twenty-five-year-old in fast sports cars – and meticulously planned his retirement.

His relations with all the partners was outwardly friendly and courteous, unless one of us unintentionally insulted him by advising a client to do something diametrically opposed to his own advice, or raised the fee of another to a level he considered bordering on theft. In the presence of strong-minded, wealthy clients he bent with the ease of a £1 note. Reluctantly, he also frequently bent to his strong-minded, ambitious partners as he folded himself tidily into retirement.

Charles – in fact, he remained 'Mr West' to all of us – was one of the kindest men I have ever known. I did not realize it then, but now I understand that he became an important father figure. Often, my wife and I spent a weekend afternoon at his house, sipping his obligatory, and too sweet, sherry, or wandering through his large and perfectly maintained garden, amazed at the precision of each orderly blade of grass. He and his wife welcomed us as friends and, away from office pressures, they exuded goodwill and tranquillity. At other times, during office hours, he and I discussed our hopes and plans, or criticized other partners' behaviour, much of which disturbed him. He said that he could 'talk more freely' with me, which was his way of admitting fears which he was sometimes too frightened to discuss with the others. Occasionally he would suggest, 'if you could', that I raise some matter or other which he was too embarrassed to.

He was the only partner with whom I could discuss tentatively how my depression felt, but he unwittingly made me erect a barrier between us by euphemistically describing it as 'your little weakness'. He balanced my little weakness by describing me as a 'high-flyer', who, 'like a thoroughbred racehorse, performs brilliantly, but needs delicate handling'. I liked the 'high-flyer' bit.

His unvarying, methodical life disturbed me. I was as disorderly as he was orderly. I poked fun at his unchanging paisley bow-ties and predictable autumn chrysanthemums, at the same time wanting him to stay as he was. He made me feel that somewhere, in a world I did not understand, was the tranquillity and certainty which I needed.

The partner with whom I had the closest creative affinity was the youngest, Gary. We were both impatient, anxious for tomorrow to arrive yesterday, and intellectually quickly grasped each other's ideas. We both rushed around more frantically than the others, and constantly felt aggravated when we had to slow down to let them catch up with us. But our relationship was close in no other way. He was my only self-acknowledged rival in the partnership, and I kept a respectful distance from him, in the same way that I never sought the company of the boy who sometimes out-performed me at school.

Like some members of the unit at Shipley Grange, there were other partners who played a less significant role in my view of the partnership, because either creatively or intellectually I felt that they had less to offer. I welcomed their lack of imagination and their inability to defy me openly. When I was with them I felt superior, and probably infuriated them by being patronizing.

Apart from Charles West, the member of my business group who influenced me most was Malcolm Saunders. Malcolm was everything I thought I was not. Thinking of him in later years I realized that I clothed him in an authoritative mantle similar to my schoolmaster, Dr Dory. He was stubborn and cautious, pedantic, slow to make a decision, but always reliable as a steady, stable colleague. He preferred conventional familiarity to unusual innovations. This insularity was typified by his incorrigible xenophobia. During my years with the firm he never strayed beyond the foreign shores of Wales, and looked at me with bewilderment when, in the early 1970s, I first discussed my ideas about how we could benefit from Britain's forthcoming entry into the European Common Market.

Administratively, he could do what I could not – accept day-to-day responsibility for mundane and essential routines, which became increasingly more critical as we expanded. I was often the partner who introduced new systems: he was usually the one who ensured that they remained in practice, leaving me to create new challenges. We admired each other's strengths and skills, and, despite enormous dissimilarities in our characters, we probably had as good a working relationship as any other two of the partners. Unlike Gary Norton's flair, which threatened my creative supremacy, Malcolm had none, or very little. In that sense, as with Charles West, he was not a competitor.

I had known before I joined the firm that Malcolm was Charles's heir apparent as senior partner; because of his willingness to undertake work which did not interest me, that presented no competitive threat, or so I thought. I had no wish to be senior partner if it meant accepting tedious and restricting responsibilities. I wanted to be left alone to create and implement my own imaginative ideas. A man like Malcolm, unaware of how willing he was to be led, and extremely competent to do what was essential for the stability of the business, felt like a valuable asset among my shaky personal liabilities.

Emotionally, Malcolm and I shared very little, but we comforted ourselves in many other ways. When we wanted to relax, and ease the immediate pressures from clients and staff, we secluded ourselves in one of our offices and talked for hours about books and writers; or, in less intellectual pursuits, fumbled through a huge selection of unblended pipe tobaccos at Bewlay's, making up our own, usually foul, mixtures. One day, having produced a lethal, black mixture consisting almost entirely of throat-choking Turkish Latakia, we decided to offer a gift of the awful stuff to Charles, as a joke. Charles looked at the proffered package with embarrassment and horror and tried not to offend us. 'Perhaps later,' he said, gracefully and dishonestly, 'but if you don't mind, I'll just have a fill of my Gold Block.' His anxious frown and polite smile repaid us for the hour or so we had wasted concocting the terrible stuff.

Malcolm and I found each other unbearable at times and seldom knew how to confront personal problems which developed between us – Father Charles sometimes succeeded in appeasing his two erring sons – but we rarely erupted into open hostilities. Our most important bond was the business, which we both treasured and needed, and neither of us wanted to damage it. He probably never understood that to me he was a frightening figure. Unknowingly, he could arouse a suppressed fury which would disturb me for days, or longer.

I recall one morning when I arrived ten minutes late at the office for our morning partners' meeting. 'Can't you get here on time?' he asked, covering his irritation with a casualness which fooled neither of us. I could not tell him that I had hardly slept the previous night, and had had to make a tremendous effort to get out of bed, let alone arrive on time. He never knew the hatred I felt towards him when he said that to me. I knew that he was attempting to demonstrate his own infallibility, but he had hurt me, and, like most hurts inflicted on me, I could not forget or forgive.

From the day I became a partner I was obsessed with the business. Unlike Malcolm, who slept like a log, or Charles, who said, 'I forget about business when I leave the office, and don't think about it until I shave the following morning', I could not get it out of my mind. As soon as I developed one new idea, or finalized the negotiation of another acquisition, my mind raced ahead to create more demanding challenges. Like my relationship with Dr Dory, it was not enough that the business was *good*: it had to be *excellent*. If we increased our fees by 10 per cent one quarter, I thought it disastrous if we did not increase them by 20 per cent the next. If Malcolm and Charles thought that we needed three more staff, I argued that they were only thinking of the immediate future, and demanded six. When Charles suggested that we should consolidate our growth I felt furious. To me 'consolidate' sounded like going backwards, when I was desperate to rush pell-mell into the unknown future.

I expected my clients to share my hunger. I had no appetite for clients' affairs which had become staled by age. Accountancy work relating to financial periods which had their place in history gave me business indigestion. I wanted to create flamboyant trading feasts with clients who were as greedy for the future as myself. Essential ingredients when choosing my clients were that they should include the most exciting, fast-expanding and highest fee-paying names on our practice's list. For those who offered what I wanted I prepared the tastiest professional dishes I could.

My wife accused me of loving my business more than my family. 'Rubbish,' I replied angrily, worried and confused because she was right. My insomnia and headaches worsened. It was not uncommon for me to work until 3 or 4 o'clock in the morning on a thrilling idea for expansion, or a demanding client's latest urgent request for advice, gulping a couple of pain-killing tablets every hour to relieve my tension. At night, secreted away with my over-activity while most of the world slept, I became increasingly desperate for continual change. There had to be something new happening. If there was not, life seemed to stand still; and when it stood still, I did not know what to do with myself. Yesterday's success was quickly forgotten. I wanted to be the firm's star, radiating brilliance. When I knew that I needed to 'consolidate', to take time off to enjoy what I had, I did not know how to. Always, at the back of my mind, was the fear that if I did not do immediately what I wanted to, a dark bout of depression might engulf me in physical and mental isolation.

Living with my own personal failure – my little weakness – was like being emotionally handcuffed to an invisible partner. I tried to believe that the more successful I became, the less reason there was for me to become depressed. When those foggy periods descended, and people near to me suggested that it was because I had been overworking, I did not know whether to agree with them, and so imply that it was a new experience, or disagree, and explain that I knew that it went beyond my working life. I covered up the first bout or two, after I started in partnership, by getting my wife to say that I had a bug, or the old standby, 'flu, but that became impossible after two or three recurrences.

When I had to explain that I suffered from depression – still having no understanding of the reasons – I felt shamed and furious. One month I was a resplendent flagship, sailing into an uncharted and exciting future; the next, I was sinking. My slight consolation was that by then I had learned that depression was not as unique as I had believed. Encouraged by that knowledge I stopped feeling that I was mad – at least for a while. When I returned to the office after a week or two's absence, I wanted to shut myself behind my office door, and work, and work, and work, to make up for lost time, and to prove how valuable and indispensable I was to the partnership.

Those were periods of exuberant activity when I felt as elated as I had been the first time the awful fog had lifted when I was a teenager. Believing that my depression had vanished, I felt refreshed and ready to recommence my conquest of the world. I wanted to forget my little weakness and to be certain that I was still admired and respected by my partners. The merest hint from one of them that my latest idea was not perfect could send me into fits of suppressed fury. Then I became convinced that they believed that I was useless and incapable. At times I hated them all: Charles West and his regimented springtime daffodils, Malcolm Saunders and his reliable time-keeping, and Gary Norton for being there to shine in my absence. Most of all I hated them, and the other partners, for not being depressed or suffering from continual headaches and insomnia.

The post-depression periods, as I then thought of them, were as frightening as the foggy memories I wanted to forget. I could not understand how I produced so much work, or why everyone else seemed to be so slow. On a Saturday morning, a few days after I returned to the office after a fortnight's absence, I decided to examine the files of all my clients. I resented that other partners had looked after them, and was anxious to re-establish contact. I dealt with any unanswered letters, brought up to date outstanding administrative matters, and issued numerous fee accounts, using a dictating machine.

On a typical day, if I was in my office, and not visiting clients, I usually filled up less than one tape, which gave my secretary a morning's work. This, plus her other duties, was sufficient to keep her fully occupied. On the Monday morning after my frantic Saturday's work, another secretary, with a worried frown, came into my room. 'Lynn's in her office, crying,' she told me. 'I thought you ought to know.' Lynn was practically having hysterics, I discovered. She had gone home on Friday exhausted, she explained between choking sobs, after I had given her an enormous amount of work. When she sat down at her desk that Monday she had seen the results of my weekend work — fourteen tapes — and collapsed in tearful frustration. I arranged to have her work shared among the other women, feeling sorry that I had upset her and angry that my work was being delayed. My partners told me to slow down, and that made me angrier.

We opened several branch offices. One, in Surrey, I visited weekly, driving as fast as I dared through the countryside, breaking speed limits, cutting-up drivers who got in my way, convinced that I had to be where I was going so that I could leave as quickly as possible to move to where I was not, but wanted to be. On the last Thursday in November 1968 I drove there after lunch. During the afternoon an employee mentioned that a thick fog had descended. At four-thirty I told everyone to go home, pleased with myself for being such a considerate employer. I thought of my drive home, through low, damp countryside, and decided to work on, hoping that the fog would clear. By 6.30 it was worse. From my office window I could not see across the street. I locked up, and made my way to the car park, barely able to see more than twenty feet, not looking forward to the drive ahead. Usually the journey home took forty minutes. That night, I thought, it could take a couple of hours. I slowly manoeuvred my car through grey-black streets, out of the town, and joined twisting, tree-lined roads, where it was impossible to see either the road's edge or oncoming traffic. After a few miles I stopped the car, climbed into the back seat, wrapped myself in a rug and went to sleep. I remember feeling comforted by the silent, eerie fog.

I woke up three hours later, immediately realizing that my wife would be worried. I continued my journey, knowing that I did not want to go home. Despite the dangerous driving conditions, I wanted to stay inside my car, cocooned by the surrounding fog. I eventually arrived home at midnight. My wife rushed to meet me, having spent several worrying hours wondering where I was. I went straight to bed and slept, exhausted after my long day.

I had no idea that that Thursday was to be my last full day's work for nine terrifying months, or that it would be more than a year before I visited our Surrey office.

Social climbing

Ben, my teenage son, recently asked me about life in the 1960s. 'It must have been amazing to grow up then,' he said wonderingly, 'with the Beatles and hippies and Rock and the Vietnam marches. What was it like, Dad?' I thought for a moment or two and replied: 'For me, the most important thing was that young people could do then what would have been impossible a few years earlier. I felt that I didn't have to be forty-five before I could get what I wanted. My generation started the sixties with Harold Macmillan's assurance that we'd "never had it so good".' He continued enthusiastically: 'But it must have been great being a hippy and listening to Bob Dylan. And what about drugs?' I explained that my energy had gone into my business, and that there were not many more hippies strolling through the streets of London then than there were punks doing the same today, and that neither myself nor my friends and acquaintances had anything to do with drugs. 'Wish I'd grown up then,' he said wistfully, dreaming of hippies. 'I enjoyed the fifties more,' I replied.

My teenage years encompassed more than depression, headaches, insomnia and studies. They included the fascinating experiences of living in the centre of a huge city. We moved to central London in 1952, when I was ten, and I left home a decade later. Throughout those years, however miserable I felt at home, I could usually comfort myself with some new thrill which helped me escape from family tribulations. Large though it was, and remains, London, my London, quickly acquired the atmosphere of a small village.

Lord's cricket ground, which I visited regularly, unable to believe that I was really seeing Denis Compton batting, edged its northerly borders. Hyde Park, where I could swim on hot summer afternoons, or stand transfixed by the vociferous harangues at Speakers' Corner, sloped gently southwards, towards Buckingham Palace. Regent's Park, my favourite, with its rowing boats for hire, and the Zoo, provided entertainment in the east; and Bayswater, edged by a wide, tree-lined avenue leading to infinity, completed the village's geographical rectangle. Snuggling comfortably inside was my school, Piccadilly's garish lights, cinemas with rising electric Wurlitzer organs colourfully illuminated by more garish lights, and the unending shops in Oxford Street, spread out like hungry mouths at a sumptuous banquet, the most greedy of which was Selfridges, the retail lord of my local manor. A penny bus ride took me to the river Thames, Whitehall and the famous museums and art galleries. Anywhere beyond was foreign territory.

Ugly, crumbling, war-damaged craters, fenced in by secretive shuttering and mountains of climbing scaffolding, were temporarily filled with noisy compressors and unseen gangs of builders. Months later the gruesome legacies of destruction emerged as a new generation of cement-and-glass office cubes and neon-lit shop windows. Something American called a supermarket opened and people said that they'd never use it because there was nobody to serve them.

In the streets, austere black motor cars with hunched backs at the beginning of the decade were replaced by gaudy, shiny-winged streamlined bodies, sometimes painted in the same shade of salmon pink as men's shirts advertised in the newspapers hawked at most corners by men who shouted 'Star, News, Stan-dard!' After the building gangs, news vendors, office workers and shop assistants had left for the day, neolithic punks called Teddy boys, dressed in jackets with shoulders spread like black flags, and trousers which drained into pointed shoes, lounged aggressively against telephone kiosks in nearby Edgware Road. I could not decide whether they frightened me more than the rouged prostitutes, enticingly banging handbags against stockinged thighs, who strutted past them in stiletto heels.

Teddy boys and prostitutes disappeared from the pavements within a few years: the broad-shouldered Teds replaced by casually-dressed flower people; the pros, forced to shelter indoors from stormy legislation, settling comfortably into massage parlours and strip-joints. (Twenty years later, Edgware Road, the roughest area in my village when I was a teenager, was identifiable by burnoused arabs luxuriously housed and fed in smart, renovated apartment blocks and elegant restaurants.) Other strange people appeared in the 1950s, and remained. In 1952 I ran to my mother shouting excitedly that I'd seen my first black man. Six years later, violent racial riots broke out a mile or so away, in Notting Hill, which became London's first *no-go* area for worried whites.

Twelve months after I entered my village I dressed up in a colourful tunic and held a cardboard trumpet to my lips, heralding my junior school's celebration of Queen Elizabeth's coronation. While class-mates waited in the wings to perform their celebratory set-piece, I proudly announced members of the British Commonwealth to parents and staff: 'And now we visit Canada, land of the maple leaf' (and several other countries, including Australia and its kangaroos, and, still coloured red in my atlas, South Africa, 'land of the veld'). For several months I knew the words of half a dozen national anthems. The day before the coronation I strolled through Hyde Park watching men hurriedly erecting the last wooden benches for lucky people who had seats along the processional route; three weeks later I waved enthusiastically as Her Majesty and Prince Philip drove too quickly in their open-topped landau along streets lined with flag-waving children. On the day itself I watched the procession and service on a neighbour's new modern black-and-white television set.

The first television I had seen, three years before, was hand-made; a bulky mass of polished oak, in the top half of which was inset a small seven-inch screen. In front of the screen, the man who built it positioned a large, curved magnifying glass on a stand, so that if I sat a few feet from it I could see enlarged smart-suited grown-ups saying things I did not understand. In 1954 my parents bought ours, an elegant piece of mock-georgian furniture, which looked like a cocktail cabinet, with closing doors and brass hinges. A year or so after that we acquired another wonder of the age – a stereo record-player, which made music come simultaneously from two different parts of the living room. I commandeered the old, out-of-date clockwork gramophone, which used wooden needles, and tried to make sure that when I played equally old, out-of-date seventy-eight records they didn't moan to a growling halt because I'd forgotten to hand-wind the machine.

With some birthday-present money I bought a small circle of plastic with a hole in the middle, and listened to an American named Bill Haley sing *Rock around the Clock*; and a cousin confided that she was in love with Elvis Presley, Johnny Mathis and Frank Sinatra, all of whom sang on bigger plastic circles, which I couldn't afford, and which, astonishingly, played music continuously for more than twenty minutes on each side.

Sometimes, on Friday evenings, if I could squeeze through jostling Soho crowds, I heard Tommy Steele's voice coming from another innovation from the 1950s – the coffee bar. He played his guitar and sang at The Two I's, but I preferred the ghoulish La Macabre, a few yards away, where the noisy, cramped room with black walls was lighted by a few white candles, and espresso coffee was served in black cups which black-skirted waitresses put on black coffin-shaped tables.

Half a mile away Chris Barber played his trombone at the 100 Club better than I had played mine at school. At the recently-built Royal Festival Hall I queued hopefully for hours, and saw Otto Klemperer conduct Beethoven, without the hisses and scratches which accompanied my treasured collection of old Furtwängler seventy-eight records. When the BBC announced a special midnight radio performance of the music from *My Fair Lady*, I already knew the songs because some friends of my mother had brought a copy of the record from New York. Before that I had seen the films, and studied the musical scores, of *Oklahoma!*, *Carousel*, *The King and I* and *South Pacific*, but none of them affected me as powerfully as *West Side Story*. I spent £2 on my first long-playing record, and saw the show five times on stage at Her Majesty's – the theatre, that is. Apart from *Macbeth* and a few poems, I seldom memorized literature, but I knew every lyric of my favourite musicals.

Customers gave my mother wads of complementary tickets for the theatre and BBC radio and television shows. Usually the theatre seats, complementary because they couldn't get rid of them any other way, were not worth having, although I enjoyed *Five Finger Exercise*. Visiting the BBC's Paris Theatre for late-night jazz concerts was better than attending the live television shows, where red lights flashed 'AP-PLAUSE' and we were expected to clap and clap . . . and clap.

Watching television at home was an uncertain amusement: family scenes were often more eventful than the programmes. When I did watch, Norman Wisdom fell on the floor, Benny Hill, a nearby neighbour, sang rude songs, and, after the set was suitably converted, I saw my first commercial advertisements. Financed by the independent network, famous Hollywood stars like Bob Hope and Lucille Ball were only a few feet away. I enjoyed radio more than television, and joyfully listened to Tony Hancock, *The Goons* and *Take it from Here*, awed that the programmes were being transmitted from so close to where I lived. Among other entertainments, Gerard Hoffnung did peculiar things with vacuum cleaners, and Tom Lehrer wrote grisly lyrics which brought a special meaning to 'almost died laughing'.

But, more than radio or TV, which I had to listen to, or watch, in the living room, I preferred my bedroom, where I studied or read the piles of books which I borrowed from the local library. By the time I'd got Billy Bunter, Biggles and Captain Horatio Hornblower out of my system an exciting plethora of books about the Second World War was available. After I exhausted the war books I moved on to Georges Simenon, Dickens, Maupassant and John Steinbeck. Most weeks I read at least four books, often with the help of an illicit torch-light under my sheets during the hours I couldn't sleep. When I had the money I rummaged through local market stalls and bought dusty, second-hand volumes which I proudly stacked on my shelves.

Often, out walking, I saw famous faces. Harry Secombe drove past me in his Rolls Royce and winked. A few years after that I had tea with him when he visited a children's holiday home where I was working as a voluntary helper. I stood outside Bob Monkhouse's office, opposite my school, wanting to knock on his door and ask for his autograph, but was scared to, and had to make do with Richard Murdoch, who I literally bumped into.

One afternoon a friend and I were listening to records in a record shop's booth – long since removed – having no intention of buying anything, when the door opened and two men asked if they could come in. I assumed that they wanted to throw us out, but no, they said politely, they were from the BBC. Could we spare them a minute or so to tell them which records we were buying for Christmas, a few days away? My friend and I made a few dishonest noises, and several hours later a cousin telephoned to tell me that he'd fallen off his settee when he heard my name and voice on the evening's radio news.

The day I got my bicycle for passing the Eleven-Plus my father told me where not to ride, so I promptly disobeyed him, and had an accident around the Marble Arch. Two men helped me up from the road and treated me to tea and cakes at the Cumberland Hotel. I almost accepted their invitation to go home with them, but was too worried about my scratched present. I didn't know what a homosexual was until several years later.

I was walking with a friend through Hyde Park one evening in 1956 when a prostitute asked us if we wanted 'a nice time dearies'. She angrily declined our facetious offer of two-and-sixpence, and shouted, 'I'll set the boys on you!' We flew away faster than the startled pigeons. Two years later I spent a Saturday night at the Jermyn Street turkish baths, and in the steam room I felt a man's hand touch my knee. I hurriedly escaped to a clear, dry-heat room to cool down and never again went on my own.

In 1958 I dressed up as an Edwardian gentleman, complete with whiskers, and, sitting in an old, open-topped London bus, waved graciously at a television crew filming the Easter Parade in Hyde Park. Six weeks later, at Whitsun, to please a girlfriend, I joined the march organized by the Campaign for Nuclear Disarmament, and jostled with tens of thousands of young people crammed into Trafalgar Square, to listen to the pacifists' angry speeches.

I mercilessly dragged my sister to most of London's museums and a few art galleries. When there was trouble at home I stole money so that we could go to the cinema or visit the Zoo. She preferred her outing to see *Giselle* and I liked hanging over the rails in the gallery of the Albert Hall getting my half-crown's worth of Promenade concerts.

I spent the last hours of the 1950s – dressed up as a Chinese coolie, at a New Year's Eve fancy-dress party – discussing Pasternak's *Dr Zhivago* with a group of under-graduates I didn't know, and was relieved that, like myself, they could not remember the names of most of the characters in the book. I kissed in the New Year with a girl who opened her mouth so wide that I couldn't find her lips.

Every experience excited me and it seemed unimportant whether the excitement was fearful or pleasurable, provided that something, anything, was happening. Until I was fourteen, apart from outings with my sister, I did most things on my own. At school I told lies, describing an imaginary circle of friends, because none of the boys I knew appeared to spend as much time on their own as I did. At home, when I went out, I often told more lies, telling my parents that I was meeting a friend when mostly I went alone to the cinemas or parks. Some days, during school holidays, I bought a ticket on the Underground, and for a few pennies I travelled for hours from the beginning to the end of each separate route. Provided that I never left the stations, and merely crossed from one platform to another, it seemed like an interesting way to cure boredom. I forced myself to believe that it was exciting, travelling for five hours in different directions, ending up where I'd begun. I created a private existence, silently entertaining myself, and fantasized about each small event until it developed into a big, exciting drama.

When I went out with a friend I felt that I had to prove what a good companion I was. Solitary days exploring my village became an asset. I knew each street, every cinema and theatre, and where all the winding pathways in the parks led. Even if I had only walked passed the London Palladium I'd say nonchalantly, 'Been there, went a couple of months ago.' If we had to travel from one destination to another, I not only knew all the interchange stations, I also knew the short cuts through archways marked 'No entry'.

At night, when I reluctantly switched off my bedroom light, or my torch battery became too dim to read by, nothing felt exciting. I just felt alone. If I'd spent an afternoon with a friend I worried that he, or she, might not want to see me again; or, if I hadn't spent an afternoon with one, why I had no friends. I could not understand why each adventure – whatever it was, even when it made me happy at the time – quickly turned into disappointment. The answer seemed to be to keep finding more things to do.

Among my greatest worries was girls. Other boys had girlfriends, why didn't I? Must be my spots, I thought, scratching my latest facial eruption. Or maybe it's because I can never remember any of the jokes I hear, or because I prefer Beethoven and Brahms to Elvis. How do you find a girlfriend? At fifteen I had never had a regular girlfriend, but had lost my virginity.

Sex was not discussed at home. It seems unbelievable now, but until I was twelve years old I had no idea what sexual intercourse was. I learned about *it* one afternoon returning from school, when a friend told me exactly how babies were made. I spent most of that night energetically masturbating, wondering what *it* was like. After that I surreptitiously bought the *News of the World* most Sundays, and occasionally smuggled a rude photograph into the house. Alberto Moravia briefly became my literary idol when I read *Woman of Rome*, and I laboriously copied out several pornographic short stories which circulated at school. I was terrified that the girls who worked in my mother's shop would know what I was thinking when I stared at them. Occasionally, once I started going out with girls, my mother made an oblique remark about 'being careful', but by then I had pre-empted her embarrassed attempts at sexual education. 'I know, I know,' I said diffidently, more embarrassed than she was.

Among its other characteristics, my home provided practical courses in geography, European and human. From the year my mother started her business we had au pair girls to look after my sister and I. I carried luggage, ticketed from towns I had not heard of, up three flights of stairs: months, usually weeks, and, on two occasions, days later, I carried them downstairs. Then more luggage arrived. In four years I must have heaved several dozen suitcases up and down stairs and in and out of bedrooms. We had a fat girl from Barcelona who barely spoke English, but cooked delicious *leche frita*; a thin one from Utrecht who cried for three days after she arrived before telling my mother that she was pregnant; an Austrian blonde who, my sister told me with a look of bewilderment on her face, had jet-black pubic hair; a beautiful, shy one came from Milan, but couldn't cook and hated London, and several came from France. I knew the location of more foreign cities than British ones. I can't remember the exact number, but during a four-year period I functioned as porter for at least ten au pairs. A girl from Paris taught me more than the geographical location of major European cities.

Monique, nineteen years old, with a fiancé in Paris, survived with us longer than most. Through my young and sexually-opening eyes she was fabulous, gorgeous, sexy, adorable, funny, sophisticated and enticing. I usually offered to show our au pairs, particularly the attractive ones, London: they provided welcome company, and I was proud to bask in my village's glory. But Monique did not wait to be invited: 'Pleeze, you take me to So-ho to-nayt, weez all zee pro-stee-toots, oui?' she said on her first evening with us. We became good friends, and many of my trips to coffee bars or music clubs were with her. I could not believe that a girl four years older than myself wanted to spend so much time with me.

On Christmas Eve, when I was fifteen, after we had spent the evening out together sipping coffee and listening to a three-piece combo playing modern jazz, we returned home and I sat talking with her in her bedroom. I amazed myself by voicing a desire which had made me rise and sink from the day I met her. 'I'd like to go to bed with you,' I said nervously, wondering where the voice I heard was coming from. Surely it couldn't be me saying *that*. 'Go a-way, and geeve me feyve min-oots,' she replied. Three hundred nerve-racking seconds.

My detailed tours of London were haphazard and neglectful compared with what she showed me of herself. 'Doz zeece surprayze you?' she wanted to know, explaining that she had shaved off her pubic hair because her fiancé asked her to. I nodded, wondering what sort of pervert she intended marrying. When I tried to remove her bra, which she'd pulled up to her neck, she pushed my hand away: 'Ay ol-wayze wear eet dans le lit to keep may boo-zam ve-ree strrong.' Damn! I thought, she's not supposed to do that. I wanted to kiss her, but, although she was prepared to open her legs for me, she kept her lips resolutely shut. 'Ay keeze on-lee may fiancé,' she told me. Another Damn! But I discovered to my proud delight that I could do *it*, and one of life's great mysteries became a sexually exciting, secret experience. The following morning Monique came into my room and gave me a silk tie: 'Eer eez your se-cond Chreece-mazz pre-zont,' she laughed. One had been enough.

An important part of that night's pleasure was that my parents were asleep in their nearby bedroom; and, as far as I knew, none of my friends had been initiated.

But I still did not have a regular 'see you on Saturday' girlfriend.

The best meeting-place was at parties and, with invitations from school friends, I gradually joined a party circuit. Before my father returned home I had to battle with my mother to get out of the house at weekends. If she heard me going out I was doomed, summoned to her room, where I would be told that I should be at home looking after her. When she grudgingly let me go out, she demanded a telephone number where I could be contacted. Once or twice I gave her the required number and she telephoned, insisting that I return home because she had been taken ill. Then I gave her false numbers, so God knows who had to explain that no, there wasn't a party, and no, they'd never heard of me. Eventually, I refused to even tell her where I was going.

On Saturdays I rarely came home before 2 o'clock in the morning. If she asked me what time I had returned I said 'about eleven', hoping that she'd been too drugged to know. Able to get away with that, I occasionally stayed out all night, returning home at 9 on a Sunday morning, loaded with the newspapers, so that if questioned I could say that I had got up early to buy them.

A few weeks after my unforgettable Christmas present from Monique my mother discovered that I had the regular girlfriend I had dreamed about. We commenced a new battle. She constantly wanted to know what my plans were, and accused me of ignoring her in favour of 'some stranger'. Christine supervised a Brownies pack and I introduced my sister to it. Her involvement enabled my mother to contact Christine, whom she invited home for tea. Within minutes of her arrival, my mother shooed me from the room, saying that she wanted to speak to her. Half an hour later, furious and worried, I interrupted the 'girls' conversation. They seemed to be getting on like old friends, and I felt delighted. 'She's a very sensible girl,' my mother said approvingly to me later, 'she has no silly ideas about getting married.' I looked disbelievingly at her, and silently vowed that in future I would keep my girlfriends to myself.

Most of my friends went out with a girl for a few weeks and then found someone else. I was like my mother – possessive. If I liked a girl, I wanted to be with her all the time, and when I was not, I thought about her obsessively. A week felt like eternity, but I was equally possessive about my accountancy studies, which meant that weekday socializing was not normally possible. Sex disturbed me. Visions of Monique would not go away. Two of my 'one-nighters' satisfied my desires, but sexual needs, while always with me, seemed not to be all that I wanted from females.

I wanted to love a girl, and when I thought that I did, my fantasies took over. There we were, the two of us, happily married, living in our lovely home, with our lovely children and lovely car. Christine was one of my loves and it lasted nine months. My friends told me that I was crazy, going out with one girl for so long.

When I was seventeen I met Jill. Six months later we were talking of getting engaged. The only person I told was my grandfather, who said, 'Well, if you love her I suppose it's all right, but what about your studies? And your mother?' Yes, what about my mother? To my surprise, at first she seemed to like Jill, but I quickly understood that what she really liked was the opportunity of meeting my girlfriend's parents. They were there, innocently paying their quarterly telephone rentals, unaware of the impending overuse about to enter their lives. Often, as soon as I left the house to meet Jill, my mother telephoned Jill's house and was chatting away when I arrived, and still chatting for half an hour afterwards. Jill's mother grimaced, I felt acutely embarrassed, and her father suggested that they change their number.

A year after I met Jill I knew that I did not want to get married, but was too frightened to tell her. Suddenly, as if I had turned off a light, I switched feelings, and what little of me she could see was cold and distant. I assumed that she would realize how I felt, but she kept telling me how much she loved me. I hated her for making me feel guilty. One weekday I telephoned her and said that I did not want to see her again. 'I knew you'd come to your senses,' my mother said gaily, 'you can do better than that.'

A few years ago I unexpectedly met Jill's parents in a hotel in Guernsey, where I was visiting an advocate on business. When I asked about Jill her mother smiled sadly: 'She's never married, you know. She never got over you. But she seems to be friendly with a doctor now, and we're hoping that at last she's found someone.' Jill was then thirty-five.

I felt sad, ashamed, guilty and pleased. In my hotel room that evening I thought of Jill and her family. When I was desperately unhappy at home they had welcomed me into theirs. When I walked through their door I felt that I belonged with them. I had never seen a family so united. Her parents obviously adored each other, but could argue without throwing chairs and saucepans. They were financially secure. And they seemed to like me, despite having to contend with my mother.

Jill was an intelligent, jolly, caring replica of her petite mother; she exuded warmth and allowed me to indulge my male-dominating role. When she told me that she loved me I felt confused. Why did she love me? How could she love me, not knowing the bad feelings which occupied so much of my days? What was love? When I told her that I loved her, too, I felt dishonest. My inner voice insisted that I did not know what love was.

We went to parties most weeks, laughed and danced a lot. She left school and started a career as a trainee buyer at Harrods'. I progressed with my studies. For a while I believed that I had found the girl whom I wanted to marry. But always I nagged at myself 'What is love?'

I felt sexually frustrated. I did not know how to behave. I knew that Monique and my 'one nighters' were exceptions. Jill was different. I wanted her sexually, but was too frightened to discuss my feelings. We kissed and cuddled for almost a year, no more than that, and I became angry at my sexual fear of her and myself. I needed to touch her body, not just fantasize about it.

Her parents gave a family party one night and Jill and I washed up the dishes in the kitchen. My sexual needs felt uncontrollable and, for the first time in our year together, I put a hand inside her blouse. She quickly pushed me away and began crying. What I had thought was my love turned instantly to hatred. Her rejection made me feel ashamed and guilty. We parted that evening in a gloomy silence. During the following week my guilt became fury. How dare she make me feel guilty for doing something which to me had felt a true expression of love!

When we met the following week she told me that she still felt upset. I apologized for something I felt I shouldn't have had to, and felt angrier. I knew that her sexual rejection was not the real cause of my anger, but I could not understand why, knowing that, I felt so bitter towards her. Her parents tried to help us recover our lost friendship, but my feelings were too extreme to want anything to do with any of them.

The day after we finally ended our long friendship, and I felt that I had escaped from a lethal trap, I went ice-skating with a group of friends, assuming that Jill, who knew of the outing, would not turn up. But she did. During the evening she slipped and fell on the ice, severely hurting her arm. I was skating round the rink with a girl I had just met. 'Is that someone from the club?' the girl asked me. 'Yes,' I said, feigning disinterest. 'She looks as though she's hurt herself,' the girl said. I glanced at the small group of people surrounding Jill. 'She's being looked after,' I replied. I wanted to go and see how she was. Then I didn't want anything to do with her. I felt ashamed of myself, and furious that she'd come skating. She knew that I would be there: why hadn't she stayed at home and not fallen on the ice! I felt that I was the one suffering, not her.

When her parents told me, so many years later, about Jill's feelings for me which stayed behind after I left her, I felt pleased. I liked the idea of a woman not forgetting me; perhaps, after almost twenty years, still loving me. But the pleasurable thrill was brief. My shame at rejecting her when she hurt herself at the ice rink had not vanished. In my hotel room I wanted to see her, to tell her that I had not forgotten her, either. I wanted to tell her about the chaos in my life after I left her, and to let her know that had we married she would probably have suffered from more that a temporarily broken arm. I wanted to see her, and talk, and apologize for my past behaviour; and I had an obsessive desire to make love to her.

I could not understand why long-forgotten fantasies which had exhausted me so many years ago returned so vividly. I hoped that at thirty-five years of age she wouldn't cry if I put my hand inside her blouse.

That was before I went to Shipley Grange; before I understood my desperate need to control, and before I understood that sex was as much something I wanted to control as everything else.

If I could meet her now I'd be able to explain that, during the hours we spent dancing and laughing and drinking her mother's gin and tonics, the one thing I never did was talk about how I felt. I'd be able to talk about my fear of rejection. And about feeling angry every time I left her home because I had to return to mine. And about my always wanting to be in control. But I suspect that she would find it difficult to understand the devastating effect which rejection then had, and still has, on me.

I wanted to be in control at the club I joined when I was sixteen. A fellow articled clerk introduced me to it. He gave me a telephone number. When I dialled it a few days later, a cheerful female voice gushed cheerfully how nice it was that I had 'phoned and how much she was looking forward to meeting me and yes of course they'd love to see me and did I know where they were and why didn't I come to the dance next Sunday and say hello and don't worry about not knowing anybody you'll soon feel at home so be sure to come along. I almost didn't. The fear of walking through an unknown door to meet unknown people worried me for several days after I accepted the invitation.

The Circus Club occupied premises a ten-minute walk from where I lived. Its activities sounded marvellous: weekday coffee evenings, Sunday rambles in the country, monthly dances, study groups, weekend trips, house parties and much more. On my first visit I felt like a frightened stranger as I nervously opened the club's imposing wooden doors. By the end of the evening I had been invited to two parties, and asked to help organize a dance. A year later I was elected the club's treasurer, and the year after that its vice-chairman. Had it not been for my studies I would have accepted the chairmanship which I was offered. I liked the idea of having my name inscribed in gold leaf on the 'Past Chairmen' board.

Throughout my late teens and early twenties the Circus provided a social roundabout from which I did not want to get off. I made friends who became my first professional clients. I mixed confidently with people many years my senior – the club's age group was sixteen to thirty – accepted responsibility for organizing club events and, had I wanted to, could have spent most nights of each week with several of the many names which increasingly filled my address book.

The majority of the club's members lived in expensive apartments in St John's Wood or large houses in Hampstead. I was invited into homes which dazzled me with their opulence. My ambitions took a gigantic leap forward. I saw before me not the uncertain visions of success which I had previously fantasized about, but the specific particularity of what I wanted. I wanted what they all had. I wanted their possessions, their security, their respectable background, their settled families. I enjoyed the responsibilities I accepted at the club, and the authority which accompanied them. I enjoyed being known by so many people, and thanked for my hard work, and invited to weddings and parties and weekends away. Above all, I felt a sense of belonging, a security as relative as the security I felt at school. It was not enough, but it was more than I had had, and I wanted more.

But I suffered. What would they think, I wondered, if they knew the sort of crazy home life I came from; if they knew that my parents, while not destitute, never managed their finances so that they knew from one day to the next what their commitments were? What would they think if they knew that I had regular bouts of feeling mad, and not being able to work? What did they think when they saw that I did not have a car, or heard that I had only been to a tip-top state school, instead of Harrow, or Stowe, or Clifton or St Paul's?

So much wealth, which I interpreted as security, worsened

the fear I had that I might fail my examinations. I *had* to qualify quickly. How else could I acquire what all those new people had, and took so much for granted? They and their possessions juxtaposed in every conceivable way with the life I wanted to forget. It seemed that if you had a large house and a good business it was not difficult to make a happy family. These fantasies may have been nonsensical, but I believed in them.

At home, during my late teens, I felt like an unwelcome lodger. I stopped studying in my bedroom. Each weekday evening, after I finished work at the office where I was articled, I went to St Marylebone library where I could study in peace until 9 o'clock. When I finished my evening's work I sometimes went on to a club function, or walked through the West End until I thought that the house would be quiet and I could go straight to my room.

When I was eighteen my mother left home, and although physical violence went with her, she left behind a house which seemed empty, partly because she sent a van to remove much of the furniture. I wanted to leave too, but to afford rent I needed a proper income. As an articled clerk in those days I received little more than pocket money. To leave home meant giving up my articles and finding a job which paid a proper salary and offered a less promising future.

Every week was hectic: office work to gain essential and valuable business experience; studies, and an occasional coffee evening at a friend from the Circus, in the evenings; parties, trips into the countryside and girlfriends at the weekends. On Saturdays I worked in my mother's business, then managed by my father, and when I could, I did part-time work for accountants to earn extra money. Mixed into the week were my responsibilities as a club officer. Apart from the few weeks each year when I was incapacitated by depression, my waking time was fully booked. I was too overcrowded to question what I was doing.

The girl I held by the waist as we skated round the ice rink, the night I let others help Jill, was Helen. We gelled immediately. She was lively, laughed gaily, talked easily. I was so impressed by her that I could not stop myself mentioning her to my mother: 'Oh no, not another one,' she moaned.

Helen and I saw each other regularly, and one night, a few weeks after we met, we went to see *Oklahoma!*, a film I had loved since my early teens. I slept through most of it, and realized that I was about to enter another period of depression. I felt close enough to her by then to explain how I felt, something I had been unable to discuss with any previous girlfriend. I told her about my difficulties at home, and she seemed amazed. She could not understand the chaos I described.

After a few weeks her parents insisted that they meet me — she was seventeen, and her father was suspicious of any predatory male. They lived in a pleasant house in the outer suburbs of London. By then, after my introduction to Hampstead mansions, I was not particularly impressed by the house. But, as with Jill's family, I was deeply impressed that she had a real home, with parents who spoke to each other, and sat down for meals together and seemed not to want to fight and threaten. It seemed to be the ideal family I had dreamed of for myself: financially secure, comfortable surroundings, and parents who cared about their children. As more weeks passed, and I visited her home more frequently, I met other members of her family — aunts, uncles and cousins — and I could not believe what I was seeing. A family, not restricted to parents and children, who obviously cared about each other and enjoyed each other's company. Why couldn't I have had a life like that?

These experiences — the excitement of living in the centre of a great city, the relief of finding a social group with whom I could enjoy myself, the self-esteem which grew as I advanced successfully towards a respectable career, and my relationship with girls, especially Helen — enabled me to escape from my family. When I was twenty-two years old I felt very, very mature. And I hoped that I had discovered love.

I knew about hate, but could still not recognize love. When Helen asked me if I loved her, I replied, 'Of course I do, at the moment.' She wanted to know why I added the last three words. 'I don't know,' I replied, and I didn't. Alone at night, restless and unable to sleep, I struggled to decide what love was. When I thought of family love I thought of my sister, and my aunt and my grandparents, but it seemed to have nothing to do with how I felt towards Helen. Love, married love, went beyond those relationships. I understood that I had not loved Monique, as I had once believed I had: she had been a sexual meal of glorious animal lust, richly spiced with infatuation. Jill had made me feel trapped, not because she was frightened to have her blouse unbuttoned, but because I had never admitted to her my miserable periods of depression and the unreality they represented; besides, I had met her when I was seventeen, and I felt that I was ageing faster than time, and that she was not. Her sweetness when I met her seemed like indigestible childishness a few months later.

I idealized married love into a cosy, comfortable relationship; as cosy and comfortable as the apparently ideal families I had met through friends at the Circus, or fanciful visions which I created in waking dreams. Love, the love I wanted, possessed a private key which opened a door leading into a private home, where nobody could disrupt blissful tranquillity, and where I could offer and receive protection. The protection I wanted to offer, and to have accepted, was to be a provider, of care and financial security. I wanted to work hard and prove that I could do what my parents could not. I wanted to be respected and admired for my efforts, and in return I expected to assume all the conventional responsibilities of a Victorian husband. My wife, the one who would help me understand love, would give me what I had never known – a stable home, where I would not be frightened to use my key when I reached the front door, and inside which would be certainty, the certainty that there was always someone there who wanted me.

Despite my hectic social life, I knew that I was more relaxed and content when away from crowds and noisy people. I needed to be part of a small group, and the most satisfying group I met in my teens consisted of two people, Helen and myself. But even being with one other person made me doubt myself: my head buzzed with desires and worries which I was too frightened to discuss. I did not want to admit them, because if I did, I admitted that I could not resolve my own problems – and that implied that I could not be a responsible husband.

Two beliefs helped me hope that I had found the love which met my ideals: Helen and I had known each other for four years, and as each year passed we enjoyed being together more; and, not knowing how to define love, I relied on my bad feelings to guide me – there seemed to be fewer of them when I was with her.

We had many wonderful times together, and agreed that the best of them were when we were alone. And we had some terrible times, mostly inflicted on us by my mother, who, among other excesses, once charged at us both, wielding a bread knife. Instead of slicing us apart it brought us closer together, but the antagonism between the two women created another jagged triangle in which I felt trapped.

We were married three months after I left home.

I gave Helen two promises not in the marriage ceremony: that I would not let my mother interfere with our life; and that I would not travel on business, as her father did most weeks of the year. The first was as much for myself as for her; the second seemed important to her and irrelevant to me, so I gave it willingly. I had found the person who would give me what I needed, nothing else seemed more important than that.

But I still doubted if I understood love.

The night before our wedding day I knew that I should not be getting married. Something was wrong, but I did not know what. If only I knew what love was, I thought, as I tried to sleep. I slept well that night, and when I awoke the following morning the sky was clear and bright, the early morning August shadows sharp and clean. How could anything be wrong on such a glorious morning! I was absolutely convinced, when I made my marriage vows, that my new wife, new home, new friends and new business were all that I needed.

Our first years of marriage were happy ones, happiness for me being constant change and excitement. I quickly realized that the last thing I wanted was a 'cosy' or 'comfortable' existence: I wanted thrills. I needed them to make up for my irregular periods of depression, continual headaches and worsening insomnia, so I comforted myself with the new pleasures in my life.

Two years after we were married Helen said that she wanted a baby. I willingly agreed. Having children fitted as neatly into my idealized picture of family life as a jig-saw piece needed to complete a puzzle. On the evening Ben was born, I had the same soaring feeling of elation which I had enjoyed on the day I passed my professional examinations. I could not believe it. Wasn't I clever, not only to have had no problems in being a partner in conception, but also managing not to faint as I watched him emerge into the world. A healthy new-born baby, with the correct number of fingers and toes. A magical son! I felt so happy and proud that for the first time in three years I contacted my parents. I wanted to share my joy with them. I could not think of past hatred and misery. They were grandparents and I wanted them to know. My mother sent a loving telegram, a huge bouquet of flowers, and a note asking when could she see 'her grandson'.

For a year or so after Ben's birth I felt that I was well on the way to achieving my teenage ambitions. I had an attractive and loving wife and a beautiful baby boy whom I adored; my business prospered; we had moved to our second home, luxuriously furnished, on an award-winning housing development, and I owned two cars. I enjoyed regular holidays, ate in expensive restaurants, bought suits three at a time, began collecting antique scientific instruments, and possessed an impressive selection of credit cards. Socially, I had a wide circle of friends, although, as at school, few of them felt close to me because I only shared with them the *me* I wanted them to know. Bank managers invited me out to lunch, building society managers sent me Christmas presents and clients willingly offered me any perks they could. Arising from my involvement with a government-sponsored property company, of which I was the financial director, I had been in the newspapers, I did honorary work with two charity committees and gave a series of six lectures each year, on financial management, to architectural students at a college. My latest interests included gardening and studying architecture. Most important of all, my periods of depression descended less frequently.

But I worried constantly, mainly about money. I had been financially impulsive whenever I had cash as a child, anxious to spend whatever I had. As an impecunious articled clerk earning £3 a week, I thought nothing of spending 10 shillings on a weekend taxi ride or 10 guineas on a sweater. I always seemed able to earn enough extra money to support my social life, and if that meant having to survive on spaghetti and chips during the week, I accepted it as a necessary evil. I drank little, smoked an ounce or so of tobacco each week, and never gambled, except on the stock exchange. (Sometimes, more by luck than financial astuteness, I made profits on my casual speculations, but when I lost several hundred pounds of our savings I was too frightened to tell my new wife until the week after our honeymoon.) When I bought my first motor car I never considered a second-hand one, and each new home was, at the time I bought it, sufficiently expensive to make my stomach churn. In addition to my income, my running-mates in this economic hundred metres were bank overdrafts, bank loans, hire purchase, credit cards, charge cards, cash cards, a mortgage several times higher than the national average – and worry.

However much I earned – and once I was qualified, my earnings were always high – I never *had enough*. I could advise clients wisely and, when necessary, cautiously, but I could not exercise self-discipline. I wanted to accumulate capital, but as my income increased, so, too, did my dashes into material possessions. If a month passed and I displayed no new award in my home, I felt defeated. Every month, when my well-trained bank statements or credit card accounts overtook me, I made a fresh start, determined to save, not spend; but then, to thrash worry, I dashed out and bought something else.

I felt a fraud. Wasn't I supposed to be a good accountant? Why, then, was I submerged by personal financial mis-management? Why, when what I wanted most of all was to accumulate some financial security, did I impulsively spend so much, and allow Helen to do the same? I was not stupid, was I?

In 1968, when I was twenty-six, I could not meet my monthly commitments. I reluctantly borrowed £1,000 – the equivalent of most people's earnings for about six months – from Helen's father, knowing that it would give him immense pleasure to have his forecast of my financial incompetency prove right. I could have made arrangements through my business, but I did not want to admit my ineptitude to my partners. I promised to repay my father-in-law within two years, but did so in four months, by careful reorganizations and out of bonuses I drew from my increasing business profits. That'll show him, I thought. The debt was cleared in September. Two months later, in dense November fog, I drove home from my branch office in Surrey, and went to sleep.

Sinking

Times change. *Nervous breakdown*, once a whispered colloquialism to express the inexpressible, has achieved formal linguistic recognition. A recently published dictionary defines a nervous breakdown as '(an occurrence of) a disorder in which worrying, depression, severe tiredness, etc., prevent one from coping with one's responsibilities'. When I read that I felt angry. How could anybody understand such an imprecise definition? Apart from someone who has actually experienced a nervous breakdown, who could realize that the most important word in the definition is 'etc.'? I knew that I was being unfair on the dictionary's compilers – after all, it was a general publication, not a medical encyclopedia – but I was remembering months, years, of my life when I had wanted people to understand what was happening to me, and did not know how to explain it to them myself.

At first, when I arrived home, having driven through the November fog, long ago in 1968, I just felt tired. A day or two later I knew that yet another period of depression had descended. The dictionary's definition was accurate, as far as it went: I worried (about not working), slept continually (for several days), and wanted to forget all my responsibilities. For most of December I felt abnormally normal; that is to say, the feelings I had were similar to those I had experienced since a teenager, and, while frightening, they were sufficiently familiar to be recognizable. People close to me sympathized and were anxious to help. My wife patiently let me rest, and waited for me to recover; my partners, through Charles West, told me, through my wife, not to worry, to have a good rest, that everything at the office was under control. Friends and staff, hearing that I was unwell, telephoned to wish me better.

Everything in December revolved around Christmas, a time of happiness, of joy and gaiety. Christmas! I had always loathed it, and that year thinking about it felt the worst of my responsibilities. It loomed ahead like a blank wall. My partners advised me not to return to work until the holidays had passed, assuming that by then I would be better. Helen, in her usual meticulous way, planned menus, bought and wrapped dozens of gifts, which I unenthusiastically agreed looked very pretty, with their colourful bows and ribbons. I knew that she, too, expected that Christmas, cheerful and oozing goodwill, would bring with it the most welcome present of all – my recovery.

Christmas arrived, and I felt guilty. If everyone expected me to have had enough time to have overcome my depression by then, I thought that it was wrong of me not to meet their expectations, so, for a few days, I tried to act out feeling better. A new year was coming, what could be a more suitable time to show how much better I really was? Christmas passed – one less worry. The first day of January stared at me from the new cookery calendar hanging on the kitchen wall, like an unspoken accusation that I had been malingering and should stop making a fuss about nothing.

January. I remember little about December, but cannot forget that January, in 1969. January meant that, to meet my scheduled recovery date, I had to feel as well as I had pretended to feel during Christmas. Shame and guilt made it essential that I regained my lost energy: my partners expected me at the office; my wife and son needed me to perform my husbandly and fatherly duties; the building society, larder, garden, credit card companies – they all needed me to keep them healthy; friends needed me to accept invitations to dinner; clients needed me to help them with momentous business decisions; staff needed me to keep them employed; the car needed me to have it serviced; books and newspapers needed me to read them, and private correspondence was begging to be filed away. I had no choice but to be better. There was no reason why I should not feel better, I had had four weeks' absence from work and family responsibilities – a week longer than any previous period of depression – so the time had come to do nothing else except feel better.

Four weeks of being unable to relax in my own home, or work, or enjoy other people's company seemed like a lifetime. At the end of those four weeks, when January arrived, I had never felt so helpless and hopeless.

The first shock, in that shocking month, was that after my Christmas pretence at recovery I knew that my familiar awareness of depression had been replaced by something which I did not recognize. My old, unfriendly mental fog – the one which I believed symbolized my madness – deserted me. In its place I experienced an awful clarity. I felt and thought so clearly that I believed that nobody, my wife, my partners, nobody, should be allowed near my frightful self. I started living in the state annoyingly described by the dictionary as 'etc.' – a state of anarchy and remorse, hatred and guilt, suspicion and pain, shame and isolation, and dreams about death. January, cold and wintry, introduced me to these bitter realities more chillingly than at any other period of turmoil during the previous fourteen years. But I did not feel mad: I felt terrifyingly real.

Guilt. I felt disgusted with myself. My partners had been kind and considerate: 'Take a break until the New Year,' they'd said. But I could not repay their kindness and consideration; nor could I meet their expectations. I could not go to work. The thought of entering my office horrified me: so many people – partners, staff, clients, bank managers, lawyers – all wanting to speak to me, saying things which I did not want to hear, threatening me with their normality. I lay silently in bed, curled up in guilt because I was disrupting the lives of those responsible and decent people by remaining in bed when I should have been feeling better. I wanted to apologize, to confess how sorry I was to have failed them. Silently, to ease my guilt, I asked them to forgive me, and when I decided that they never would, I hated them.

And more guilt. I felt guilty that I was such a despicable failure as my wife's husband and my son's father. I didn't want to see either of them; when they entered the bedroom I pretended to be asleep. Please forgive me, I muttered to myself, please forgive me for not wanting you.

Yet more guilt. Why had I been such a terrible, uncaring son that my mother accused me of ruining her life, of wishing her dead? Why, after I left home had I not been good, and not apologized for my awfulness, and not given my parents the love and respect which parents deserved? I wanted to be forgiven: I wanted not to feel guilty.

But feeling guilty was not my sole preoccupation in January. Most of the time I did not feel guilty. Most of the time I wanted to be dead. Death felt like an intimate, trustworthy companion secretly lying by my side in bed. When I was not feeling guilty, or fantasizing about death, I survived on hatred. I hated everyone and everything, and that made me feel guilty, and that made me want to be dead.

When I could not return to work I became suspicious of my partners, creating in my mind imaginary meetings between them, from which I was excluded. I mentally prepared detailed scripts in which each partner expressed an urgent desire never to see me again. I imagined them talking: 'He's more trouble than he's worth. Let's get rid of him.' In my destructive fantasies I heard them demanding my resignation from the business; gloating over innovations which I had introduced and which they were changing in my absence; enticing away clients, and explaining to staff that I would not be returning to the office because I was incapable. At times these fantasies seemed so real that I expected a letter to arrive, telling me that I was no longer acceptable to them, that I was no longer a partner. I pictured myself as unemployed and penniless, a useless ex-partner, lying in bed for the rest of my life, until I found a welcome relief in death.

Eventually, after I exhausted myself with fears of a conspiracy against me, I remembered what Helen had said Charles West had told her: 'He does more work in a day than most of us do in a week. Tell him to rest. Everything's under control.' They do need me, I gulped tearfully, trying to believe those words; but I could not, and my suspicions returned. If everything is under control and I am not there then how can they still need me? In the middle of the month, when partners' monthly drawings were credited to our personal accounts, I wanted to telephone my bank, to check that my usual money had been received, but that meant speaking to people who knew me. The fear of speaking to anyone was worse than the suspicion that my income may have ceased.

When Helen suggested that I speak to Charles, or another partner, I angrily shouted that I would not, could not, and then felt guilty because I had lost my temper. I didn't speak to them until early summer, but they kept telephoning to ask Helen how I was. I hated those messages of goodwill: each one increased a debt which I knew I could never repay. I wanted them to understand that I could not return to the business, because I would soon be dead. But I also wanted them to continue transferring my monthly income, to telephone Helen, and to need me.

The telephone. I hated the telephone. It seemed to continually ring: it startled me when I was awake, and woke me up when I was asleep. Who was it now, for God's sake? Was someone asking about me? Why didn't Helen come to tell me who it was? When she did come I often pretended to be asleep. I told her that I would speak to nobody, but once, when she passed on a message from a friend, I yelled at her that she should have called me, so that I could talk to him. I lied: I didn't want to talk to anybody, but I kept needing to shout and attack, and Helen, sometimes with tears in her eyes, tried patiently to accept my tantrums. I did not want her to accept them: I wanted her to be angry with me, to shout back; and when she did not, I felt cheated, and angrier – until I felt guilty at my unprovoked attacks. But anger returned quickly and sullenly.

For more than nine months I refused to answer the telephone. When Helen was out of the house I took the receiver off the hook, hoping that she would not notice when she returned. I had a dreadful secret about the 'phone: it was a clawing, outstretched hand, an inanimate symbol of my mother. She had never stopped assaulting me with telephones: internal ones, which rang incessantly when she was working and insisted on disturbing my school homework because I had done something to anger her; external ones, fired at me when I was out of the house as a teenager, or aimed belligerently at my home after I married. I hated the telephone when it rang, and I hated it when it did not. I wanted to destroy it. Sometimes, during the early months of my breakdown, I wanted to telephone her, to tell her that I needed her, that I knew that she was the only person who could help me; but I knew, too, that she would disappoint me, and my hatred worsened.

Each day's mail frightened me as much as the telephone. I heard unseen letters rustling and dropping quietly onto the hallway carpet, and immediately wanted to rush downstairs to open them. Instead, I silently fumed because Helen sometimes made me wait until she next came upstairs. One simple request to her, or a few seconds out of my bed, would have solved the problem, but I did nothing – except become more angry. I expected that every letter would bring bad news, or forgotten, unpaid accounts. When they eventually arrived at my bedside, usually on a meal tray, I held them in front of me, unable to concentrate on their contents. Figures on electricity bills meant nothing to me; catalogues from book clubs might just as well have contained blank pages. I pretended to read my correspondence, frightened to admit that nothing was decipherable. If a parcel arrived, usually containing books, unless Helen was in the house I preferred to let the doorbell ring until the postman went away – and felt furious with her and the postman for not giving me what I wanted. Each letter, each ring on the front door or telephone, intensified my fears.

Any hint of normality infuriated and upset me. Sounds from downstairs, when Helen had a friend sipping our coffee, aroused suspicious thoughts. What were they saying? Why were they whispering so that I could not hear their words? Who were they laughing at? Me? I wanted to know everything and nothing, and curled up more miserably under my bedclothes, furious and hopelessly alone.

Downstairs! Downstairs, a few feet beneath my bed, was enemy territory. People, familiar or unknown, but particularly the familiar ones, threatened me when they sat on my chairs or walked through the living room. Echoes from cupboards and doors opening and closing heightened my fear. Who was doing what? Why so much noise? Why so much silence? Downstairs was as terrifying as my feared office, or thoughts of driving my car. Downstairs was a place I only visited when I was physically alone in the house, or when Helen and Ben were asleep. I hated downstairs and telephones and letters, and postmen, milkmen and refuse collectors.

February. By February I had created a routine which reconciled a few of my worst fears. I slept much of the day, or pretended to, and late at night prowled inquisitively through the house, examining jars of pickles, or neatly-stored eggs in the refrigerator as though they were newly-discovered curiosities. I never made myself a cup of tea, or a sandwich, because I did not want Helen to know of my undercover excursions into alien territory. I wanted to see but not be seen.

I remember one night when I got up and went downstairs. I wanted to read a book. Knowing that I wanted to read made me feel that I must be getting better. I selected a paperback history of Mao Zedong's long march through China. I sat down and during the night read the whole book, perhaps 250 pages. I felt that the depression was almost over, finishing that book; but when I woke up the next day I couldn't remember anything that I'd read. I sank into deeper depression, wanting to explain to Helen how terrifying it was to read a book and not know what it was about the next day. But I couldn't tell her that. She probably thinks I'm mad already, I thought.

Another night I felt guilty that correspondence remained unanswered and bills unpaid. I attempted to organize my mind so that I could organize my papers, but it was one more vain sally into painful responsibilities.

When I was alone, and the house silent, I experienced a dreadful peace. I felt safe, free from unwanted intrusions. No telephone, no mail, no suspicious sounds to arouse my distrust – no people. But feeling safe disturbed me. I could not forget that beyond my garden walls existed a world which I feared and needed. I interpreted this distant world as a thing, or many things – my office, my undriven car, distant streets, clients' factories. The things I feared I wanted to destroy. I fantasized that I would sneak into my office and set fire to it, eliminating one unwanted responsibility; and that I would pour sulphuric acid over the garden lawns, so that I could stop fretting that spring, and essential garden chores, had almost arrived. You can't mow dead grass or update burned files.

Like December, February announced a time of celebration: Christmas changed to my birthday. But by then I could not even pretend to take any interest or acknowledge any pleasure when cards and gifts were caringly given to me. I felt guilty that, once again, I was not satisfying other people's expectations. I wanted to shout out angrily that I felt too sad to enjoy anything, especially a birthday, with so many memories of childhood disappointments.

Most days I planned to return to work – soon. Hours passed slowly but weeks rushed by. After almost three months' absence from work I wanted, or thought that I wanted, to return to my office. 'Another week or so,' I said regularly to Helen, 'and I'll be back.' At the beginning of February I decided to return in March: at the beginning of March I decided to return in April. As each intended date of my proposed return to the office came close I secretly shuddered, terrified by responsibilities which I believed I should accept, and by the realization that, despite hopes of recovery, I remained incapable and unwilling to do anything.

I could not understand why, as time passed, I felt worse, not better. Attempts at rationalization failed: my partners, my long-suffering partners, seemed to want me, and my suspicious fantasies vanished; my finances, if anything, improved, because staying in the house meant that Helen and I spent less on entertaining, and shopping expeditions were out of the question. I stopped worrying whether my monthly income would be credited to my bank account. More attempts at rationalization failed: Helen still cared for me, despite my withdrawal from her, and she used every device she could to reassure me that soon I would feel better; Ben seemed as bright and bouncy as ever, and I felt less of a failure as a father; we had our home and comforts, and the days were sunnier and warmer as spring arrived. There was no reason, I argued with myself, why I should feel so bad.

Some days I did not feel so bad: more frequently I felt hopeful, even cheerful. Time, I persuaded myself, time was what I needed. Occasionally, after I began leaving my bedroom during the day, I pottered in the garden, excited by early spring crocuses and trumpeting daffodils, and thrilled that delicate fuchsias had survived the winter frosts. Often, by early evening, I could not believe that a few hours earlier, when I had woken up, my first thought had been that I wanted to die. Ben, whose gurgles and laughter had irritated and angered me a few weeks earlier, became a source of optimistic energy. For his sake, I told myself, I must get better. I played with him in his playroom, and regretted how quickly our hours together passed. When he went to bed I felt lost.

Once or twice I agreed with Helen that we should accept an invitation from friends to visit them, but then I immediately panicked, and told her to cancel the arrangement. More guilt, and shame, at my weakness. My hopes for recovery continually crumbled. Invariably, when I thought that my breakdown was coming to an end, some tiny, apparently insignificant event burst into an internal explosion which I did not know how to quell, and did not feel able to discuss with anyone.

Springtime. In March Helen persuaded me to leave the house, and we began going out for drives in her car several afternoons each week. I sat in the passenger seat, trying to pretend that I welcomed those trips, when we usually went out for tea. But I worried. Supposing we met a client, or one of my partners heard that I was up, dressed, treating myself to car trips and buttered scones, when I should have been working? I resented being driven. I was the one who should be driving, not my wife. I should be in control, not her. Each trip ended, or started, disastrously. I kept my frustrated feelings bottled up inside me, trying not to pour out my fury. The slightest emotional shake and I exploded. If Helen changed gear too early when driving the car, or I convinced myself that she had, or a waitress took too long to bring our tea to the table, or I convinced myself that she had, or Ben . . . and so on . . . I uncorked my awful feelings, trying at the same time to suppress the misery which ruined any contact with people. I withdrew into silent fury and wanted to escape, run, flee from everybody, to sleep, or preferably to die.

I tried explaining to Helen some of my worst feelings. They were all connected with my mother. I did not admit that week after week, when I hid myself under bedclothes and cried, memories of my mother flooded into me. I wanted to see her.

I wanted to repair our damaged relationship, to forget bitter memories of the years since I left home, of days when I had travelled to London, on business. Days when I knew that my mother was nearby, and needed me as much as I needed her. Often, after I left a meeting, I drove to St John's Wood, near Regent's Park, where she lived in a small flat, and parked my car opposite her apartment block, wondering if she was in, trying to decide whether or not to go and knock on her door. I never did, and never told anybody what I had done. Fear kept me away, but fear, too, made me want to be with her. My hatred of her comforted me: it helped explain why I wanted to be dead. I always felt closer to her when I thought of being dead.

But I could not satisfactorily discuss my mother with my wife. After one attempt we had a furious row. I stormed from the house and for the first time in four months drove my car at night. I was wearing a shirt, trousers and slippers. The night was bitter. I wanted the cold air to freeze me to death. I drove to the M4 motorway, intending to kill myself by crashing the car – a fantasy I had been planning for years. I joined it at one of the Maidenhead junctions and drove towards Slough. My foot was flat on the floor, pushing the car to its maximum speed. Lights flashed at me from oncoming traffic. I wanted to twist the steering wheel and never see or hear anything again. Then, suddenly, I knew that I did not have the courage to do anything, and I felt ashamed of my weakness. I slowed down, and drove carefully, returning home less than an hour after I had vanished. 'Where did you go?' Helen wanted to know. 'Just around the lanes,' I lied. I never told her about my death fantasies.

By April, acknowledging that I was suffering from a major breakdown which I did not know how to repair, I believed that nobody could help me. It's up to me, I said to myself, it's all up to me, to get better, to work, to stop wanting to be dead. Support from family and partners seemed to be teasing deceits: when I accepted what they offered I hated myself for needing it. Accepting help felt like indulging myself in luxuries which I could not afford. The time would come, unless I killed myself, when I would have to repay them all, and I did not want to have to repay anybody for what I did not want. But I did want what they offered, and that contradiction made me more angry and more guilty. Being helped was a punishment: the more I accepted help the less capable I felt.

Not even Douglas helped, and he was a doctor, a general practitioner.

Douglas Allison was a client of mine, one of three doctors practising at a modern local medical centre. He knew that I was prone to depression. A year or two earlier he had sent me to the psychiatrist who helped me by telling me how common depression was. Douglas had looked after Helen when she'd had asthma attacks after our financial crisis, and had pulled Ben from her a few months earlier. He and his wife were friends of ours. I balanced his books of account; he balanced my family's health. It was a mutually comforting relationship. 'I couldn't do the things you do,' he once said to me, admiringly. 'I can't do the things I do,' I replied cryptically, envying his calmness and placidity.

We saw each other, as patient and doctor, a few days after I had first felt unwell, in December, and after that at regular intervals. I resented his visits, but offered welcoming smiles as he sat next to my bed. I wanted to be alone. Douglas, and Helen hovering behind him, were unwelcome intruders in my dark world. I wanted them to go away. 'I'll be back at work next week, Douglas,' I said, 'been overworking.' I wondered what he would have done had he known that the thought uppermost in my mind was the wish to be dead.

In March, Douglas suggested that I could visit him at his surgery on Wednesday mornings, after he'd seen his other patients, when we could have a cup of tea and a chat. I didn't want to, but I agreed to go and see him.

Then I felt sick, and worried that I could never leave the house. His surgery was a ten-minute drive from where we lived. Except for my wild drive on the motorway I hadn't driven a car for months. I worried about the commitment every day.

Helen wanted to drive me to him, but I refused. I had to do it myself, I said. Douglas and I began a routine which was to last for several months. Each Wednesday I drove to see him, and we chatted about how I was feeling. He persuaded me to try some anti-depressants, but they made me feel worse. He changed the prescription, and I threw the pills away after taking them for a week or two. After I left him I used to cross the street and buy six or seven packets of chocolate, and eat them greedily. I started buying one pound weight boxes of chocolate, and hiding them away so that I could eat them during the lonely hours of my sleepless nights. That was the most enjoyable part of visiting Douglas, buying goodies for secret pleasure.

Gorging myself with chocolate merely helped increase my weight. Drugs hadn't worked; neither had Douglas's attempts to help me. Eventually, I think as surprised as I was that I showed few signs of feeling better, he suggested that I see a psychiatrist. I was feeling desperate. Nearly five months had passed since I stopped working, and, although sometimes I felt calm, generally I felt isolated and confused by my inability to rejoin society. Perhaps, having refused to visit a psychiatrist for several weeks, I should accept Douglas's advice?

I dreaded going to see a psychiatrist more than I had feared my first weekly trip to Douglas's surgery. I did not want to have to go to a hospital where everyone would know that I was suffering from a nervous breakdown. Helen wanted to come with me, but I said that I preferred to go alone. I did not want to go alone but refused to ask anybody for anything: when they refused me what they didn't know I wanted, I felt a bitter hatred overwhelm me.

'What's wrong with you?' the psychiatrist asked.

'I feel depressed.'

'Why?'

'I don't know.'

After a few more questions he stunned me by asking if I had ever felt suicidal. Nobody had ever asked me that before.

'Only once,' I lied. He wanted to know how I intended killing myself. I told him about my idea of crashing the car. 'What about the people you might have killed or maimed?' he asked. I told him that I hadn't thought of that, which was another lie, because I had, and it had worried me. 'What gives you the right to kill other people?' he wanted to know. I hated him, and distrusted him. He wasn't interested in me, I thought, he's more interested in other people who aren't here.

I had hoped that seeing a psychiatrist would help, but it didn't. I spent the next two days in bed, the first time for several weeks that I had not got up during the day. 'Perhaps I should have sent you to someone else,' Douglas said, when he came to see me. 'He's got a reputation for being aggressive. It works for some people.' I never trusted Douglas again, and refused to see another psychiatrist.

During May I felt less withdrawn, and begain mixing with people more often, but when I did, I wished I hadn't. I did not know what to say to them. I wanted to explain how I had felt, but instead pretended that nothing bad had happened. I had been overworking, I said, and felt betrayed when they believed me. The only contact I wanted was with my partners, not for themselves, but to rebuild my self-esteem. I decided to return to the office at the beginning of June. Douglas suggested not more than two days a week to begin with, and no late nights.

Summertime. As soon as I had fixed a definite date to start working again my recent improvement vanished. I worried that I would not be able to work properly, or concentrate. I kept thinking of the book I had read, and not remembered. What would they all think of me? How could I convince clients that I was capable of handling their affairs? I drove to the office one night, when Helen was asleep, and wandered through the building. My desk was as tidy as it had been when I was last there. Why was there no correspondence? Who had dealt with it? What had they said to my clients, and the staff? I examined a few files. Nothing seemed very important. I searched for the latest monthly trading figures, but couldn't find them. I felt sick. May passed into June, and I could not decide whether I wanted to work or not. I postponed my return until July.

At the end of June, Charles West personally delivered a cheque to the house, my half-yearly bonus. When Helen told me that he was hoping to speak to me I refused to see him, but then changed my mind, and went downstairs – the first time I had spoken to one of my partners since the previous November. I told him that I'd had endogenous depression, Douglas's diagnosis. Yes, Charles said, he understood. He'd had a long chat with Douglas, and hoped that I didn't mind. I felt furious that things had been going on behind my back, and relieved that they all seemed to care about me.

Another month passed before I felt confident enough to face my other partners. I returned to my office one Tuesday morning in August. Everybody seemed pleased to see me. By lunchtime I felt that I could burst into tears at any moment, and nobody seemed surprised when I said that I was going home. I returned two days later

Within a few days I wanted to work full-time. Then the depression returned, and I believed that it would never go. More weeks dragged by until, slowly but hopefully, time seemed to produce the only cure. In September I went to the office most days, but after a few hours' work I felt exhausted. Often, instead of saying that I had to go home, I sneaked away from the building, hoping that nobody had seen me.

Autumn. I worked my first full week during October. I resigned from several business activities which had required evening work. I left the office earlier, usually by 6.30. I decided that the breakdown had been the best thing that had ever happened to me. My year's suffering was what I had needed. It had got out of my system desperation which had been bottled up since I was thirteen years old. Provided I accepted that I had my limitations, nothing like it would ever recur. Satisfied with my conclusions, I felt no embarrassment admitting to other people that I had had a breakdown. I had grown up, buried my past in the graveyard I had mistakenly believed I had consigned it to when I left home, and thankfully, while still young enough to recover, had learned how to cope with my life.

By the end of October I believed that I had liquidated depression and established a new *me*. I had previously been undercapitalized by a lack of self-control. Now, in my embryonic new venture, I knew how to trade profitably with myself. It had been a costly experience, one which I could not afford again. Occasionally I nagged at myself, confused as to why such a disaster had occurred, but, Hell!, what did it matter, I had survived, hadn't I? And so, a year after my November fog, I persuaded myself that I was better.

Which was a pity, because, just when I thought that I was soaring high into my rewarding future, I was sinking more deeply than ever into emotional insolvency.

5 Self-destruct

Introduction

At one of our weekly meetings during my year-long break-down, Douglas, my doctor and friend, spreadeagled my personality on a plain sheet of paper. He drew a straight line: 'That's how most of us live,' he said. 'We have our ups and downs, but the downs are little bumps below the line, soon balanced by the ups above it.' Then he drew a large *U*-shape, bisecting the straight line, the *norm*. 'That's you, see-sawing high above or far beneath the way most of us live.' I studied my *U*. What he said made sense. I nodded wisely. All I had to do was to straighten myself out. But conforming to the norm, while vaguely an attractive idea, seemed to imply that, in some uncertain way, I should cease to be myself. The straight line looked stable and orderly — and as interesting as a twelve-inch ruler. On the other hand, the *U* looked exciting, bouncing across its duller, rigid neighbour. I wanted to retain the excitement I craved, and eliminate the misery. So I compromised. I'd stay straight most of the time, but every now and then to break the monotony, I'd find something to uplift me. Not too much, I told myself, but enough to avoid boredom, enough to keep me happy, but not so much that I would be in danger of dropping below the worrying flat line. I would be like a spirit-level, mainly firm and solid, with a bubble that could move about when it had to, yet never burst.

Douglas's *U* posed more problems than it solved. I tried to carve its image in my mind, hoping that it would remind me of past dangers; but, despite my new-found philosophy, and

164

the mask of confidence which I glued to myself, in quiet moments, when I was alone in my car, or lying thoughtfully in bed, a disturbing question haunted me — why did it, the breakdown, happen? I wanted, but could never find, an answer. If I can't answer the question, why couldn't others answer it for me? Surely someone must be able to tell me what really caused such chaos? People had been kind, patient and sympathetic, but nobody had helped provide an acceptable answer to my question. Douglas presumably hoped that he had provided me with a simplistic explanation which would enhance my self-understanding. Charles West continued calling me a 'high flyer', and agreed with me that I was sensible enough to store my little weakness tidily in a permanent, personal reference file. At the same time, he advised me not to work too hard, thus contradicting himself, and irritating me. Helen told me that I should be proud of my achievements, and spend more time with the family.

Only Malcolm Saunders, my future senior partner, voicing his thoughtful and practical opinion, uttered words which truly reflected how I felt. 'I've thought about you a lot,' he said, shortly after I returned to the office. 'I'm sure it's nothing to do with work. We all work long hours. You've got to stop rushing in all directions, and decide who you are.' His words fell on deaf ears, because if I had one intention above all others, it was to prove to them all that I was stronger, not weaker, as a result of my breakdown. Instead of trying to understand what he meant, I interpreted his comments as a challenge. I rushed in every direction I could think of, unaware that by doing so, I eliminated any chance of discovering who I was. I knew that my unspoken decision 'never to feel depressed again' was nonsense. The words merely reflected my fear that I might never stop feeling depressed.

I did not know why, but to my amazement something remarkable occurred. I stopped suffering from the foggy and frightening periods of depression which had plagued me for so many years. Six months passed, no depression; a year, no depression; two years, still no depression. Aren't I clever, I

congratulated myself, to have become so strong and determined, to have levelled out so well? How weak I must have
been, giving in to those silly, misty bouts of confusion.

Birthday wishes

From the day I left school, my thirtieth birthday appeared
ahead of me like a distant summit. By then I expected to have
fully achieved my ambitions. I thought of the years between
as a fascinating, mountainous challenge, beyond which my
thirtieth birthday rose high and dignified, a glorious, majestic
peak on which I could display my personal flag of success.
For a while, during my breakdown, I had an accident, fell
from a precipitous emotional edge into an unexpected chasm;
but soon I recovered, and from my clumsy fall I learned to be
more cautious. That was why, three years after falling, I
climbed proudly to my ambitious peak — my thirtieth birthday.

People told me how lucky I was. Married couples,
hopelessly trying to salvage themselves from the wreckage of
their marital disasters, came to me for advice. 'If only I could
be as contented as you,' they said enviously. One husband
visited me at home several times a month for a while. 'This is
the one place where I feel peaceful,' he said, drooping
miserably into an armchair, and comforted by a too-full glass
of malt scotch. Another apologized for coming to the house
so often. 'I knew you'd understand,' he said just before he
burst into tears, and told me that his wife was having an
affair with a business colleague. I felt sorry for them, and
proud that I had what they did not — a contented, well-
adjusted marriage.

Other couples suffered the agony of not being able to
conceive. While they visited doctors and consultants, and
struggled to plant a family, mine blossomed. Ben seemed
intelligent and happy, and enjoyed his new private school;
and Vanessa, born the year after my breakdown, attracted
admiring strangers, who stopped to tell me what a beautiful

baby she was. Hers had been a worrying birth, unlike her brother's, but they both entered the world healthy, and remained so. By the time Vanessa was due to start at her private school, Ben would have moved on to another, in readiness for the day he started at public school. When I heard of anxious, childless husbands and wives, desperate for boisterous kids, I felt sorry for them, and proud of my son and daughter.

Family and friends came to see us in the new house we bought, a year after my breakdown, and admired the décor, and the extension we built, and the small but pretty garden. 'I don't know how you do it,' they said, 'all this moving. What is it, your third now, in six years?' I showed them my growing collection of antique scientific instruments, and the latest paintings hanging on the walls; and when they left I snuggled comfortably into an armchair in our family room, surrounded by a thousand or so books. Two years later, the same family and friends visited us in another house, and sometimes I felt embarrassed because it was so large, and theirs was so small. I showed off more paintings, especially the one I had personally commissioned from a local artist, and my latest eighteenth-century theodolite, protected inside an enormous, glass-cased, floor-standing display unit, and took them round the rest of the house. 'Where did those gorgeous tiles come from?' 'Portugal.' 'Isn't that a lovely set of cabinets?' 'Yes, we had them hand-made by the same man who did the settees and chairs.' 'Look at your kitchen!' 'From Harrods', took four men three weeks.'

The house was large, five times larger than the first home we had lived in eight years earlier; and the acre or so of garden — 'It's more like a private park than a garden,' my father said when he first saw it — was magnificent. On fine days we played croquet on the wide-swathed lawn, which I mowed with my sit-on mower. Twice each week Bert the gardener, husband of Elsie the daily woman, vanished into the distance, to superintend the vegetables, or lop branches from overgrown trees. I worried slightly because the sweeping oval lawn would soon be smaller, when the drawings for the proposed swimming pool were transformed into concrete and liquid reality. To the north of the house I paced out the size of the extension which had recently been approved by the local council; to the east, beyond the winding gravel drive which hid the house from a narrow country lane, I rested my arms on an old fence and watched sheep grazing on National Trust farmland. The best investment I've ever made, I thought to myself. And worth about a third of a million pounds in 1986, it would have been — if I'd stayed there.

Most Saturdays, if we weren't entertaining at home, Helen and I went out to eat; if the bill was less than £20 — a decade and a half ago — I thought that we'd been quite economical. I had to drive the baby-sitter home at the end of the evening, to her tiny terraced cottage house which she couldn't afford to redecorate, and felt sorry for her, but proud of my newly-built *Country Life* home. On Sunday mornings the doorbell often rang before I was up, and I had to lob the garage key down to young Andy, who came each week to clean the cars. Fancy having to get up so early, I thought, hoping that he wouldn't scratch the bodywork.

At the theatre I always sat in the centre of the second row of the dress circle; after a morning's shopping at Harrods' I took the family out for lunch at the Churchill Hotel. One Friday I telephoned Helen from the office: 'Let's go to Paris next week,' I said. 'What about the children, I can't send them to my parents again?' she replied. I spent the afternoon rushing about to obtain a temporary passport for our baby-sitter, so that she could come with us, to look after Ben and Vanessa.

When I drove to see clients they wandered inquisitively towards my car. 'Never seen one of those,' they said, 'what is it?' 'A Bristol,' I answered, explaining that only seventy or so were hand-made each year. When some clients, unable to afford luxurious saloons because their businesses were struggling to survive, wanted advice about liquidation, I felt sorry for them, but proud of my expanding and profitable business.

Everyone, either in words or looks, told me how lucky I

was. I told myself how lucky I was; day after day I told myself that, and tried to believe it. After all, I had achieved my teenage ambitions, more than achieved them, despite past depression and a nervous breakdown.

On the morning of my thirtieth birthday, chilled by a bitter February frost, I walked into the large front garden, and looked round at the material proof of my success, while waiting for Ben to come tumbling from the house, so that I could drive him to school. I looked beyond the leafless trees, and, as though a stranger was quietly calling to me from the damp mist, I said aloud, 'I've had enough, it's too much.' Behind me stood the great house, with its slanting Canadian-style roof — and its horrendous mortgage; the keys in my hand unlocked the immaculate Bristol — financed by the bank; Ben came cheerfully across the drive — and I saw more than a decade of future school fees; Helen and Vanessa stood by the front porch, waving goodbye as I drove off, and I waved enthusiastically back — thinking of the expensive summer holiday which I had just booked.

At work, I told nobody that it was my birthday. I shut myself in my office, and told my secretary that I had some important work to do, and did not want to be disturbed. A client had an appointment with me during the morning. I cancelled it. Thirty years old, I kept repeating to myself, thinking of the people who seemed to admire my achievements. Why doesn't anybody understand how little it all means to me? Thirty years gone, thirty more to go before I retired. Thirty more years of being responsible for a family and business and clients and employees. Thirty more years of worrying about money. Thirty more years of headaches and sleeplessness and trying to persuade myself that I was one of the lucky ones. Thirty more birthdays, probably more, of laughing and saying how wonderful my presents were. Thirty more years of lying in the sun by the side of luxurious swimming pools overlooking the Mediterranean, wondering why I felt so wretched. 'It's gone on for too long,' I said, still speaking aloud. 'I can't face this for more years than I've lived already. I want to be dead.'

I had fantasized about death for almost twenty years. Sometimes, when I was alone in my car, listening to music blaring from the stereo, I thought that it would be wonderful, surrounded by fresh fields and cheerful music, to die, at that very moment, when I felt safe and secure and content. On other occasions, my wish to be dead felt like a deep shame, an awful release, a shocking, irresponsible neglect of my duties. But that day I felt different. I knew that I was not depressed; my mind seemed so clear and logical. I was not hysterical. I was calm, realistic and precise.

I did not recognize it then, nor for many years afterwards, but at about 10 to 9 on the morning of my thirtieth birthday, while I waited in my garden for my son to come out of the house, I experienced the first of what I think of as my 'triggers'. Something happened, I did not know what, but suddenly I had all the answers which I had vainly searched for from my teens. I felt that I had clicked into position. I knew what to do.

My old, foggy type of depression had indeed ceased; but something new had taken its place.

Trigger-happy

I knew what to do, and felt excited, elated, relieved, and sad. It was all so logical, I told myself. I should have understood sooner, and would have, had it not been for my past periods of foggy depression. At those times my mind had been cloudy, but not now. Now it was perfectly clear. I just needed a few hours to myself, shut up in my office, to work things out.

I could never be happy, that was obvious; how stupid of me not to have accepted that simple fact years ago. What a ridiculous fraud I was, pretending to other people that I loved life, when I strolled along office corridors, whistling cheerfully; or when I enthusiastically made plans for my family, knowing that I had no future. What a relief, finally to admit that I had no future. So many problems could be resolved. So many questions answered.

Such a pity, to have used up so much energy on other people, when, if only I'd thought more about myself, I might have realized sooner what a fraudulent waste my life had been. Still, at least I was only thirty. A less logical mind could have taken much, much longer to come to the obvious decision. I had to vanish: it was as simple as that. I had to remove myself from the people I threatened, the people who thought that they knew me, but never had, and never would — the people who told me how lucky I was. Perhaps, after I had vanished, they'd understand that by killing myself I was saving them; perhaps, at last, they'd accept that I was not as lucky as they believed me to be. Perhaps they'd feel guilty for their mistake.

I sat quietly in my office, and worked hard. I had to make preparations. I had to protect my family. For an hour or so I concentrated on money. I listed my assets and liabilities and decided that with careful planning Helen and the children could be well protected. But there were two problems: my business and my life assurance policies. Because of restrictive clauses in my partnership agreement, which I had helped draft, it was not possible to withdraw substantial sums if I resigned as a partner; but if I died, the position, for me and my family, was better. And, because of suicide exclusion clauses, unless I was very careful, the large sums for which my life was insured might not be collectable after my death. I studied my financial calculations more carefully. There must be enough money, after I was dead, to support my family. There had to be.

At about 11 o'clock that morning I left the office. I drove slowly along familiar roads, mentally noting each dangerous bend, every steep hill where a car might accidentally drive over an edge. Isn't it sad for them — my wife and children — that I should have to be doing this, but they'll understand that it's what I have to do. I brushed away tears, surprised that I should be crying, when I knew that I was not depressed. Some time later I parked the car, and walked through stark, winter countryside, examining remote corners where a body might lie hidden for weeks, undetected by weekend ramblers.

Then I remembered that my death had to be accidental. I can't die accidentally in a field. It will have to be the car. I can do it, I persuaded myself, I can arrange my death so that it will not be suspicious; the insurance companies may be big and powerful, but I can beat them at their own game. I have to. I must.

Then, as suddenly as my trigger had been cocked, ready to fire, I released the pressure. Well, perhaps, one day, but not yet. In the meantime there were preparations to be made.

At home, I began throwing away old correspondence, and kept only what I thought would be needed after I was dead. I went to see Douglas Allison and told him that I needed something to help me sleep, and secreted the pills away, as part of my contingency plans. In the office, I transferred responsibility for several clients to one of my junior partners.

Thinking of suicide kept me going; without it I had nothing to look forward to. But, until it happened, I had to cope with the people closest to me. Ben disturbed me most. How would he survive without me? He needed me, he was so young, he should not have to lose his father, but if I remained with him I was only prolonging the agony. He was young, he'd survive. He would suffer more if I lived than if I died. Everybody else, except my daughter, who I hoped was too young to remember me, slotted into a different category. They were the ones who stood silently by my graveside, feeling guilty because they had told me how lucky I was. So many of them, all thinking about what they had done to me. Hopefully, some of them would even shed tears, and miss me.

While these fantasies – which to me were starkly real – occupied my night-time thoughts and wide-awake dreams, the rest of my life continued as though nothing unusual was happening. Occasionally, I wondered if I was depressed, but because I did not feel exhausted, and because my mind felt wonderfully alert, unhampered by my frightening fog, I dismissed the idea as ridiculous. Quite the reverse, in fact. I felt surprisingly energetic. I may have my own plans, I thought, but I must not ignore my responsibilities. I must keep busy, so that nobody will suspect that anything has changed.

In the office, I worked harder than ever. At home, I indulged the family in unending treats. In 1972 I worked, and played, and embraced suicide, with equal determination.

Charles West, my senior partner, retired that December. The remaining partners discussed how to commemorate this important event. We decided to present him with some silver at a farewell dinner. I had another idea. Why not write a history of the practice, and present copies to all partners and a few important clients? The other partners hummed and hahed, and said they did not have the time. That was what I wanted to hear. It was my idea, and I wanted to implement it, me, no one else, so that Charles would understand that the relationship between us went beyond our business interests. I thought that it would be a labour of love, that I was doing it for him, as a special, enduring gift.

I have a copy of the book by my side while writing these words. It is a sumptuous production, thirty heavy-quality folios of history, statistics and illustrations. During my years with the firm we acquired seven other practices, some of which, though small, had interesting histories, details of which only became known when I started my research. I discovered, for example, that a long-dead partner in one practice had written a definitive book on accountancy systems, and had been a founder member of the Institute of Chartered Accountants; another had been a driving professional force in the development of, of all things, the veterinary world, and seemed to prefer horses for clients; and a third added up his figures on a seventeenth-century set of Napier's bones, which he later donated to a national museum.

In the concluding paragraphs of our history I wrote optimistically about the firm's vision of the future – a future, my words assured its readers, in which our expertise and their entrepreneurial skills would merge into unfettered success. I included a few words of caution – about inflation and world competition — but the emphasis was upon wide-ranging global opportunities, including advances in technology and communications. As a flag-waving exercise for our business it identified everything about the future which I thought I believed in . . . but . . . at the same time I was longing for death. Thirty copies of the book were printed, one of which was inscribed to me by Charles 'with very happy memories'.

Nobody, including myself, understood that the dedication and time I invested in the book was not really for Charles. It was my personal farewell to a business I had once loved but had grown to hate. I believed that Charles's departure was a signal to me: the green light forward had changed to red. I had to stop. I had had enough.

As the day of his retirement came closer, I felt my good feelings towards Charles change to bitterness and resentment. He was leaving me. Didn't he understand that without him I could not survive with the other partners? The sense of loss felt appalling. Who would I be able to talk to? Who could I telephone to say I needed a day or two at home, who would not ask questions, but would understand why? Who was left in my business group to trust? Most of them were as remote as any other person in my life. I conditioned my death wish. If I escape from the business, perhaps I can survive. I wanted to talk to Charles about my fears, but I was conscious of his preoccupation with his own affairs, and frightened to trust him with too many of my worries. For six months I wanted to tell him that I, too, intended leaving. Instead, I listened to his optimistic and precise plans for the future, and fumed silently, dreading each new day at the office.

I behaved at the office as I behaved at home — outwardly so normal, so cheerful and so enthusiastic, that nobody suspected that I was slowly releasing the safety catch on my trigger. When I fired the first shots they were encased in a silencer, and nobody heard the noise. My partners didn't hear the screams of agony inside me while I energetically bombarded them with more ideas for expansion; nor did they realize, when I insisted that I deal with fewer clients —

because, I explained, my most important ones needed all my time — that I was stemming the flow of my responsibilities; and they never understood that I had secretly dressed my business wounds with soothing absences from the office. I organized my working life in such a way that I was seldom in the office for more than one day each week. Whenever I could, I travelled — far away, and for as long as possible, from infested ambitions which had to be amputated.

I aimed myself in all directions. It made little difference to me where I went, or why, so long as I discharged myself at new targets. During a twenty-four-month period I travelled, on business, to New York, Washington, Dusseldorf, Frankfurt, Paris, Madrid, Rome and, most months, to Jersey and Guernsey. I spent many nights unnecessarily away in England, under any flimsy pretext. If a client asked to come and see me, I told him that I would be near his business, and that it would be easier for me to visit him. My partners sometimes questioned the amount of time I spent away from the office, but I persuaded them that it was for the good of the firm. Although I was intentionally vanishing from them, I nevertheless worked so effectively that the high fees which I earned allayed incipient suspicions.

While I manipulated my working life, I also ensured additional absences from the home which I knew I had to leave, by planning lavish and regular holidays with the family. In the same period as my hectic business travel I managed to take my wife and children to France (several times), Greece, the Canaries, and away for a few weekends in England. They were some of the treats I wanted them to enjoy.

There were others: a birthday party for my son, with fifty children prancing and dancing noisily on the floor of a private suite in a hotel; imported French clothes for my daughter; furs and jewellery for my wife. I was too far away to let them see me, but I wanted to see them happy and well-treated. At the time, the irony was lost in my clear, incisive mind.

I assuaged my bad feelings — feelings which I shuffled into

a worthless hand of guilt, sadness and loneliness – in other ways. At night, when I could not sleep, I began drinking great tumblerfuls of smooth, heart-burning brandy, and to my delight discovered that they helped me forget that I wanted to die. But that was a short-lived pleasure. I had never drunk much alcohol, particularly spirits, and despised myself for having to sink so low. I don't need artificial stimulants, I told myself sternly, unaware that I had been intoxicated for most of my life. I had never gambled much, either, not in the casino, horses or dog-racing sense – even my occasional flings on the stock market were modest; but, mainly because I had never done it, I visited a casino once, and lost £50 in not many more seconds. Gambling's not for me, I decided, unaware that almost every act I performed was for far higher stakes than a few pounds. But I discovered one pleasure I did enjoy – other women.

For eight years I had been a physically faithful husband. I had overcome, despite temptations, several itches, but I willingly scratched my sudden rash. Memories of my teenage shyness with girls had stayed with me, and when a female client offered herself, literally, I was astonished. I shouldn't have been, because I had been mentally snaking towards her for weeks. Booze and bets didn't give me what I wanted, but she, and others, did, fleetingly. Like all my other excesses during this period, they remained exhilarating personal secrets.

Although today I can interpret my behaviour as belligerent, while this frantic period was actually happening, I felt that I was on an exciting and frightening helter-skelter. At times I knew that I was rushing down into a trough that left me gasping. How could this be, I wondered, constantly assuring myself that I could not be depressed, because I recognized none of the old, familiar patterns. When I rose dizzily upwards, thrilled at what lay ahead of me, I laughed scornfully at myself. How could I even think about depression, when my thoughts and plans were so clear and unalterable! As I hastily rushed up and down – like an unending series of my doctor's explanatory U-shaped portraits – I drew further away from people and groups.

On several occasions I tried to discuss my feelings and worries. When I most wanted to explain to Charles West that I could not remain as a partner, I filtered my words through a personal code, in the same way that, when I played *alter ego* at Shipley Grange, my true thoughts were disguised. 'Oh!' I sighed wearily, 'I wonder where we'll be this time next year.' 'Looking for another practice to take over, I expect,' he replied enthusiastically. Why can't he understand how bad I'm feeling, I thought angrily, expecting him to decode my message. When I told Helen that I was feeling restless in my career, and could do with a change, she said anxiously: 'But they know you, and understand you. Look how good they were during your breakdown. You need their support. Why give it all up and risk the unknown? What will we live on?' I was furious. Just because I had not explained that if I did not leave I would kill myself, surely that was no reason for her not to understand.

All my relationships were similarly disguised. I had no intimate friend, and did not want one. Those friends I had, mostly from my days at the Circus Club, visited us for lavish dinners, or invited us to their homes every month or so. During those evenings my conversation roamed into safe subjects, like business, the theatre, holidays or gardening. Sometimes, aware of the inner battles raging inside me while I joined in shallow discussions which felt unreal and irrelevant to my life, I goaded people into arguments, intentionally saying things which contradicted what I had heard them say, even when I agreed with them. These intellectual attacks, which I hoped would at least raise the social temperature, achieved nothing, except to provide further proof that nobody could decipher my emotional mayday signals.

My conviction that I was a social fraud crystallized into another reason for ending my life: I was a threat to other people. I did not acknowledge that they were threats to me.

Then, for a few months, I shared my menacing worries with hundreds of millions of people.

In the autumn of 1973 the Middle East erupted into the

'Yom Kippur War', when Egypt launched an unexpected attack on Israel. Arab States, resenting what they interpreted as the Western world's failure to support their cause, cut off oil supplies. Within a few weeks fuel prices soared. Petrol rationing became a probability. In Britain the miners were on the brink of a major strike. Power cuts began, and the lights went off in Piccadilly. At the end of the year the government introduced the Three-Day Week. By the new year the country's commercial and industrial life was in chaos. A bitter miners' strike, and an indecisive prime minister, contributed to what the media agreed unanimously were the worst social upheavals since the Second World War. All my personal fears were justified; I was right, there was no future, not for me, or for anybody else.

At a time of universal turmoil, I felt better. If the world was so depressed, then my own feelings, reflected in the gloom of candlelit shop windows, felt normal; if national and international aggression in 1974 had led to the Third World War, I think that I may possibly have felt content.

I have often wondered how I would have felt and behaved in time of war. As a child, I heard personal stories from adults who were just recovering from one, but, apart from the tears in her eyes when my aunt told me about an RAF friend of hers who was killed during an air-raid over Southampton, most people seemed to laugh at their memories, or tell me exciting tales of adventure. War was terrible, they said, not enough food, blackouts, children sent away from home, bombs and fires, Hitler and gas-chambers. But my family — parents, grandparents, uncles and aunts — continued to impress me with what sounded like happy memories. The war enabled my father to leave home and escape from the misery of long, tedious days in a sweat-shop; because men were away fighting, my mother was able to become the manageress of a clothes shop; my aunt met dozens of Yanks who fussed over her; the same Yanks helped increase my grandmother's savings. Heroic war stories published in the 1950s — *The Dam Busters* and *Reach for the Sky* were two of dozens – left me wide-eyed in admiration and wonder. 'I hope you never have to live through what we did,' adults said to me when I asked questions; but their words seemed to contradict what I understood. I grew up believing that war was awful and serious, but exciting

The only thing I did not like about war was that when I entered my teens young men were still expected to serve two years' mandatory conscription, which to me meant twenty-four months of unrelenting physical exercise and discipline, both of which I loathed. Fortunately, conscription was abolished before I left school. At about the same time, pictures of a mushroom-shaped cloud appeared on the front pages of national newspapers. The hydrogen bomb sounded so unreal – yet exciting – in my adolescent mind that I agreed with the majority opinion: it was so fearful that it could never be used. But I still had a strange feeling that I would enjoy a war.

By the beginning of the 1960s I had changed my mind. Someday, somewhere, I believed, someone would press the button. If that meant my certain annihilation, then the most intelligent philosophy was to enjoy myself for as long as I could, with as much as I could. I discovered the word *hedonist*, and respected my maturity. There were people of my own age who argued bitterly against this reaction, convinced that nuclear explosions were realities too horrific to be ignored; but few of them moved in the circles I mixed with. Most of my friends and business colleagues were absorbed by explosions of a different kind – rising profits, soaring pleasures and swelling bellies full of sons and daughters.

Other explosions – like unemployment and inflation – belonged to history, or the unexpected future. I cannot recall meeting one school-leaver or university graduate who could not find a job; and inflation was an abstract subject dealt with briefly in my accountancy studies. When trade unionists announced a strike, which they did with increasing frequency, we said: 'What this country needs is a few more unemployed'; and when we bought our first homes we paid 4½ per cent interest, assuming that it would remain unchanged.

My son's enthusiasm for the decade he never knew, the one he smothered with 'the Beatles and hippies and Rock and the Vietnam marches', bore little relationship to the one I knew. He would have laughed contemptuously at the movements I gingerly made towards the awakening changes. I marched rigorously into my career, and stepped firmly into my conventional family commitments. Reports of peculiar groups of people of my own age advocating and practising unmarried family relationships shocked me; and when I understood that these same groups smoked drugs and criticized the Conservative party, I despised them. Until I represented several music and entertainment clients in the last years of the 1960s, I had never met anyone who took drugs, or admitted that they did. The only meanings I knew of dope, hash, score, shit or pot were those defined in dictionaries. And as for the Beatles, well, I liked some of their music, more of it than I expected to, but it was at least five years after they first topped the charts before I believed that they were anything other than an enjoyable, but brief, musical inter-lude. I thought that I had been fully initiated into their cult when they released their *Sergeant Pepper* album; but not until recently did I learn — from my son, naturally — that songs which I had enjoyed simplistically had a deeper meaning. 'Really!' I said to him, astonished to hear that 'Lucy in the Sky with Diamonds' had less to do with cellophane flowers and Plasticine porters than with LSD. By the time he'd finished patiently redefining lyrics which had buzzed innocently and melodiously in my head for more years than he had been born, I began wondering where I had been in my twenties. To regain some credibility I emphasized that I had worn skinny ties with floral patterns, and that for three years or so I changed my Tony Curtis hair-cut so that both ears and part of my shirt collars were hidden. He laughed sympatheti-cally.

I laughed — I laughed so much that my stomach muscles

ached – when I went to see *Beyond the Fringe*. On Saturday nights, noisy party-goers creased foreheads, worried in case the host refused to turn on the TV at 11 o'clock, so that we could all sit down and watch, with delighted amazement, the virulent satire introduced by David Frost. On *Panorama*, Robin Day said unbelievable things to cabinet ministers and business tycoons; afterwards, when the shock of hearing and seeing Authority flattened on the TV screen had passed, I wished that I had the influence and perspicacity to cut through my own suspicions about smiling politicians and powerful industrialists. When, during a TV discussion about censorship, Kenneth Tynan said 'fuck', I rushed from the room to tell my wife, wondering if I had misheard. I felt shocked and elated. Such freedom: what was happening in the world! Satire and confrontation stabbed complacency, and I enjoyed the gaping wounds.

Enjoy seems a cruel word to describe death, but, perhaps because death and history have always been important to me, I enjoyed the sadness of sharing President Kennedy's assassination and Winston Churchill's funeral. On both occasions I felt that I was part of a momentous event. I wanted to be closer than a newspaper headline or a television screen. On the Monday after Kennedy's death, my wife and I joined the trailing, silent and subdued queue outside the American Embassy in Grosvenor Square, and felt part of history when eventually I signed the Book of Condolence. Somewhere, stored in a distant archive, are the few words which I wrote and have now forgotten. In January 1965, I joined another silent queue, and walked through Westminster Hall, past Churchill's catafalque, while blue-uniformed RAF officers stood to attention, clicked heels and changed guard. How could one man do so much, I wondered. The Kennedy queue was predominantly a young gathering, the majority close to my own age: at Westminster Hall I felt out of place, everyone near me was so much older.

My reactions during the 1960s to signs of change felt as contradictory as my feelings about myself. I shared the thrill of youthful economic independence, and the freedom which enabled me to regard an older generation as older, but not wiser; but I worried when I heard that same generation ridiculed and mocked. Kenneth Tynan's four-letter word seemed to say everything. It was marvelllous not to feel restricted, but who was going to define the new rules?

I stood on the social and cultural sidelines, uncertain about which team I supported, and decided that I wasn't sure that I supported anyone. I retreated to the easier familiarity of my family and career, and evolved most of my beliefs from the necessities of my personal existence. In an unemotional sense life *was* easy. I did not have to go without a wife, or children. I knew that, provided I worked hard, there was no reason for me to fail in my career. My days were spent with similar-minded people. Optimism opened the decade. To balance this with my depression and worries I instructed myself neatly. So long as I'm happy 50 per cent of the time, I persuaded myself, life is good.

Clients whom I had grown up with, and who, like myself, expected to get bigger, got bigger, and bigger. Banks were desperate to lend money. (One bank manager telephoned me in 1970, asking me to borrow as much as I wanted for any business scheme which he could properly recommend to his district office.) New markets, both for goods and overseas, were available to those who took risks. But as the decade advanced, the half-life I expected to sparkle began to show signs of dimming. As each year passed, more problems arose. Inflation gradually moved out of my textbook and into my office. Profits by the end of the 1960s often only increased on paper because of rising prices. Unending strikes decimated production schedules. By 1973 my light had disappeared, at times literally, due to the Three-Day Week.

I had one client who made engine parts for British Leyland. Steel comprised less than 10 per cent of his raw materials. One year he could obtain no steel, another he could obtain steel, but his finished products were refused admission to a factory in Oxford because British Leyland, yet again, was on strike. Each set-back involved a trip to the bank. Overdrafts and loans increased in real money values, profits did not.

During the Three-Day Week his business finally collapsed, not because of too little steel, which was difficult to buy, or because the customer was on strike, but because the bank, which had previously assured him that it was as reliable as a partner, suddenly, without notice, demanded a large reduction in his borrowing.

That Three-Day Week! It took me out of myself. For a while I was too busy attending crisis meetings with clients – clients who for years had been the blood of my working life – to remember that death was my priority. I felt depressed, they felt depressed, everybody felt depressed; but it was a depression which made sense, based on reality and tangible anxiety and worry. We were all so depressed that we cheered each other up. I understood the cheerful twinkle in people's eyes when they spoke of the misery they lived through during the Second World War.

By April 1974, the twinkles had gone. Working weeks were back to normal. Six months of chaos ended. Clients and friends behaved as if nothing had happened. I hated them all for bouncing back to their straight line, because I could not cope with normality. I was at the bottom of my *U*, and crashing down on top of me was the 50 per cent happiness I had temporarily regained, when everyone felt as bad as I did. The 1960s? – a disaster; the early 1970s? – worse; April 1974? – pull the trigger.

I did.

Confessions

My initial experience at Shipley Grange was like the recent British Rail television advertisement: two unseen trains, travelling in different directions along lines coming from infinity, each with an arrow at its head, speed towards the centre of the screen. Clickity-click, clackety-clack. Rushing, whistling noises: clickity-click, clackety-clack, faster, faster. Suddenly, they meet. Wham! Splat! Shudder! Blaring crescendos from the music department. Is-it-a-crash, is-it-a-smash? Of course not! cues an encouraging message, as the crashing timpani softens to gentle, reassuring strings: 'We're getting there.' End of advertisement. Turn off the TV. Rush out and buy an Awayday ticket to your nearest psycho-therapy unit.

After my two engines, heaving behind them overloaded emotional compartments, had rattled along for four un-reliable weeks, I arrived at a group junction, convinced that my past was about to smash into head-on collision with my future. If I wasn't careful, instead of staying on the rails, I would topple over and crash – and get nowhere. From my past I had travelled into a possible future, but I still could not decide whether I was getting anywhere.

At the end of my first month, I was formally shunted into a maintenance yard, to be scrutinized by the group, to decide if I was functioning properly. Each member, including myself, had to appraise, inspect, and report on my progress. Was I in danger of breaking down; were my feelings well-oiled; could I effectively ease the brake on my behaviour without whip-lashing my passengers? Did I take any notice of danger signals? And what about my compartments: were the doors into them open or closed; and once inside, could we all sit down comfortably, or would I vandalize my own furniture? While we all anxiously prodded, probed and tested my reliability, I hoped, fervently, that I would not be consigned to the psychotherapeutic scrap-yard

Everyone agreed that, although I had not arrived, I was 'getting there'. I had been checked and approved, and certified as fit to continue my travels. Such unanimity hurt me. I knew that to prove that their confidence in my future was well-judged – to prove that I could 'get there' – I had to offer more of myself to them than I had previously been prepared to. The time had come to convert myself from shaky local diesels into inter-city expresses.

My two separate, but related, journeys had begun from the day I joined the group. On one journey I had chugged steadily through my past – some of it – and stopped at childhood and teenage stations, and then hurried through a few narrow cuttings in my adult years. The second journey travelled towards unclear horizons, through boggy fields of sinking group feelings and rising group anger. Yet, despite my halting stops and starts, and the uncomfortable bumps and jerks I had given the group, they wanted me. But would they still want me if they entered dark, threatening tunnels, in which I opened up compartments as uncomfortable as cattle trucks, and about which they knew nothing?

During the weekend after my first review I felt ashamed of myself. How could the residents – the staff had notes from confidential meetings – think me safe, when they had only been admitted to those compartments which I felt ready to unlock? How could I have allowed them to inspect me, and at the same time hide from them my most defective parts, the compartments which I had secretly hitched behind my engines, barred as 'out of order'? I felt that I had to open these doors, to let them crowd in, to confess and say, 'Look, see what you missed, now say that you still want to travel with me.' My fear that I may not have the courage to open the doors into my reserved compartments grew so alarmingly that at one point I decided that I could not return to the unit on the following Monday. But I needed them to hear what I had to say. My worst fear was that they would be so disgusted at what they discoverd that they would change their minds, demand a second review meeting, express their fury that I had misled them, and shame me into breaking my journeys.

'I want to stay,' I began by saying on Monday morning, 'but if I do, I have to say something.' I spoke, uninterrupted, for seventy-five minutes, and only stopped when Stuart pushed his chair back, and stood up to indicate that the formal meeting had reached the end of its allotted time. When I sat with the other residents in the living room, during the mid-morning break, I felt suspicious. What did they all think of me? Did they regret their Friday decision that I should stay with them?

Barbara, the woman I had reduced to a huddled, hysterical heap a few days earlier, when I accused her of being a cock-teaser, broke the silence. 'I'd never have believed you, if I'd heard that anywhere else,' she said. I couldn't decide if she felt sympathetic, nauseated or terrified. 'I didn't have time to say all that I wanted,' I replied. Cathy said she was hungry, and left the room to make a sandwich. Is she really hungry, I wondered, or does she need to get away from me?

In the evening, Barbara and I went out together, to a local pub for a drink. She, more than any other resident, seemed to understand that I had not recovered from my morning's confessions. I needed to talk more about them, not in the presence of a dozen people, but more intimately, so that I could believe that one person, at least, still wanted me in the group.

'Something snapped. I didn't understand it then, and I don't understand it now,' I told her. 'That's one of the reasons I'm here.' *Then* was 1974; *now* was 1981.

I did not use the word 'trigger' until a counsellor introduced it into a discussion about my behaviour, long after I left Shipley Grange. We were talking about my experiences in 1974, the same ones Barbara and I were chatting about over our lagers. 'Something snapped,' I repeated. . . .

The sensation felt as precise as the sound of a dry twig breaking, or the click from an electric kettle when the water has boiled. Before I snapped, or clicked, my mind had been fuzzy, clouded by dozens of conflicting thoughts; and my feelings, which I did not recognize as feelings, were as clouded as my thoughts.

The trigger, snap or click which occurred on my thirtieth birthday took place at about 10 to 9 in the morning. I have experienced four major ones since then, two of them associated with the confessions I made to the group that morning. Each trigger was preceded by extended periods of sleeplessness. Unexpectedly, after each one, instead of feeling drowsy, and in need of rest, I felt alert, clear-headed and energetic. Fuzzy thoughts vanished, cloudy feelings blew away. I felt that a force had spent itself, and left behind the calm stillness of death.

In April 1974, after the Three-Day Week ended, I received

a telephone call from my friendly bank manager, Jim, the one who had almost begged me to borrow money from his bank a few years earlier. 'I hope you don't mind my asking,' he said pleasantly, 'but do you still need your overdraft facility? I have to send in a report on balances that aren't reducing, and yours is one of them. No problem,' he assured me, 'just more paperwork. Hope you don't mind my mentioning it.' He sounded almost apologetic. 'Oh, don't worry, Jim,' I replied cheerfully, 'I wanted to clear it this month anyway.' 'There's no need to do that,' he said, obviously relieved. We chatted about a few mutual clients, and ended our conversation with an agreed lunch date. I slowly replaced the receiver. I felt sick. How was I going to find £10,000 within a month?

I had not overcome the perennial difficulty of controlling my personal expenditure. I could not really afford the large house which I had purchased, or the luxurious and expensive additions, which had increased its original cost by one third. I knew that my financial affairs were as out of control as the escalating international oil prices. The time had come, as Charles West would have said, to 'consolidate'. A few months earlier I had explained to Helen that we would have to take care, the future was uncertain. She suggested that we should sell the house. 'Impossible,' my *alter ego* said sternly, 'That's a bad thing to do, and bad means failure, and you mustn't fail. What would people think?'

Resulting from my bank manager's diplomatic request, I examined my finances. I needed £15,000 to pay off all my commitments, including the overdraft, and excluding the mortgage. Fifteen thousand was a lot, but not such a lot that I could not arrange to settle it, and reorganize myself financially, as I had had to do a few years earlier, before my year-long breakdown. My annual income was more than that. And I had learned from my past mistakes. This time I'll talk it over with my partners, I thought – well, with Malcolm Saunders. I don't want them all to know. I went to bed, satisfied that I had made the right decision. Helen, lying peacefully asleep beside me, knew nothing about my humiliation that a bank manager had asked me to settle an overdraft; or that, downstairs, filed away in tidy bundles, were unpaid bills which I had marked 'urgent', 'within one month' or 'wait'. Yes, that's what I'll do, I thought when I settled under the covers, I'll speak to Malcolm, and discuss a satisfactory, temporary arrangement. A loan perhaps?

That was one of the last sensible thoughts I had for fifteen months.

Within minutes of deciding that I should speak to my partner, I knew that I could not do it. It meant admitting failure, of being shown up for a hopeless imposter. I was a fraud, as I had always known. How could I expect help from anybody? Why had I so cheerfully told my anxious bank manager that I would settle my overdraft within a month, when already my monthly income was fully committed?

For several hours my life, which I assessed as a perpetual series of misadventures and failures, passed through my mind like a funeral procession. I was not aware of feelings, only thoughts. Each one led relentlessly to another. Occasionally, as the mournful hours ticked by, I tried to control myself. Take it easy, relax, concentrate, try to work out what to do. And then, some time between 5 and 6 o'clock in the morning — SNAP! I knew what to do.

I arrived at my desk early that morning, and immediately began putting into practice the solutions which had clicked into place a couple of hours earlier. I wrote two long letters — one to Malcolm, the other to Helen — both explaining what I was doing. Then I filled in several building society withdrawal forms, and dictated three letters to clients. In the afternoon, when the typed letters stared at me from my desk, like criminal indictments, I wondered what I was doing. I must be mad, there's still time to destroy the incriminating evidence. But it has to be done. I've made my decision. Within a week it will all be over. A dead man is a safe man.

Accountants, like lawyers, but to a lesser extent, often hold clients' monies on deposit, for future commitments or current investments. A few months before my bank manager's unwelcome telephone call, I had negotiated the sale of a business, on behalf of three directors who owned an engineering company. A taxation liability for capital gains arose; for a short period they agreed to deposit the funds with several building societies, each of which paid my firm commission for the amounts invested provided that the money was not withdrawn within six months. My letters, addressed to the three directors, advised them that, if they transferred their money from one building society to another, additional commission could be earned, half of which would be credited to their new accounts. All they had to do was to sign the enclosed withdrawal forms, instructing the existing societies to remit the money to our client account, and I would transfer the appropriate sums, plus their share of the commission, to another society. Within a few days, the signed forms were returned.

One day that week, during another escape from my office, I drove into central London, ate a smoked salmon and champagne lunch at the Ritz Hotel, and then walked along Berkeley Street, enjoying the mild spring sunshine. I peered through windows full of rare carpets, costly perfumes, and antiques, and at the several car showrooms selling Rolls Royces. Hadn't Helen said, not so long ago, that she wondered if we'd ever own a Rolls Royce?

An hour later I bought one, silver and grey, and two years old. 'Would you like us to arrange finance?' asked the respectful, smartly-dressed young salesman. 'No, that won't be necessary,' I replied loftily, irritated that he had questioned my financial needs. I wrote out and signed a cheque for £11,000, increasing the overdraft which I had promised to clear within a month. We agreed that the car could be collected a few days later.

Why did I do that? I wondered, as I drove home that evening. How can I pay for it, when I'm already in debt? In bed, I decided that I would telephone the salesman the following morning, and cancel the ridiculous and extravagant purchase. ('You can't do that,' implored my *alter ego*, 'what would he think of you!')

I did make a telephone call the following morning. I advised my bank manager that I had issued a large cheque, but told him not to worry, the overdraft would be settled that week, two weeks earlier than I had agreed.

My snap decision to resolve my financial difficulties, prior to dying, depended upon my clients agreeing with my proposals to transfer their money. It did not occur to me that they might refuse. They didn't. I intended collecting in the various sums, which totalled £40,000, retaining the £15,000 I needed to settle my debts, and reinvesting, on their behalf, the balance. In my letter to Malcolm, I explained that the clients would not know what I had done; and that he could repay what I had taken from the proceeds of the sale of my house, which Helen would sell after my death. It was all so neat and logical — until I bought the Rolls Royce.

When the withdrawals from the building society had been deposited in my firm's bank account, I instructed our internal accountant to send me three cheques, for the amount banked on behalf of each director. 'I'm not sure which new society they're going to,' I told him, 'so send them in blank, and I'll let you know in a day or so.' As far as he was concerned money came in one day and went out another. I knew that any day the Inland Revenue could issue a tax demand, or that my clients could ask for confirmation of the deposits, or that my partners might query the transactions, but I proceeded with my plans, convinced of my own infallibility. Fifteen thousand, I had originally calculated I needed, but after the car purchase, which continued to bewilder me, I decided to keep the lot – £40,000. I entered my bank's name as payee on the three cheques, signed them as one of the sole mandated signatories, and deposited them in my personal account. The theft was so crude and detectable that I knew it would be discovered within a week or two, when our firm's next bank statements arrived with the returned cheques. But by then I'd be dead.

I rewrote the letter to Malcolm, explaining that, if there were insufficient funds from the house sale, the balance of the stolen money could be repaid from life policy proceeds which would be received, because, of course, my death would be an 'accident'. It did cross my mind that I was involving my partners and wife in fraud, but I quickly dismissed their moral predicament. They'll want the money, I reasoned, so it's up to them.

After the money had arrived in my bank account, I enjoyed some of the most satisfying few hours for years. I settled all my unpaid accounts; sent off cheques to suppliers – for gas, electricity, telephone, rates, and so on – to cover the few months' expenses which would be incurred after my death, and before Helen could sell the house; calculated how much was left, allowing for the overdraft repayment and the cost of the Rolls Royce; and ended up with a surplus of £14,000. Isn't it wonderful, I thought, now I can die in peace, knowing that my family will have no unpleasant bills to worry about.

My partners? Well, they'll be surprised, but really, I've helped them. They'll get the money they need to open the building society accounts, which the clients think already exist, and, apart from a little administrative inconvenience, they'll save a fortune, once I'm dead and no longer drawing my high income. The only losers will be the life assurance companies, and who cares about them? I had not yet worked out what to do about the Rolls Royce.

Meanwhile, I had another idea. I took Helen for a week's holiday, to the South of France. While she enjoyed sunbathing on the private beaches, I pretended to sleep, wondering how to explain the treat I had arranged. 'There's a surprise coming,' I finally told her, the day before we returned to England. I explained that business was so good that I'd paid for the Rolls with a bonus. Surely, I thought, she must realize what's happening. Perhaps she'll speak to one of the partners, or their wives. Someone must find out soon . . . surely.

After our short holiday in France, and my acquisition of the Rolls, I had to return to the office. Had they discovered the theft? Would I walk into the board room, and be confronted by grim accusatory faces? No. They asked me if I'd had a good week. Wonderful, I replied enthusiastically. The Rolls? Yes, it's mine, got it on the cheap from an uncle. Why was everyone so blind!

I began complaining to the partners that I was fed up with

work, fed up with tedious administrative duties, fed up with petty squabbles. Malcolm and I had earnest discussions. We blamed a recently-introduced partner for much of our discontent. Why hadn't they discovered my theft? Why, having planned to kill myself as soon as I had settled my personal debts, was I discussing business problems, as if nothing had changed?

Weeks passed: April led unexpectedly to May, and May, amazingly, led to June, and nothing happened. I was still alive. My plans were going wrong. I wanted to die, but that surplus money lay there untouched in my bank account. I felt sad that I would be leaving my children. They must have something to remember me by, Helen too. A holiday. A long, glorious holiday: a final treat for the family I did not want to leave, but had to; something for them to remember.

At the office, surprised that I was still there, I began surreptitiously tidying up. I passed more clients to a junior partner; for the few I retained, I dictated lengthy memos, so that after my death another partner could immediately familiarize himself with their affairs. Every few days I added notes to my two letters — Malcolm's and Helen's — and then hid them carefully at home, behind the first volume of my set of Samuel Pepys's diary.

For some inexplicable reason, my theft remained undiscovered.

I planned a detailed itinerary for our intended family holiday; and went on regular shopping sprees. I bought Helen a large, and very expensive, diamond ring from Kutchinsky's in Knightsbridge, and another mink; as an afterthought, to keep her company, after I was dead, I added a second television. Surely now she'll start asking questions, I thought. When she did, I brushed aside her doubts. Really, business is terrific, I told her.

And, still, the partners did not discover my theft; the clients did not ask about their non-existent investments; the Inland Revenue demanded no tax. I felt powerful and brilliant, but kept wondering why I was still alive.

Each week I drove up to London, and, through a call-girl agency, hired a girl for an afternoon or evening. (I had avidly read the inside back page of the *New York Herald Tribune*, Paris edition, since my thirtieth birthday.) The girls, all of whom were attractive, and a few intelligent, earned their money by sitting opposite clients in elegant restaurants, and lying next to them in expensive hotel bedrooms. They cost £100 a night, £50 for an afternoon, excluding meals, champagne and occasional gifts. Eventually I met Tina, whom I liked enough to make my own private arrangement with. To add some security to our relationship, I booked a permanent suite at what was then the Carlton Tower Hotel. Once, then twice, weekly, sometimes more often, we shared a small but delightful bedroom and living room on the tenth floor.

At the end of July I visited my doctor, Douglas, and complained that I was feeling depressed, which I knew was untrue – although I had begun to wonder what was wrong with me. I wanted his support to explain to my partners that, rather than suffer another year's breakdown, I needed a long rest. 'You'll have to stop travelling around so much, and spend more time in the office,' one of them said sympathetically.

In August, four months after my theft, I packed several suitcases, two children, and a wife, into my spacious Rolls Royce, and left England. Nobody knew where we were going; nobody could come chasing after me because they'd discovered that I was a thief; nobody could disrupt my farewell family treat.

We spent a few days in Paris, at the Plaza Athenée, followed by two weeks in Cannes, at the Carlton; then we drove across northern Italy, until we reached Venice, where we stayed at the Lido, so that the children could enjoy daily trips in a motor launch into Venice city; finally, we returned to Cannes, where we stayed for a month in a family suite at the Majestic, overlooking the Croisette. In eight weeks I spent more than £10,000. Every day I expected to see Malcolm

Saunders striding angrily towards me, his hand menacingly outstretched for the return of the stolen money. Surely they must have discovered the theft!

Some nights, while the family slept after their days in the sun, I collected the Rolls, and drove into the mountains behind Cannes, determined to drive over a deathly edge. Then I worried about what would happen to my family. They'd be troubled by the police, and have to arrange for my body to be flown back to England. It seemed more sensible to wait until our holiday was over before killing myself. I began wondering if I actually had the courage to do it.

On Monday 14 October 1974, six months after I had stolen the money, I returned to my office. Malcolm greeted me coldly. 'You could have let us know what was going on,' he said, 'you told us that you'd be away for one month, not two.' Still they don't know! I told him what I had intimated to another partner before I went on holiday; that I intended leaving the business and taking a consultancy job in South Africa. No one questioned me, except to ask if I knew what I was doing. I had lost their goodwill, not because I had stolen £40,000, but because, for the first time in nine years, they realized that I could not accept their group.

We agreed that I should resign at the end of the month, and that my profits would be drawn until the end of the year. It was my last hour at the office as a partner. I was alive, but felt dead. I had destroyed one of my two teenage ambitions. When I destroyed the group mural at the unit, I remembered the day I left the partnership.

For six months I had expected to confront an accuser; for six months everybody who lived, worked or socialized with me had accepted that my life was normal, reasonable, that nothing was wrong; for six months I had not known from one day to the next what was happening to me. Gradually, the clear-headedness, which had comforted me in the early hours of the morning I made my decision to steal £15,000, changed to total emotional and intellectual confusion. Now, having coldly rejected my partners, there could be no more pretence. I had ended my business career, and given my family their last treat.

Helen, settling in after our long holiday, assumed that I had returned to work; the children returned cheerfully to school; Bert, the gardener, proudly showed me crops of luscious autumn apples. I could not believe that I was the only one who knew that it was all a huge fraud.

I spent the next day driving aimlessly through dismal countryside, trying to decide what to do. On Wednesday I told Helen that I had to stay away for a night on business. That morning I roamed through Harrods' buying clothes and toiletries, and a suitcase to put them in, and then headed south, in the Rolls, to Dover and Calais and Paris. Two days later I telephoned Helen, who by then had learned that I had left the partnership. She was frantic. 'Don't worry,' she said, 'just come home, and we'll decide what to do.' I couldn't believe that, still, nobody knew about the stolen money.

I flew back to London, leaving the car in Paris, and, reluctantly, after months of disbelief that it had remained a secret, I told my wife, and my aunt, who had been staying with her, about my theft. Abruptly, I faced, not two women, but reality. I had no job, very little available money, a family to support, and seven ex-partners who did not yet know about my guilty secret. For the first time it occurred to me that I could be sent to prison.

All the accountants I have ever met have at least one friendly solicitor, just as they have at least one friendly bank manager. David, my personal solicitor, was an old friend from the Circus Club. The day after my confession to Helen and my aunt, I sought his advice. Yes, I agreed, make an appointment, at my house. Tell them it's urgent. Next week. Don't tell them what it's about. And I'll only meet two of them. David made the 'phone call, to Malcolm Saunders, who agreed to meet us at 10.30 on Tuesday 22 October. 'He probably thinks we're going to ask for money,' I said, smiling. From the look I received I knew that David was not amused. I also knew that he would do his best to assist me, professionally, as a solicitor: there would be no more friendly lunches.

The Friday before the meeting I flew to the newly-opened Charles de Gaulle airport to collect the Rolls, which I intended offering to the partners as part of my reimbursement of the stolen money. Before I left Heathrow I telephoned Tina, my expensive human treat. We shared a bottle of champagne as we travelled, first-class, to Paris. But our party, entertained by her professional expertise and my financial largess, had ended.

I returned to London, easing the elegant Silver Shadow through busy rush-hour streets. Soon, in a few days, it would be Tuesday, time, at last, to clear up the mysterious mess I had created. I should have headed west, for home; instead, I drove across Vauxhall Bridge, towards Hyde Park. I could hardly see where I was going: tears streamed down my cheeks. 'I can't do it,' I remember sobbing to myself, thinking of the forthcoming meeting with my partners. 'I have to. I must,' I moaned.

But I didn't.

I booked into the Royal Garden Hotel and wrote a letter to my aunt, a bitter letter, saying that she was the only person I could write to. Then I set fire to all my personal papers, flushing them down the lavatory. I opened a window and gazed out at the lengthening October shadows spreading across Kensington Gardens. In the beautiful late afternoon, believing that everyone in the world was to blame for my misery except myself, I sat on the edge of my bed and longed for death.

Since my thirtieth birthday I had collected pills. When I complained to my doctor that I could not sleep, I hoarded what he prescribed, treasuring them like illicit, uncut diamonds; when I told him I felt depressed, he prescribed Valium. They went into the collection, too. By that afternoon, I had more than a hundred tablets. I think I swallowed about fifty before my throat went on strike. Then I had a drink, swilling whisky from a bottle which had kept the pills company for weeks. My last memories were of my mother, living less than three miles away.

I woke up in darkness, remembered in my drugged mind that I should have been dead, and shivered. I staggered from the bed, and closed the window, unable to understand why I was alive. By the bedside, I saw most of the undrunk whisky. That's it, I thought, the whisky. I should have drunk more of it. But I remembered its foul taste. Ugh, I can't drink any more of that. I was still shivering. In my fuzzy mind, whisky, death, coldness and heat must have merged into an idea, because I poured the alcohol onto the sheets, lay on top of them, and stretched across to a side table for some matches. I felt comforted by the warmth of fire on my thighs. At last I knew where I was going.

Hell appeared dressed in blue and holding a notebook. I don't know what, if anything, I said to the policeman who sat by my hospital bedside. Maybe he was never there. Later, a neatly-dressed man asked me how I was feeling. 'We've given you another room,' he told me, 'I'm afraid the other one is in a terrible mess.' I went back to sleep. Later still, he returned. 'Is there anyone we can contact for you?' he asked. 'What happened?' I said. 'There was a fire. I told the police that it must have been an accident.' He looked at me thoughtfully, and added, 'I thought it best not to show them the letter.'

I telephoned my aunt, who hurried to the hotel. The solicitous manager reappeared. He told her that someone had noticed smoke coming from my room. The police, fire and ambulance authorities had respectively taken statements, doused the fire and carried me off on a stretcher, not as I had expected, to the local morgue, but to St Stephen's Hospital. Subsequently, I had been returned to the hotel, because, having burned all my personal papers, presumably no one knew what to do with me. He didn't explain to her that I had written a false name and address on the registration card. . . .

I recounted these events to the group in my dullest, most monotonous voice. I felt like a talking textbook. I wanted them to know what had happened, but as each incident emerged I felt bored listening to myself speak. They were hearing about crime, and Rolls Royces, and call-girls, and luxury hotels, and suicide. My narrative was factually accurate, but emotionally barren. I sat rigidly in my chair, staring at the wall opposite, with my legs tightly crossed and my hands digging firmly into my thighs. I remembered the terror I felt during those crazy days: but I didn't tell them about the anguish I suffered when I thought of leaving my family; or the dread of walking into my office, not knowing if my theft had been discovered; or of the days spent sunbathing on the Riviera, trying to hide my tears from Helen and the children; nor did I admit that on several days, when we drove along winding, treacherous mountain roads, I wanted us all to die; and I omitted to mention that the main reason I spent so much time with Tina was because I felt incapable of being alone. But most of all, I spoke in my tedious, disinterested voice, because I knew that, by the time I had finished what I had to say, there was a strong probability that I would burst into tears in front of them all. By accepting me into the group they may be entitled to hear my confessions, but nothing gave them the right to see me cry. . . .

The effects of my overdose had not worn off when Malcolm, and Gary, came to see David and myself on the Tuesday morning. I told David that he had better do the talking. I felt a terrible sadness, sitting at my dining-room table, surrounded by three men who had shared so much with me. I stared defiantly at Malcolm, as if to say, there, now you see me as I really am, what are you going to do about it?

David studied his notes. After explaining about the theft, he went on to set out how much I could repay. The car, of course, and some spare cash, and the proceeds of the house, and the cash from my collection of scientific instruments, and whatever else we had agreed when I visited his office the previous week.

(I sat in the room, wondering how such a catastrophe had occurred. I knew that a moment of change had taken place in April, six months previously, when I lay in bed wanting to speak to Malcolm about a loan, and had then decided that I could not. From a split second in my life, it seemed that I had changed from someone who hated life and wanted to die, but was still capable of existing, to a person who lost all sense of reality. During the months when my theft remained undiscovered, I never once thought of possible punishment. I did not think, 'I shall be dead, so cannot be sent to prison'; it never arose as a realistic possibility. From the morning I set in motion the theft, although I was frightened of it being discovered, the fear did not prevent me from hurtling forward into destructive acts which could only lead to disaster. I thought of people close to me – my wife and partners mainly – as fools, who could not see what was happening. I could not understand why my extraordinary behaviour had gone undetected. Extended periods away from my office, lavish holidays, a Rolls Royce, expensive presents and sexual escapades occupied all those days, and yet apparently I never aroused suspicion in anybody's mind: no one counted the financial cost of what I was doing; no two people who could have pieced together the fantasy I was putting into practice spoke to each other; no client complained that I was not meeting his professional needs; my secretary, who worked closely with me during the day, never suspected that anything was wrong, even when my outflow of work diminished; Helen accepted that I had drawn bonuses, which, had she used a pencil and paper, had to be improbable. In a few short months she was a part recipient in expenditure which amounted to about two years' normal income, and totalled more than £40,000 – in 1974 – and yet she never raised other than casual questions, the answers to which seemed to satisfy her. Clients, whose money I stole, never checked their accounts; partners never queried large cheques passing through the firm's bank accounts. The longer my deceptions passed unnoticed, the more it astonished me that no one was astute enough to know what was going on. I despised them all for their stupidity, and hated them for letting me get away with it.)

I heard the voices of David and my ex-partners droning on.

Documents had to be prepared, time tables agreed. When would the house go on the market? How much was it worth? Not to go into the office. Must keep everything quiet. No publicity. Keep in touch. They didn't speak to me: I didn't speak to them. David walked Malcolm and Gary to the front door, but as far as I was concerned they'd never arrived.

For three months I panicked. So many things happened between November and January, that I cannot place them in any chronological order. I disappeared one night, and my aunt came to collect me from Bournemouth; my father came to stay with us for a fortnight; Helen collapsed and went to hospital; my secretary kept telephoning; at 2 o'clock one Sunday morning I telephoned Malcolm, telling him that someone had telephoned me, threatening to report me to the police, and then wondered if it had been a nightmare; clients contacted me, asking me to join the boards of their companies; the building society wanted to 'draw to your attention' that my payments were in arrear; prospective purchasers wandered inquisitively round the house; I had a car accident; all my pension and insurance policies were cancelled; Ben left his private school; I registered a consultancy business and started working; my solicitor told me that I could go to prison for anything from three to seven years; Helen decided that she had to protect the children, and refused to agree to her half-interest in the house being used to repay my debt; my ex-partners decided to sue the bank for accepting cheques signed by me and in my favour. Finally, the day before my thirty-third birthday, I thought that some normality could return to my life.

In January, I had confided in a friend and client. He wanted to help. A meeting was arranged between us and my ex-partners. Of the £40,000 stolen, £10,000 had been repaid. The rest would be provided by my friend, for whom I would work as financial consultant. In three years or so my debt to him would be repaid, partly from my proceeds of the house sale. I tried to be enthusiastic about my new, and highly-paid job. My biggest relief was that I expected to retain my professional qualification.

And then, two days after everything had been finalized, Jim — the bank manager who was unwillingly involved in my financial manipulations, a possible claim for negligence, and, ironically, was also my friend's bank manager — telephoned, asking to see me, urgently. Like my solicitor and ex-partners, old, friendly relationships had ceased. He asked me to sit down, and called in his assistant manager, to take notes. 'I've heard that Bernie Robbins intends lending you a large sum of money, and that he's offered you a position with his company. If he does either of those things, this bank will immediately call in his borrowing facilities, and, in the circumstances, he may find it difficult to change to another bank. If I were you,' he concluded, 'I'd move away from this area, and change my name.'

I left his office with only one thought in my mind: how can I tell Helen this latest horrific news? For three months we had both lived in fear of a police car entering our front drive; we had been unable to talk rationally to each other, except when relatives or friends acted as arbitrators; our home, social life and finances were crumbling away; we had both been ill. With Bernie Robbin's support, hope had arrived. Now, hope had vanished. I had to tell her that the job, and the loan, did not exist. Until I had my meeting with the bank manager, I believed that I could rebuild my life. His final words, '. . . move away from this area, and change my name,' brought home to me the futility of what I was hoping to achieve.

The kitchen was steamy when I walked into the house. The children were eating supper. Helen looked pale. At 6.30, after Vanessa had gone to bed, Helen, holding a bottle of tranquillizers, said: 'I'm going to bed. I wish I could go to sleep, and never wake up.' And that, I thought, as she left the room, is before she's heard my ruinous news.

Ben, then seven years old, kept me company until he was too tired to stay awake. By 11 o'clock I was alone, sitting in my study. I probably sat there for an hour or so, listening to the voices screaming inside my head. There's nothing more I can do! I can't go on! I've had enough! She's had enough! She wants to be dead! So do I!

SNAP! CLICK! 'I wish I could go to sleep, and never wake up.'

I knew what to do. It's what she wants. It's what we both want. My thoughts seemed to echo inside me, as if I was in a great, empty chamber. Each word kept repeating itself like a slow, repetitive drum-roll. Each thought seemed to be suspended in a great space. I felt that I was floating above myself, listening carefully to what I heard below me. I knew what I was doing, but my actions seemed to be those of a stranger. When I got up from my chair my movements seemed mechanical and precise.

I unlocked the back door, and walked into the garden, across the wet grass, to our summer house. My voice was ahead of me, pulling me along. I remember my movements so clearly now, over a decade later, that I find it difficult to understand why I could not then stop myself. I rummaged in the darkness until I found what I wanted: a large hammer, the sort used for banging fence stakes into the ground. Slowly, as though I was reliving a past experience in an unreal dream, I returned to the house, and trudged up the stairs, towards our bedroom. I knew what had to be done. It's what she wants, I kept thinking. I'm doing this for her sake; afterwards, it will be my turn.

I hit her several times with the hammer, until she woke, screaming. Then, silence. The room was dark, illuminated only by a few unclear shadows from the porch-light outside the house. I could see nothing. In the terrible silence I felt the wooden hammer handle, still gripped tightly in my hand. I think I screamed, and vaguely remember a sudden light. I've killed her, I thought. How could I do that! Not once, in the fifteen years I had known her, had I physically hurt her.

My slow, precise feelings and movements vanished. I grabbed the bedside telephone, and hysterically dialled 999. I asked for the Police. 'I've killed my wife,' I yelled at them. They tried to calm me, and made me repeat my name and address. I dashed from the room, to the front of our driveway, waiting for the police to arrive. I remember lying on the road, screaming, 'Help me! Help me!' Lights went on in the nearest house, several hundred feet away. Then, silhouetted in our porch, I saw Ben, standing by the front door, dressed in his pyjamas. 'Daddy, why did you do it?' he called. Moments later I heard cars approaching. 'Where is she?' someone asked. I pointed to the unlit, upstairs room. An ambulance arrived. I was shaking. I wanted Ben, but before I had time to ask about him, they were driving me away, a driver, and two policemen sitting on either side of me in the back seat. I remember thinking how strange it was that I was still wearing my suit, because always, when I returned home, I changed into slacks and a casual sweater. . . .

Barbara sat next to me in the pub. Pretty, cock-teasing Barbara. She had heard my confessions to the group earlier in the day, but I knew that what I had said then must have sounded very different to what I said as we sat sipping our lagers. I wondered if she was frightened to be alone with me.

Vicious circles

A is for Abu Dhabi, adultery, alcoholic poisoning, Amman, Amsterdam, anger, Antwerp, arab sheikhs, Atlanta and attempted murder; B is for bankruptcy, barrister, Beirut, blood transfusions, Bonn and burglers; C is for a Cadillac, call-girls, California, cells, the Channel Islands, Cologne, Corfu, Concorde, consultancy work and Cyprus; D is for death and drug dealers; E is for *Evita*, employees, escapes, expensive meals and excitement; F is for fear, the French Riviera and a four-year prison sentence; G is for Geneva and guilt; H is for handcuffs, hatred, headaches, high walls and barbed wire, hospitals and Houston; I is for insomnia and IRA terrorists; J is for Jordan and a judge; K is for Kuwait; L is for Leonard Cohen, Luxembourg and loss of professional qualification; M is for magistrates, mail bags, mental deficients, Mexico, millionaires and murderers; N is for new houses, New Orleans, New York and Nice; O is for Oklahoma, the Open University and overworking; P is for Palestinian refugees, Paris, parole, police investigations, prison, private detectives, private schools, psychiatrists and the punishment block; Q is for quiet times; R is for responsibility; S is for San Diego, San Francisco, Saudi Arabia, sex offenders, social security, social workers, solicitors and suicide; T is for tears, Texas, trial and triggers; U is for unemployment; V is for violence; W is for warders; X is for the vote convicts lose; Y is for yoga; and Z is for Zurich.

If the above paragraph reads like an index, which the printers of this book have mistakenly included in the wrong place, let me quickly absolve them from professional incompetence. In a way, though, it is an index; it summarizes some of the people I met, places I visited, and experiences I lived through, during the five years between the day I attacked my wife and the day I joined the unit at Shipley Grange.

To write about everything which happened to me during that half-decade would not only be repetitious; it would require a book several times longer than this one, several chapters of which would be unpublishable. In most ways, I behaved and felt as I always had, and continued to act out one role, while desperately trying to live with the *me* I secreted away.

But some of my experiences during this period were so devastating, or, occasionally, rewarding, that they greatly influenced, and continue to influence, my life. One of the worst was having to live with myself after I telephoned the police and screamed that I had killed my wife. I didn't kill her − she suffered a hairline skull fracture, and, after a week in hospital, was fit enough to return home − but my guilt and shame became a walking nightmare. It did not matter that when we first met after she left hospital, by which time I was in prison, she held me in her arms and said that it was not my fault, that she understood; nor could anyone, including members of my family and friends who visited me, ease my terror. For more than five years, long after I left prison, whenever the memory ravaged my mind, I heard myself shout 'No!' Ten years passed before I understood, and accepted, why I had tried to commit murder. But in the immediate aftermath, while I pleaded with the police to tell me if Helen was dead or alive, I felt that never, never, should I be permitted to live with normal people.

When I was initially questioned, I wanted to say nothing, to insist that before I said anything, I had the protection of my solicitor; but within minutes I felt disgusted with myself. What right had I to seek protection? I quickly admitted my crime, and, unsolicited, told the police about my thefts the previous year. One of them wrote down my verbal statement. Two or three hours later they asked me if I was prepared to sign it. I read the pages, aware that some of what was written down was not what I had said, but I did not care. I signed. (When I re-read the statement, before my trial, I noted that the 'verbals' were not factually inaccurate; but words had been quoted which I would not have used – even when hysterical. One offensive sentence which I was supposed to have said was: 'I never done nothing like this before.')

At 4 a.m. they told me that Helen's condition was not critical. Then they locked me in a cell. Half an hour later I was taken into a cold, poorly-lit room, and charged with attempted murder. At 9 o'clock my aunt arrived, followed shortly afterwards by Douglas, my doctor. At last, after hours of frantic worry, I received the first detailed reports about Helen and the children. At 9.30 a solicitor, the brother of one of my clients, came to see me. At 10 o'clock, at a special court hearing – it was Saturday morning – I was remanded in custody until the following Tuesday. Four hours later, handcuffed to two other prisoners in a police van, I was taken to Oxford prison. During the journey, one of the policemen turned to me: 'Don't blame you for belting her,' he said affably, 'they all need that now and then, but why try to kill her, a bloke like you?'

As soon as I had passed through reception formalities, I entered the prison hospital. Two weeks later, calmer, but terrified of what lay beyond the safe doors of the quiet, clean and spacious hospital, I was moved to the remand wing, third landing, cell eighty-six. Inside were two other men, three beds (one single, two bunks), one chair and a small table, as well as our basic prison issues. We each had a bleach-stained plastic chamber pot, sheets, two blankets, one pillow-case, a plastic mug, a toothbrush, a razor without blade and a wooden shaving brush. To reach my bed, the upper bunk, the other inmates had to sit on theirs. Once I had climbed up, apart from a narrow aisle leading to the locked door, there was no spare space.

After my trial, three months later, I attended fortnightly meetings with the prison psychiatrist, an elderly, friendly man, who told me that there was not much he could do for me while I was in prison. 'But I'll arrange that you see me anyway, gives you a chance to get away from the others.'

When I explained that I did not understand why I had stolen the money, when I could so easily have sorted out what were not particularly large debts, or, worse, why I had attacked my wife, he pressed his wrinkled fingers together: 'Possessions,' he said, 'a house, or a cherished poem, won't work. Meaningfulness is what you need.' He told me that, although a Christian, he was a believer in Buddhism. 'Try breathing through your nose ten times when you can, and think only of what you're doing. Listen to the sound, feel the shape of your nostrils change. Try that. Took me years.'

Another afternoon, he told me a story about several land girls, working on a farm in Sussex during the Second World War. They were all nice girls, he explained, from good families, trying to do their bit. Their fathers and brothers, of course, were overseas, possibly wounded, or dead. One afternoon a German pilot parachuted from his aeroplane. 'They ran over to him, those nice girls, and pitchforked the man to death. Too much pressure.' He had treated some of them for psychological difficulties. 'Most of them understood what they'd done, and eventually got over it; but one didn't. She never recovered. How's the breathing going?'

We met seven or eight times before I left Oxford. I wasn't too sorry when the meetings ended. Seeing a psychiatrist was no easier in prison than anywhere else. It was bad for your reputation. Meanwhile, my guilt felt worse; my initial outrageous shock of disbelief changed to unrelenting horror.

My first letter from prison was to Helen's parents. 'Tell her that we must get divorced,' I wrote. One of the first things which Helen said to me when we met was that all she wanted was to have me back home. My guilt wouldn't diminish, but I had other confused feelings and thoughts. I didn't want to go home. I didn't want to be in prison, either, most of the time, but sometimes, to my surprise. . . .

I felt peaceful, more peaceful than I could ever remember feeling, as if a calming hand was comforting me. Uncertainties, about going to prison, losing my qualification, being made bankrupt, were all ended. I knew what would happen. The silent hospital, where I was locked in a private and comfortable room, was lonely; but once my first drug doses wore off I could read, write letters or just rest — except when recurrent, silent memories screamed 'No! Not me!' each time I thought of my attempted murder. Even in a 'three-up' cell, which, with a little generosity to the right 'con', could be reduced to a 'double', I sometimes experienced peaceful feelings.

I was sentenced to four years' imprisonment. After ten months at Oxford, I spent several weeks at Bristol, and was finally transferred to Winchester. As I wrote earlier, nothing was very different to much of my previous life. I still had to live with people. And there were several advantages: I lost three stone in weight, and felt fitter than I ever had; I attended yoga classes, and began to have some perception of what relaxation might be; during the last half of my 'time' I had a trustee job and a single cell, left unlocked from 7 in the morning until 9 at night; I read 182 books — I still have the list — as well as the complete works of Shakespeare and a sizeable chunk of the Bible; I started a course for an Open University degree; I listened to every promenade concert in 1976, and most overs of the England and Australia test matches; and I began writing. Despite the restrictive regime, I could, for once in my life, do what I wanted, not what I thought I had to do. Being locked away from the world left me unexpectedly free — sometimes.

On the other hand, there were more disadvantages than

benefits: I had to contend with violence, not necessarily towards me, but arbitrary cruelty and viciousness from both 'screws' and 'cons', often directed at those least able to protect themselves; I had to learn, painfully, to live with groups of men for whom prison was an acceptable risk; I experienced previously unknown squalor and filth; when I was not thinking of leaving them, I craved for my family; and loneliness, emotional, intellectual and physical, brought with it a different sense of isolation — I couldn't physically escape from the grim walls which hemmed me in.

I vacillated wildly between wanting to go home and return to accountancy work, and fantasizing that I would keep my release date a secret and vanish. My bank manager's suggestion that I should move away and change my name was often on my mind. During my most tranquil hours I knew what I wanted, and it wasn't to return to my family, or to accountancy.

Twenty-one months after I was taken into custody my parole was approved. Helen met me at the gate and drove me to the small, attractive home she had purchased, far away from where we used to live. The following week I managed to get a job — in an accountant's office. I enjoyed being free to walk and talk and able to plan for the future, but I felt submerged in guilt, shame and fury.

I had spent twenty-one months incarcerated inside high walls, surmounted by barbed wire, determined to create a new life; but within weeks of my release, I knew that I was spinning in a series of old, familiar circles.

My mother's release arrived three months after I returned home, when she committed suicide; her slender, green barbiturates left her dead, decomposing and undiscovered, for two weeks. When I entered her flat, after her body had been removed, I almost fainted as I breathed in a ghastly, sick, sweet smell. On the carpet by her bed I noticed small, curled bits of brown paper. I ran from the flat when I realized that the shreds on the floor were, in fact, remnants of her dead skin.

I had last seen her in John Lewis, in Oxford Street, where

she was busy buying some material and did not see me. I walked away. I tried to remember how long ago that had been. Five, perhaps six, years before her death. She had written to me once in prison, and now I cannot recall whether I replied. From the day of my wedding, thirteen years before she died, she had visited my home only once; she had seen my son twice, and never met my daughter. Two years before she died she remarried, but her husband — a step-father I never met — died within a few months, unable to cope with her, some people said.

For a day or two I could think only of practical matters: the funeral, disinfecting her flat, contacting furniture removers, sorting through her papers. On the third night, tears, great streams of them, poured from me. 'Why did she have to die like that?' I moaned, and, 'Why can't I think of good memories?'

I hoped that, after her death, my memories of her might fade, but they never have; if anything, they seem more powerful today, a decade later, than they were while she lived. And yet, with her death, came some unexpected relief. She inherited money from her second husband; my half was sufficient to enable me to settle old debts, and so obtain my bankruptcy discharge.

Three years later, her sister, my aunt, who started life as my grandmother's 'beautiful baby', shrivelled into a frightful, sad, emaciated bundle, and died from cancer of the stomach. She, too, had remarried shortly before her death.

While I was in prison on remand — when daily visits are permitted — she visited me almost every day, bringing changes of clothing, fresh food, half bottles of wine, cigarettes for trading — anything, in fact, she could think of. The week I was released, when I had practically no money, she gave me £100, saying, 'It's Christmas soon, you'll need it.' She came to my wedding, visited all my homes regularly, loved my children, and for many years lived less than fifteen minutes from my home. I saw her every day during her last three painful and despairing months. After she died I felt guilty, because I never shed a tear.

Another regular visitor before and during my prison sentence was my father. We saw each other, not often, but regularly, from the time my son was born. During the difficult weeks after I admitted my theft to my partners, he offered whatever help he could, and, at one period, had he not come to live with me I would not have known how to exist. While I was in prison he came to see me as often as distance, time and visit entitlements permitted. 'I know you,' he said, 'you'll soon be back where you were.' Unfortunately, he was right.

Within a few months of regaining freedom I had established a thriving financial consultancy business. My lost qualification, while a permanent professional scar, proved not to be the restraint I had expected. My income was less than it had once been, but I had at last come to terms with material recklessness; gone were credit cards, overdrafts and excessively high mortgages. 'Think cash, not credit' became my financial motto, one which has proved a lasting password to financial self-discipline. I did not know it then, but other times of financial hardship were not far away; when they arrived I was not burdened with unwanted debt. But my emotional balance was more overdrawn than it had ever been, because I had accumulated costly bad memories, all centred on the events which led to my prison sentence.

I actively sought work which would enable me to travel. For a few years I travelled more, and for increasingly longer periods, than I had previously. In 1980, for example, I visited, either with the family on holiday or, more often, on my own on business, most countries in Western Europe, several in the Middle East, and the USA twice. My business trips, which, before prison, were seldom for longer than three days, now often stretched to two or three weeks. If I did not have a forthcoming escape I felt trapped and anxious: I had to get away. My working hours, when I was in England, were long and tiring; for most of 1980 I went to my office seven days a week, even if only for a few hours at the weekends.

By the middle of that year, four years after I left prison, Helen seemed to have recovered from the shock of my theft.

Our standard of living was high, our commitments low. We had moved — our sixth home in fifteen years of marriage. She wanted me to be proud of my recent achievements; but I wasn't. I struggled to keep my feelings masked. I knew that she had suffered, and blamed myself. I wanted to make up for my chaotic past. I dabbed, rubbed, swathed and immersed myself in guilt. And quite right, too, after what you've done, I admonished myself. To reduce some of my moral debt, I urged Helen to have our new, and substantially paid-for, home, and our joint savings, in her sole name. It seemed the least I could do, knowing how much she had suffered from our financial chaos.

Why, I asked myself — having paid for my crimes with a prison sentence, lost qualification and bankruptcy; and then paid large sums to creditors, re-established a business career, and learned to control my personal finances — why do I feel as bad as I used to? Surely I'm entitled to some peace? I still felt a gigantic fraud, leading a life full of confusions which seemed to go round in circles which grew smaller and smaller. I could see what was at the centre; I saw it coming in the summer of 1980.

For almost twelve months before then, while remaining self-employed, most of my consultancy work was for one group of companies, owned by a wealthy Palestinian who lived in Kuwait, or Rome, or Palm Springs, or London. His main trading activity was importing luxury goods to the Middle East, particularly furniture and electrical and electronic products. His assets. which amounted to many millions, were invested substantially in properties in Europe and the USA. He wanted an advisor, someone who could organize his rapidly expanding empire, and who could represent him at meetings where it was useful to have a non-Arab present. He reeled out his financial bait, offered me many benefits, and I, gasping to re-establish the professional security I had thought impossible to achieve during my worrying days in prison, was hooked.

As far as he was concerned, he had bought me. Had I been female I'd probably have ended up in a distant harem. He, his various senior employees, and myself, were travelling in different directions – geographically, I thought – most days of most weeks. Our business heart throbbed from his London office, where five telex arteries, one for each main commercial activity, pumped a constant supply of corpuscular energy on to my desk. As his sole British advisor, he expected me – and I accepted the responsibility – to control the financial temperature.

Jamyl and I became friends: we visited each other's family, and spent hours discussing how to organize not only the business, but the world. I didn't care if he telephoned me at 10 o'clock in the evening, and asked (told!) me to hop on a 'plane to Amsterdam the next morning; or if he flew into London on a Sunday afternoon and had to see me urgently. As far as I was concerned, I was doing an important, challenging and exciting job. When I watched the digital counter rise to mach 2 inside the cabin of Concorde, I felt that I was soaring higher than I had ever soared – which, at 52,000 feet, I was, in the literal sense.

But neither he, nor most of my business contacts and new friends, knew about my past. I carried it with me every day, like contraband through GREEN, waiting for my fraud to be uncovered by an alert customs official.

I willingly worked with Jamyl for more than a year, during which time he was seldom in England for more than two or three days a month. I felt like a free agent. Then he decided to live, more or less permanently, in London. Suddenly my feelings towards him changed. To be at his beck and call, via telex messages or telephone calls, was one thing: to have him sitting on my lap was quite another.

One Saturday afternoon in June I sat in his office discussing a contract with him and a friend of his from Saudi Arabia. At about 5 o'clock I explained that I had to leave soon, as I had an evening engagement. 'We've finished anyway,' Jamyl said, 'you go and spend time with your lovely family.' Then he turned to his friend and smiled. 'You see, Mahmoud, these English, they don't work the way we do.'

I was furious, and fumed for the rest of the day. The following morning, while we untangled the lengthy rolls of overnight telexes, I told him how angry I was. He denied that he had criticized me. But it was too late: my feelings were in turmoil. I felt angry, hurt and abused. I've had enough, I thought, I can't go on.

It wasn't just Jamyl's words which sent me plummeting downwards. I had not known how to live with myself as a child; at school and at the Circus Club I felt isolated; working with my ex-partners had been acceptable, provided that I did what I wanted; marriage, one of my earliest desires, had proved difficult, partly because, in a sense, I had never really married – I had divorced my parents; being a parent created more problems – my son was in his teens, and I did not realize that I wanted to control him, but he was determined not to be controlled; and my new business life, blighted by my shameful prison sentence and bankruptcy, merely worsened my feelings of inadequacy and self-dislike.

I needed to, I had to, escape. And escape, which began as a need to leave Jamyl, and then to leave my family, finally appeared in its familiar guise – death. SNAP. CLICK.

I recognized the clear-headedness, and the same destructive feelings which had descended five years earlier. I knew that I should tell someone what was happening. Helen seemed happy, and I didn't want to upset her; Douglas, my previous doctor, lived far away, and I had never met our new local GP; my mother was dead, and anyway, I knew that I would not have confided in her; my aunt was dying from cancer. I persuaded myself that there was nobody to talk to, and was pleased, because, actually, I didn't truly want to talk to anyone. Death, as usual, had its gloomy side, but it offered some personal pleasure as well. 'That'll show them.'

One morning I vanished.

For eight weeks I travelled across the United States. In New York I bought a Cadillac; from there, I drove south, to Washington, Atlanta, and New Orleans, where I arrived a few days before *mardi gras*. After that, I moved on to Texas, and spent several days close to the Mexican border, by the Rio Grande. Eventually, after a month's driving and stop-overs, I reached California.

Often, as I headed west, towards the Pacific, I thought of my aunt, who had died several months before I vanished. She had spent two years in California, when I was a young boy. If she is anywhere, I thought, that's where she'll be. It seemed a good place to die.

The journey across the States was a strange mixture of excitement and despondency. One moment I felt elated – so this is Bourbon Street! – the next I felt ashamed that, yet again, I had deserted my family and career. When I strolled round the Alamo, in San Antonio, my eyes watered. Helen and I had seen the film before we were married. I couldn't eat in public places; they were full of mums and dads and sons and daughters, so I added several dozen McDonald's to the thirty-three billion the advertisements proclaimed had already been disposed of. I became addicted to late-night TV, because, unable to sleep, it kept me company. Several times I lifted the telephone receiver, wanting to ring England. Should I? Shouldn't I? Yes. No. No, they were better off without me. There was no aunt to write a letter to. Onward to California, excited and depressed.

During my second day in San Diego I went for a walk along the shoreline at La Jolla. I was thinking of hiring a boat and drifting into the ocean. I even enquired about hire charges. But then I entered a tea bar and met an English woman. For the next month death seemed as stupid an idea as I had ever had.

Eight weeks after I left home I decided to remain in the States – someone had offered me a job, and assured me that they could arrange a valid work visa – but, first, I had to return to England, to sort out my affairs, and bid my farewells to my family. Everything seemed right.

To my surprise, I did return to England. Jamyl and Helen had tried to find me; they had employed a private detective, who must have had a full, but frustratingly incomplete, file. I was needed, everyone said.

But it was too much: all that goodwill and forgiveness

from the family; rather too much badwill from Jamyl, and the consequent loss of my consultancy work; the imperative from them all to 'settle down'. One night I drained almost a litre of whisky into my stomach, and the local hospital drained it out. A few weeks later I vanished again, back to California.

At Los Angeles airport I dithered. Should I go north, to San Francisco, or south to San Diego, where I could meet up with my woman friend? I went north.

As usual, I mixed misery and marvel. I traipsed round beautiful 'Frisco for a day or two, wondering what it would be like to die of starvation in the middle of the Pacific Ocean. On a Saturday afternoon, I stuffed a few dollars in my pocket, and mailed the rest of my money to Helen, in England. On Main Street I bought a hamburger and Coke, a small reel of Sellotape and pack of green plastic trash bags. In my hotel room I already had a knife and a few sleeping pills. This time, I decided, there will be no mistakes. Death by pills and booze had not worked seven years earlier. Now I'll be more certain.

When I had eaten my last supper, I took two pills, merely to make me drowsy. A green bag went over my head, and I fumbled with the Sellotape to make sure that no air could get in through the twisted plastic around my neck.

It did not work. I awoke to find the plastic bag still on my head, but a gaping hole where it should have been Sellotaped. I remembered my knife, a vicious, six-inch affair, and cut as deeply into each wrist as my fear of pain would allow. Blood, more than I had ever seen, spurted from my arms. Within seconds the upper parts of my body were wet, sticky, and frightfully red. Spots and splashes had dripped on to the bedclothes. When, shocked by what was happening, I held my painful arms in front of me, streams of blood trickled down my legs and over my feet. My last act that day, one which I had not planned, and which I later bitterly regretted, was to grab the telephone, push a button, and shout, 'Help me!'

A fortnight or so later I met the man in England who asked me: 'Are you angry?'

6 *Emotional equations*

Introduction

I joined Shipley Grange believing that it was my last chance; either I would discover *me*, or I was doomed for ever. I expected sympathy for my suffering and a set of answers to guide me through the rest of my life. I wanted to know why everything I thought I had achieved had ended in disaster. Before I went there I established my own rules. It will be like an advanced study course, I decided, with lessons to learn and remember. If I had the determination and discipline to work for my professional qualification – five gruelling years – then six months should be a doddle. They'll tell me what to do, and I'll do it. If they don't . . . well, I shall have tried. I expected to learn how to overcome depression; to eradicate childhood memories which kept interfering with my life; why I had stolen money; how not to feel bad about my prison sentence and the attempted murder of my wife, and how to be a good husband and father. Helen did not want me to go there, which meant that I had to work especially hard. I expected to succeed within the month I had scheduled for the challenge; if that was not long enough then I was prepared to stay the six months I had agreed to. From the débris of unending catastrophes, all that remained intact was my family. For their sake, I tried to believe, I must concentrate and succeed. For their sake, I must atone for my crimes and get rid of my guilt. Then in one or, at worst, six months I could start again – or kill myself.

But it was not for their sake, and I knew it. I did not care how difficult it was for my wife and children to cope with my absence. I had nothing from them which made me feel good, or even less bad. I rearranged the lie I used to tell my wife when she accused me of loving my business more than her. 'I'm doing it for your sake,' I had told her many times, knowing that it was not true. Now, my lies were more desperate. 'I'm doing this for us. If I don't try this,' I told her before I joined the unit, 'I'll never forgive myself.' What I wanted to say was, 'If you do anything to stop me, I'll never forgive *you*.'

I started the journey into myself full of hope. I hoped that determination and hard work would lead to peace and happiness. I hoped that the group would give me answers which, if correctly noted in my diary, would mean that I need never repeat past mistakes. I hoped that I would stop wishing that I was dead. Within days I knew that one month would not be long enough. There was more to learn than I had expected. And, when I thought that I had progressed in one direction, an unexpected encounter with the group sent me in confusion somewhere else. I kept losing my way.

It was hard and painful, entering this new world; and exciting. Sometimes the excitement compensated for the pain, except when the pain returned, because of another attack from the group. When that happened I forgot the excitement, and converted the pain into failure. Each unexpected attack felt worse than the previous one. In my early weeks I could not accept that the attacks were not always attacks aimed specifically at me; sometimes, they were other residents' defences; sometimes they were neither attacks nor defences, but attempts to help me.

There was so much to learn, I constantly reminded myself. So many bad feelings. So many bad memories. So much peculiar behaviour. Where do feelings start, and memories end? Why do I do what I do? Daily, and nightly, contact with the group involved continuous confrontations. Usually, behaviour and feelings seemed unrelated – until we discussed them. And memories. Memories which I thought I had forgotten. I tried keeping my memories and feelings hidden in the early weeks, and my behaviour became the part of me I tried to understand first. I did such strange things, and wanted to know why. Why would I want to be nice to someone because I was angry with them, for example? Because I was frightened to face anger, they told me. But I was not angry, I insisted. I liked the people I was nice to. Didn't I? When I was angry I shouted, and slammed doors. How could I be nice to someone if I really wanted to hurt them?

Feelings which I wanted to fit into neat, orderly compartments would not go where I expected them to. 'Why don't you express your anger?' Stuart asked. So I did. I told them when I felt angry, sometimes, and, because I had done what I had been told to do, I expected to feel better. But I didn't. And I began to understand something I had never realized: feelings did not come one at a time. They had a nasty habit of tossing about in all directions at once, like a juggler throwing balls into the air. However, unlike a professional juggler, I was an emotional amateur, and I kept losing control. I had trouble deciding what I was handling. Were they balls, or cylinders; were they good balls and bad cylinders, or bad balls and good cylinders; and why wouldn't they go where I threw them? And why, when I wanted them to go in one direction, did other members of the group ruin my performance by throwing theirs in the air?

I behaved with the group exactly as I had always behaved. I tried to be all-knowing and all-powerful. I tried to take command of them and myself, as I had in my teens at the youth club, or in my business partnership, or in prison. They accused me of always wanting to be right, not considering their feelings, expecting too much from them. Those were the times when memories came flooding back. Hadn't Helen said similar things, and my partners? Hadn't my mother told me in my teens that I was arrogant? I had ignored them, but I could not ignore the group. They were my last hope, and I had to remain acceptable. So I listened more carefully, and, resenting each personal admission that they were right, I tried to change my behaviour. I tried; but I seldom succeeded.

When I realized that it was not easy to change, I became discouraged. I was failing . . . and time was rushing by.

Struggling to understand why I expected so much from myself and everybody else, I learned about expectations. I wanted to make up for what I had lost, for the miserable years of my childhood and the stresses of living with parents who never did what I wanted. All those terrible memories. Why did I have such foul parents? It was unfair. Until Shipley Grange, I had not accepted how foul they were. I heard myself shouting that I hated them.

When I learned that hate was destructive, I tried to forgive them. My mother was dead, yet I yearned for an opportunity to be with her again, to put right all the wrongs. I wanted to forgive her for ruining my life. I wanted to forgive my father for not showing any interest in me. Thank God he was alive. I could make up for all those lost years. After I wrote to him, explaining some, not much, about what I was learning, I felt that I had made some progress. Yes, that's what I must do, I told myself, forgive them. Then I'll feel better. For a few weeks, I thought that I had resolved a great problem. I thought that I had forgiven them. But I hadn't, and when I realized that I did not know how to forgive them, I hated them more. If it were not for them, I moaned, I would not be here, in a mental institution. When Stuart asked me if I was going to hate them for the rest of my life, I hated him. Didn't he understand! Who else could I blame?

Memories brought me back to the present. I began to understand that what I was doing in the group was the same as what I had always done − screamed for attention. I want you to give me something. Now. Do exactly as I say − or else! Then my memories threw me backwards. Wasn't that what my mother used to say to me? And how many times had I yelled silently at my father, 'Why don't you *do* something?' I could not separate the past from the present. Yesterday was today, and I hated yesterday. In group meetings I often heard myself speak, but my mind was not listening. It was far away. Memories. Wasn't that how I'd always felt, as though there were two of me? But I knew that I had met my stranger, my secret enemy, so how could there still be two of me?

'You won't trust your feelings,' they told me. 'But I don't know what I'm feeling,' I replied helplessly. 'How are you feeling now?' 'Angry,' I replied. 'Why?' 'I'm remembering my childhood.' 'Is that where you want to be?' 'Not likely.' 'Then why do you stay there?' 'Oh, for Christ's sake, leave me alone.' 'Is that what your mother used to say to you?' 'Yes.' And I felt angrier than ever. How could I ever forgive them, any of them, parents or the group or . . . no, that could not be possible. Not her. I needed her, and she needed me. She kept telling me how much she needed me, every night on the telephone she cried, she needed me so much. (One weekend, after I had been at Shipley Grange for about two months, Helen fainted. She was ill, she said. I'd have to leave the group, and come home, where I belonged. I told her that she reminded me of my mother.)

I verbally expressed more hatred at the unit than I had during the previous forty years, and the more I expressed it, the worse I felt. I began to understand that my behaviour and memories and feelings were in a hopeless embrace. I wanted to separate them, so that I could get back to my studies, and work out how to control each small act, forget all the bad memories, and feel better. Often, after a private, comforting hug with my diary, I did feel better, and said so in the group, to prove that I could do what the other residents could not. That'll show them! But, just when I thought I had resolved a problem, someone would do or say something which infuriated me, and I could not remember what I was supposed to do or feel.

I felt that I was suffering as I had never suffered before. The journey backwards into my past had lasted several months. During the week at the unit, and each weekend at home, I tried to believe that it was worthwhile; that out of the terrible memories I had relived, would appear hope for the future. Staff at the unit kept telling me that I was angry; as I listened, and attempted to understand what they meant, I began to agree with them. Yes, I was angry; but why would nobody understand how sad I felt? It all seemed so terribly unfair.

They wanted me to admit that I was angry. I had admitted it, hadn't I? Why wouldn't they admit that what was really upsetting me was that I felt so sad?

The other residents told me that they suffered more than me. To prove it, they came to me with their problems, as if I had all the answers. They thanked me, and said how amazing it was that I understood them so well, and how amazing it was that I could explain things which they had never understood, and how amazing it was that whenever there was trouble, particularly at night when we were on our own, I was always there to comfort them. I exhausted myself comforting them. Stuart said I did it to forget about myself. 'You don't do it for them,' he said, 'you do it for yourself.' And my hatred increased. I had never done it for me, I told myself. Looking after my sister, to protect her from my mother; helping my employees, when they had a personal problem, and I should have been earning fees; chasing round southern England to find a home for my grandfather when my aunt refused to let him live with her: how could any of that have been for myself? On top of everything else, I fumed in a tearful rage, now I am being accused of not caring about other people.

'You'll do anything to get attention,' they said to me. 'You need it so much, you don't care how you get it, so long as you get it.' Memories, more memories. Hadn't I said that to my son, when his form teacher accused him of disrupting the class, and I had to go to see her? 'Of course, you'd rather have approval *and* attention, that's why you work so hard to be liked.' More memories. Working until 3 o'clock in the morning to meet an urgent deadline for a client. 'I like your sort,' he'd said flatteringly. 'If there were more of us about, this country wouldn't be in the state it's in.'

I listened to what I heard about myself in the group, wrote in my diary, and felt better. I discovered that I could understand much more about what the others were doing, and told them so. Once Stuart said, 'You've the most difficult problem in this group.' I was horrified to hear that, but excited. It felt good to know that I had a bigger problem than anyone else; and bad, because I did not know what he meant. Another day he said, 'You don't trust anybody in the group. You don't trust yourself, so how can you trust us?' Memories. The day I told my mother that I had stolen a pound, and she told my father, after promising not to, and he tied me to a bed and beat me. I cried, not because he was beating me, but because *she* had told him. How could I trust her after that? It was hard not crying in group meetings, when memories flooded into my mind, but I managed not to, except once. Only once in six months, when most residents did it most weeks. 'I'm not stopping until you stop crying,' he'd said to me as I lay on the bed. Why did she tell him! She promised not to.

'Why don't you stop talking, and feel?' they said to me during a meeting. Didn't they know that if I did that I'd probably burst into tears in front of them. How could I do that! Instead of making me feel worse, why wouldn't they give me the answers? Then I could leave them, privately read my notes each week, and feel better. It would be like going to church on Sundays.

Weekday advance

The summer of 1981, when I started at Shipley Grange, was hot. Clear, bright days of unending sunshine, and warm nights with cloudless skies, made me want to believe that my future, too, could be bright and clear. I spent much of my free time during the day lying on my back in the sun, sucking in long, slow breaths of country air, gazing upwards at the thousands of leaves on the horse-chestnut tree which dominated the garden, like an old, protective guardian. In the evenings I usually set aside more private time, sometimes walking a few yards to a delapidated wooden gate, where I leaned on its rickety posts and tried to find comfort in the twinkling stars. I needed those quiet hours to recover from the harsh realities being exposed inside the house, where, day and night, I felt threatened and defenceless. My time with the group felt as confined as the agonizing days in prison, five years earlier. There were no black, iron bars, or high, barbed-wire walls, to keep me away from society, only my desperate need to learn how to rejoin a frightening world. Away from the group, neither sun nor stars helped. I felt as alone as I had when travelling across America earlier that year.

Pressures of living with a group, any group, had always disturbed me; but I had to experience shock and attack before I realized even that simple truth. Now, the pressures were different, because whatever pretences had supported me in the past were torn from me, until, eventually, I covered my nakedness with new understanding. However much I wanted to believe it was not true, I needed help, and the help, when it came, proved emotionally exhausting. I continued travelling from one unknown destination to another. Behind me were grim memories and confused failures. Ahead was . . . what? The group was a chaotic emotional junction, with hidden signposts to places I had never visited. When I rushed in the one direction I knew, backwards, to the self I recognized, relief temporarily made me want to stay there. Then I forced myself to admit that I had not changed direction at all. I had come to the unit to leave the past, but seemed for ever to be returning to it. When I lay stretched on the grass, or stood studying the stars, I wanted to scream, 'Let me out! Let me out! Anything but this.' And then I would remember some small sign which had become visible as I struggled to understand what was happening to me, and, reluctantly and hopefully, I returned to the real world — the group.

One of my earliest paintings was *silence*. I had believed silence to be 'golden', a time to meditate and make sensible decisions. How could I depict silence on a sheet of paper? I sat on my stool trying to decide where to start. A minute or so passed, and I could think of nothing. Unable to find an answer, I felt angry, and from that anger came the new-born picture. I painted a thick, black arc across the bottom left-hand corner of the paper. Next to it I added another, in red, then another, in purple. I liked what I saw: a powerful, unconventional rainbow. In the larger area of paper, above the arcs, I began jabbing my brushes, and with no ideas, no scheme, the jabs became wild, uncontrolled meteors, attacking my arcs. The paper was full of black, red, purple and orange; but those furious meteors could not penetrate the tough arcs they attacked. A small white area remained in the bottom left-hand corner, no larger than a clenched fist. That, I thought, must be a good place to be. I painted in a bright, friendly yellow, and had finished. I was ready to join the group circle and discuss what I had painted, but, when I stood up and looked at the threatening picture, something made me reach down to the bright yellow and tear it from the paper. I had lost my peace.

I was surprised, but not confused, by what I had painted, and angry. Why had it taken me so long to realize that I hated silence? I began reliving some of the destructive thoughts which attacked me when I thought I was at peace with myself, in silence. I remembered long walks in the country-side, or hours spent gardening, when I expected to feel happy, but could not stop thinking about people who annoyed me. I remembered the hours of misery, when I had stood silently in front of my mother, hearing but not listening to her dreary and self-pitying complaints and accusations, and wished that she were dead. I understood that I felt threatened by silence. How could I get rid of the threat?

Another art subject was *secrets*. I drew this in charcoal, the one time I did not use vivid paint. Secrets, I thought, what secrets do I have? I thought of the business I had helped create, and the destructive theft, and my black Samsonite briefcase, and drew it in perspective, like a three-dimensional rectangle. Then I added a padlock and keys to its handle, protecting them with thick, metal chain-links, until the briefcase was partly hidden. I thought of prison, and pencilled a great cage, with bars, behind which the briefcase and chains were almost obscured. Finally, I drew a wide, black border round the edge of the paper. In the discussion circle someone asked me what was in the briefcase, pad-locked and fastened by chains, inside my prison cage, enclosed by the black border. 'I don't know,' I said. Other people in the group had drawn or painted explicit, tangible secrets. One showed a huge mother cuddling a tiny child. Another had two ghastly heads eating each other. We discussed those, and others; but, after my 'I don't know', nobody questioned me further, and I felt ignored, and angry.

Why wouldn't someone tell me what to do, I thought? Why can't I make my silences good, and my secrets clear? What am I doing here, if nobody will tell me what's wrong with me? I never said those thoughts aloud, but raged inwardly, not understanding that I was withdrawing into silence and hiding my secrets. I discovered some answers, not in myself, but through other residents. Other people's silences infuriated me. Why won't they talk, I wanted to know? I learned to talk, and occasionally, in between the unending advice I gave to other residents, I let out a secret; or, forced into defending myself, someone else prised it from me.

The hot, comforting summer ended. Prickly conkers fell off the horse-chestnut tree, and powerful winds gusted through the draughty house. Autumn thunderstorms excited some of us, and terrified others. We turned on the central heating, ordered extra blankets to keep ourselves warm, and trudged along slippery, icy pathways to collect our food from the distant kitchens. It rained throughout November; in December early snow layered the hedgerows in beautiful, undisturbed whiteness. The seasons changed, and so did the group. Time was passing, but my fears and bad feelings refused to melt away. Instead of moving steadily forward, like the hands of the clock on the living-room wall, I was in a whirlwind of past and present. One moment I sat talking, discussing a new revelation; the next, I was seven years old, suffering from a pain I had not known had been festering inside me, like a malignant cancer. Clinging to that early memory, on the verge of discovering a hidden truth, I hurtled into my twenties, wincing at another unexpected twinge, before rejoining the discussion I had left. I knew that unless I stopped storming everywhere at once I would never settle down and discover the answers which I needed. Nothing was what it seemed to be. Christmas was coming, and the New

Year, and finally, in February, the end of my six months. All that seemed to grow during the barren winter months was my anger. How could I get rid of it?

I was learning to recognize anger, and waited anxiously for it to disappear. Because I could recognize it more easily I expected that I would change, that from each new scrap of information a new *me* would slowly emerge, like a caterpillar discarding old skin for new. I wanted to crawl out of my furious past, clothed in a new, protective cover of peaceful understanding. But there was so much to learn, and time, like the group, was running away.

I had been at the unit for more than two months before I grasped the single, most important piece of 'intelligence' which was available to me; and I did it in a group meeting, not in the secret world of my diary. I had been lost in history, but was living in the present. I suddenly understood that to live with myself, and others, I had to comprehend what happened, great or small, as it was happening. There, at the unit, if I could work out what I did, and how I felt, and not try to explain it away by blaming my past, was the answer I wanted. Through the members – residents more so than staff – I could understand myself. They were facing the same problems, experiencing the same angry feelings, and reacting as I did. If I stopped trying to escape from them, perhaps I would feel better. So much passed between us, that it is not possible to write about it all in one book – several volumes could be filled. The essential point was that when we were together something was always happening. One day I thought I had recognized a new feeling, the next I discovered that one feeling was with me, and another joined it. One of us would recall a memory, and a mountain of group memories and feelings would emerge. I understood many things at different times, and slowly they began to evolve into a new self-portrait. I still could not control my feelings, but I was learning to recognize them, and that helped. Bit by bit, despite feeling bad most of the time, I felt that I was 'getting there'.

Val

When I started at the unit, the group member who threatened me most was not Jim, our Baby, or Barbara, the Temptress, or any of the residents, but Val, the staff nurse. I disliked her immediately we met. At my vetting meeting she had said, 'You won't find it easy.' That had sounded like an attack. Was she implying that I was incapable? She was in her thirties, scruffily dressed, not pretty, and her hair hung in untidy ringlets, as though she had forgotten to comb it. I was certain that she disapproved of me. During my first weeks she seemed to dominate the group meeting room. When I spoke, I felt her eyes staring at me, and dreaded her responses. But the expected responses never came. She ignored me. I was right: she disliked and despised me. If, when I spoke, she changed position in her chair, or shut her eyes, or played with her straggly hair, I felt that she was saying to me, 'Why don't you shut up.' Outside group meetings she laughed with other residents, but ignored me. I hated that most; that she laughed, brightly and frequently, often telling dirty jokes, falling backwards and clapping her hands, as the peals of laughter echoed inside me like gloomy proofs of my own misery. I could not laugh like that. What right had she to laugh, when I felt so bad? To protect myself from her silent attack, I tried to ignore her; but her silence towards me in meetings, and her gleeful laughter with other residents afterwards, infuriated me.

She knew how I felt about her, and I knew that she understood more of me than I wanted her to. After a few weeks trying to pretend that it did not matter, my resentment poured out during a meeting. I wanted to attack her, but was frightened to. She was punishing me, and I wanted it to stop. I spoke apologetically, hoping that she would realize how much she was hurting me. 'I don't understand it,' I began. 'I don't seem to be able to talk with you, Val, and it's worrying me.' It had been difficult, saying those words, and I expected the difficulty to be understood, and the problem solved.

'Don't try to control me,' she replied in her Midlands accent. I felt furious and deeply hurt. I had tried to make peace; she had prolonged the war. More than ever, I wanted to hurt her, but did not know how to. I was right, I persuaded myself, she is a threat. How can I progress in the group with her sitting near me, mocking every word I say, by ignoring me? She had not listened to what I'd said. Why would I want to control her? She was the one who wanted to control me.

Weeks passed. When I spoke to her, I tried to avoid further rebuffs by matching her bluntness with my own. To gain her support, I listened to what she said to other residents, and tried to understand what she expected from them. I felt better knowing that I was not alone; many of the others were frightened of her, too. Often she said cruel, hurtful things to us all, but even though I thought her a bully at times, most of what she said to the residents sounded reasonable, coming from somebody who laughed a lot and was so confident. It's all right for her, I thought angrily, it's easy for her to criticize us. She hasn't got our problems.

I wanted her to like me. She obviously did not like what I was, so I tried to discover what it was about me that she did not like. I never asked her, and she never told me. Through her, I believed, I could find some of the answers I wanted. Without understanding why, I began to realize that often, in group meetings, we reacted similarly to particular members. Once or twice she said that she agreed with something I'd said. Things were looking up; I still felt that she disapproved of me, but in a less threatening way. I did not understand what was happening, but I liked it. We spoke together more often outside the group meetings, but I remained wary. For a woman, she seemed too damned confident, and laughed too much. Sometimes, I laughed with her. One day I said, 'Val, what I'd like to do most, is to get a brush and comb your hair. It drives me potty.' 'What's wrong with my hair?' she demanded. 'It looks like a jungle.' I moved over to her. 'Gerroff!' she laughed. When, some time later, she came to the unit after visiting a hairdresser, she asked me what I thought of her new hairstyle. 'I like it,' I said. And I noticed that she had a lovely smile.

In November, we were told that she was being transferred to Birmingham. I felt sad that she was leaving, but accepted that she was doing a job, and if she had to be transferred, so be it. It would make no difference to me.

When a member of the group left, we held a final review meeting, provided that, if they were residents, they had completed their six months. At this meeting the member leaving was expected to describe how they felt towards the remaining members, each of whom replied. When I heard Val was leaving, one of my first feelings was fear of what she would say to me at her review. I never forgot her harsh, 'Don't try to control me.' On the Friday she left, we sat in our circle, and I waited anxiously. She began with the resident on her right. I counted quickly. Three more, then me, But she moved haphazardly around the circle, and I cursed her for being so unpredictable. She said encouraging things to one or two residents, but was not 'nice' to everybody, and several residents looked hatefully at her, or thoughtfully studied the floor. I wanted my attack to come. Waiting for the unknown felt worse than taking my punishment. She looked at me, and I tried not to lower my eyes. I thought of our exchanges during the past months, and of how she seemed to find fault with so much that I said or did. I remembered our time joking and laughing together. It's all been a charade, I thought. She just got bored in the meetings and needed some light relief.

She turned to me, and I tried to appear calm and unconcerned. I heard words that shocked me – 'the resident I'll miss most', 'like your sense of fun', 'reliable', 'accepts responsibility'. I could not believe my ears. What was worse, I could not stop tears streaming across my cheeks, the only meeting in six months when that happened. When my turn came to reply, I wanted us to be alone, and felt angry that I had to share her with the other members. My eyes were burning, and I was frightened to say too much, in case I started crying again. I choked out a brief 'goodbye and good luck'. I felt cheated. What I wanted to say was 'I wish you weren't going'; but I felt ashamed that I had cried, and dared not risk another display of weakness.

I could not understand why I had cried. It worried me throughout the day, and into the night. How could a stranger have that effect on me? I hated crying in front of other people, and yet a scruffy, noisy woman who never stopped threatening me, had made me cry in front of the group. I felt the shame more because not everyone else had cried. Specifically, Jim had remained dry-eyed. Alone in my room, I tried to remember when I had last cried in 'company'. Memories. Four years earlier, three nights after I heard that my mother had committed suicide, I cried in front of Helen. They had been cries of fury. 'Why did she have to die like that?' I had moaned. 'Why can't I think of any good memories?' More memories: of times I had seen my aunt, after an absence of several months. 'How are things at home?' she would usually ask me. I remembered how, until late into my teens, each time I saw her, I clasped her tightly, and burst into tears, wanting her to understand how bad I felt.

My aunt had died eighteen months before I joined the unit. I had been shocked that, after she was dead, I had never cried. She was ill, I reasoned with myself. She had cancer. It was better that she died, and stopped suffering. Death was a blessing for her, I told myself. But I could not understand why I never cried for her, or even missed her. I had thought about her when I made my Odyssey across America, heading towards California, but I couldn't remember missing her. Now she was gone, and I had to accept it. I remembered a day she had visited me in prison.

'Do you regret these past years?' she asked me. I sat opposite her, in my grey uniform, not knowing how long it would be before I was released. Before I answered her I recalled the thrill of visiting new countries, the excitement of taking risks, the pleasure of power, and replied, 'No, I'd do it all again.' She tried to smile, but I had shocked her. While I was on remand, she had been visiting me daily, travelling thirty miles each day, bringing me comforts. I think she wanted to be thanked, and for her that included a guarantee that she was doing good. If I was unreformed, where did that leave her? She forced a smile, but I knew that I had hurt her because I had told the truth as I felt it at that moment.

When I returned to my cell, and remembered what I had said to her, I felt furious. Of course I did not want to do the same things again. I wanted the punishment to end. I wanted to be released, never to return. I wanted to tell her how frightened I was, how desperate I was to be safe and free, and to understand why I had attacked Helen, and stolen money. I wanted to wrap myself in her; but by deceiving her, I had sent her away, not knowing how helpless I felt. I wanted to tell her how much I missed her. I wanted her to comfort me with more than fresh yoghurt. Instead, I had pretended to be in control of myself. I could not tell her that I still needed her. She believed me when I told her that I would do everything again. How could she believe that? Didn't she understand my coded message?

Val had disappeared from my thoughts. All I could think about was my dead aunt, and the precious times we had spent together when I was a little boy. I felt that I had to be with her. Why had she died before I could tell her how much I needed her?

In the privacy of my room I cried out desperately for the only person I wanted. It had taken me eighteen months to cry for her. Eighteen months to admit how badly I missed her. I felt relieved after I cried. I owed her those tears, I thought. And then I remembered how our last years had felt damaged. I believed that it went back to the day I had told her that 'I'd do it all again'. By the time I had calmed down, in the early hours of the morning, I felt angry that those last years remained in my memory. Tears were one thing, they had come and gone, like a flood-tide, but my anger remained. I wanted to remember the good years, not the bad ones.

After Val left, we discussed how we felt now that she had gone. I admitted that I would miss her. Stuart asked us if we felt angry that she had left us. 'No, I don't feel angry,' I said, like the other residents, 'but I'll miss her.' By then, I had forgotten my night of misery, crying for my lost aunt, and it did not occur to me to link Val, a stranger, with her. When I admitted that I 'missed' Val, I felt neglected; but the more Stuart tried to insist that I felt angry that she had left the group, the more I felt angry with him. Who was he to tell me I felt angry, when I did not? If I felt anything, it was sadness.

Years later I thought I understood, when I began to examine how I felt when I admitted 'sadness'. Often, I realized, I was not sad. I was angry; angry at losing what I needed. I had always wanted my aunt to be my mother. Val had frightened me, like my mother, and helped me, like my aunt. My fear of distrust for a staff nurse had lessened once I trusted her a little. Then, when I wanted her, she had been whisked away, killed off from the group. I had lost someone I needed — my mother.

Billy

Billy had no home. His mother had a boyfriend, and neither of them wanted him, except for their sexual excitement. His relationship with his father remained an enigma in the group. One weekend Billy would stay with him, the next he was back in a lonely bed-sit, and we did not know why. During the week Shipley Grange was a refuge to him, as it was to us all. But unlike the rest of us, he refused to join our war. On several occasions he fell asleep during meetings. Stuart, voicing our exasperation, gave him an ultimatum: 'Join the group, or leave.'

Although I tried to shrug off our early 'father and son' relationship, I discovered that it was not as easy to do as I had expected. I was old enough to be Billy's father, and wanted to believe that I could help him, or, as Val might have expressed it, 'control' him. He was eighteen and reflected many of my own memories from my teens. His refusal to learn from my mistakes infuriated me. I recognized through him my own rejection of authority. I told him that he reminded me of many of the young prisoners I had known, and tried to frighten him by saying that soon he would join them, if he was not prepared to change. He pretended to listen. One day, after a period of continuous attacks, not only from me, but from several other members, he admitted that he had been discussing the group with a nurse who worked in one of the nearby open wards.

'Your problem, Billy,' I said, 'is that all you want from here are free meals and a bed.' He sat in his chair, legs sprawled untidily in front of him, a vicious grin spreading across his face. 'It's all right for you,' he said, 'you've got a home, and your wife comes to collect you in your new car on Fridays.' His stumble towards me started an avalanche of accusations. 'You don't know when you're well-off,' someone added. 'Look at your two kids, they love coming to see you.' 'And you'll have no trouble getting a job when you leave.' 'I've never had a holiday, you've been everywhere.' 'You're not queer.' 'You've never been on social security, I've never been off it.' 'You should hear yourself speak. That posh voice.'

I was horrified, at what they were saying, and at the looks of hatred which glowered at me. 'If you think any of that helps, you're mistaken,' I replied, trying to hide the pain I felt. Stuart came to my rescue. 'I think we're talking of envy and jealousy,' he said. I realized that I was not certain of the difference. Envy? Jealousy? How did they differ? I decided to look up the two words in a dictionary as soon as the meeting ended. No one seemed to understand that behind my mask of calm indifference I was furious. Billy's just a stupid kid, I persuaded myself, trying to make the rest of the group dislike me.

When the meeting ended, I quickly escaped to my room, wanting nothing to do with any of them. How could they not know that family and possessions added to my misery? I had given them my trust, shared with them some of my worst fears and feelings, and they accused me of being better off than they. Hadn't they heard Stuart say that he thought I had the most difficult problem with the group? Their ignorant accusations confirmed my expectations. They could never help me. They hated me because I had worked hard to build a marriage, and father two children, and owned a house and a car, and went on holidays, and ... they were disgustingly jealous ...or was it envy?

I searched for a dictionary, and found a battered, dog-eared book in a cupboard. '*Envy*: jealousy.' '*Jealousy*: envy.' That proves it, I thought angrily, there isn't even a decent dictionary in the building to help me. I was furious at the group, and at myself for not knowing something as straight-forward as the difference in meaning between two common words. Stuart had implied that of the two, jealousy was most destructive. I decided that all of them, even those who had voiced no accusations, wanted to hurt me, so they had to be jealous. From the violence of their words, I knew that their feelings threatened me. Until that day, I had never considered that other people's jealousy could be a threat to me, and, mixed with my anger, I felt excited at the discovery. If other members of the group suffered from jealousy towards me, then presumably so had people outside the group. My ex-partners probably, and members of my family, and friends. No wonder I had so many relationship problems, if everyone felt like that. Thank goodness I was not jealous!

Jealousy: a frightful sounding word, one to be avoided. I knew that I was not jealous. I thought about it, and wrote about it. If I suffered from anything, it was ambition. I had learned that I was competitive, too competitive. That was the closest I was to being jealous. Too ambitious and too competitive. That was why I resented people who had bigger houses and more luxurious cars and longer holidays. All I had to do was control my ambition and competitiveness, and I would not need big things. I might be envious, I decided. Envious of residents who were younger than me, and lucky to have come to the group in their early twenties; and envious of friends who had mothers and fathers they liked: but, of the numerous accusations hurled at me at different times in my life, jealousy had never been included.

In the privacy of my room I wrote in my secret diary and discovered, slowly and inexorably, that another cherished belief about myself was about to be buried under that morning's accusations. I attacked myself. I remembered how, each time I moved into a bigger house, I resented those that were nearby, the really big ones, the ones owned by people who had been to a public school. I thought about Jamyl's dollars, earning more interest in a week than I earned in a month. I mentally flagellated myself, trying to force memories of past resentments into my mind, ticking them off one by one. Yes, I had wanted what other people possessed. I had wanted £100,000 in the bank and a few investment properties, to make me feel secure. And, yes, I had hated anyone who had what I wanted. If that was part of my problem, then understanding it would help me overcome it. The glaring eyes and twitching mouths of the residents in the group that morning haunted me. If I had become like them because I was jealous, learn, learn, and stop making the same mistake.

Once a week the hospital held a social evening in the main building. I kept as far away as I could from it, to avoid seeing the deranged mental patients who went there to dance and enjoy themselves. Cathy went from time to time, and one evening came and sat next to me in the living room. 'I've got a problem,' she told me. (Another secret — good.) I waited for her to tell me about it. 'It's Billy,' she said. 'We were dancing, and when I was close to him I fancied him . . . you know, *that* way.' Unusually, she seemed confused and indirect. I discussed it with her, trying to remain detached and objective. 'I know how you feel,' I said calmly. She lowered her voice. 'I've felt that way before,' she continued, 'about you.' I wanted to tell her that she was not the only one, and was pleased at her admission, but she had made me . . . jealous. It was one thing to hear her say she wanted me; quite another to bring Billy into the conversation. I advised her that if it worried her she should discuss it in the group. When she did, she only mentioned Billy. I was relieved that I had not been forced into a discussion involving myself; but at the same time, I did not like the idea that the group thought she fancied Billy more than me. I wanted to let the group know that she had discussed how she felt with me the previous evening, so that they would learn that she had fancied me too. I remained silent. Billy, the dishonest kid who seemed to have least to offer the group, became the centre of attention. He was becoming too much of a threat.

The unit had a small weekly cash allowance from hospital funds, which financed occasional outings, farewell parties and extras for the house. Five pounds had gone missing. A group meeting was called. We sat in an embarrassed silence. 'One of us wants to hurt the group. What should we do about it?' Stuart asked. We decided that every member should explain how he or she felt about the theft.

When Billy's turn to speak arrived, he accused us of suspecting him. He was right. No direct accusation was made, but he was the prime, probably the only, suspect. The matter remained unresolved. When we were alone, I told him that I was convinced that he had stolen the money. His vicious grin appeared. 'I know you are. So is everyone else.' He had tears in his eyes, but my need to hurt him would not go away. 'Think about it,' I advised him. 'You won't be thrown out.'

The atmosphere of suspicion in the group was heightened by the theft. Discussions veered wildly: from deceit to trust; from revenge to shame; from rejection to intolerance. 'Why do we feel the need to take?' Stuart asked. But we wanted to answer a more tangible question. Who swiped the petty cash?

Then something happened which I had not expected. In a group meeting Billy accused me of always being 'right'. For several minutes he told the group how he felt about me. I enjoyed making him feel bad, he said, and never believed him. I made the rest of the group distrust him. He wanted me to stop telling him what to do. 'I don't see why you're in charge of this group,' he said. 'It's about time someone else took over.' I smiled, trying to hide the fury I felt at his attempted *coup de main*. Everyone in the room except Billy remained silent. 'You're a thief, so what makes you better than me?' he asked. 'Well, if I am,' I replied, 'at least I didn't steal the group's cash.'

I had scored a bullseye. He stopped staring aggressively at

me, and directing his voice at the carpet, denied that he was the culprit, but another resident said that we all thought he was. Stuart explained that stealing the money was a way of getting attention, and I felt angry that my attack had moved from Billy to us all. I knew that I would never forgive him for criticizing me in the group. I also knew that several other residents had enjoyed what he had said to me. Somehow, I would make him suffer.

Billy became more restless. He vanished for hours to his friendly nurse. One morning he was missing at the group meeting. He had vanished, permanently. I felt elated: his going eliminated another competitor. I felt angry: he had escaped before I had been able to hurt him. I felt guilty: was it my fault that he had left? But most of all I felt relieved. The group was getting smaller.

Jim

By my fifth month, December, Jim was the longest surviving resident. Four more weeks and he would have completed his six months. Since August, I had been confused by our relationship, but, as the weeks passed, I knew that if I could understand what was happening between us another secret would be revealed. Despite periods when we talked and admitted the barrier between us, we disliked each other more, not less, after each polite attempt at mutual acceptance. After Billy left, he and I were the only male residents in the group. The competition which raged between us had to be resolved, and I had four weeks to find the answers I wanted.

When a resident came to the end of his fifth month, an assessment meeting was held. It was Jim's turn. He looked serious and preoccupied before he began to speak. I assumed that, like us all, the ordeal of a specifically personal meeting was worrying him. He began talking. I wanted to hear what he thought he had gained from the unit, and waited expectantly. Christmas was coming, and we all had reasons for dreading it. Weekends at home were difficult for residents, suddenly unable to communicate as we could during the week. A ten-day absence from the unit, to enjoy Christmas and the New Year, felt like a death sentence. Jim was a symbol of stability, and through him I assumed that I would feel justified in remaining with the group.

During the whole of my time at Shipley Grange, Jim's personal assessment was the most devastating rejection I experienced. He told us that he had thought about it carefully; that he believed he had made a dreadful mistake coming to the unit; that if he had had any idea of the torment, humiliation and distrust he would encounter, he would never have offered himself as an applicant. He thanked us all for putting up with him, and hoped that we would not feel as ill and disillusioned as he did. He understood what a burden he had been to us all, and felt deeply ashamed of the spectacle he had made of himself, and quite appreciated that we had every justification for becoming angry with him. He concluded by stating his intention of leaving that morning, immediately after the meeting. We were all stunned. He had identified the doubts and feelings of all residents. I regarded him contemptuously, not wanting to accept his feelings.

We tried to persuade him to stay. I felt that, if he realized how much he was wanted, he would return after Christmas, and complete his six months. He was adamant. He had expected us to make him change his decision, but it was unalterable. Someone asked him what he was going to do. He was uncertain, he admitted. His first priority was to have a rest, and try to forget the nightmare he had lived through since the summer. He wanted to spend Christmas with his family — the family he had spent five months berating; after that, he said, he hoped that he would feel better, and fit enough to look for a job. He thought that he might be able to work in the administrative offices of his local hospital. 'What do you think about that?' he asked me. 'I'm not your bloody father,' I snapped at him. It was our last verbal exchange. To avoid having to say goodbye, I escaped to the kitchens, or somewhere, as soon as the meeting ended. It was a bad start to Christmas.

Too many changes were taking place, at the unit and at home. Everywhere I felt betrayed. I wanted to feel gain: I felt loss. The group was disappearing; time was vanishing; and I did not know where I was going.

In October, I had visited Terry — a friend and client from my years in practice — at his factory in Reading. I wanted to make plans for when I left the group, and it seemed essential that I had a job to look forward to. Terry had been thrilled at what I was learning about myself. He had experienced a similar metamorphosis a few years earlier, but I had not understood what had happened to him. Now I did. He was one of my last remaining links with my lost business. He had been one of the first to visit me in prison and offer encouragement and hope for the future. I wanted his approval for what I was enduring.

I asked him for a job. It had been difficult, summoning the courage to do so, and I feared that he might find a pretext for refusing me. 'If you want to come, you're welcome,' he said. 'I know you'll do what's right. The only thing is, I don't want to be under attack from you.' Helen and the children had come with me, and after seeing Terry, we drove through the countryside looking for somewhere to live. Working for Terry meant another house move, but that seemed a small inconvenience compared with the security of a job. We agreed that February, after I had completed my six months' psychotherapy, was the best time to move.

For a day or two I felt that I had made the right decision. Then doubts began to torment me. Terry had frightened me when I accepted his help after being released from prison on parole. I remembered the headaches and tension which came every week when I drove to see him; and his question — 'What are your fears?' — and my confident reply — 'I don't have any. (Did I say that!) I remembered the anxiety I felt, because I suspected that he knew something about me which I did not; and his refusal to answer me when I asked him to explain his enigmatic smile. And I worried about his conditional offer of employment — 'I don't want to be under attack from you.'

I tried to compromise between my need for employment and my suspicions of him. For weeks I struggled with doubts about the proposed move. I remembered that even on the day I had visited him in October, my head had throbbed painfully. But I wanted a job, desperately, and his offer was the only one I had.

When Jim assaulted the unit on the day he left, I felt frightened. He had voiced fears I had been battling with for weeks. That weekend I wrote to Terry, and told him 'that I knew it would not be right'. I did not say what I was feeling; that I could not work *for* him, and I could not work *with* him; that if I could not be in charge, the job was worthless. I had not admitted to myself that I was frightened of him. Terry and Jim were disturbing me at the same time, apparently for different reasons. Neither of them were giving me the answers I wanted; and both of them had made me angry.

I tried to work through my feelings towards other men I had known. Dr Dory, Malcolm Saunders and Jamyl Marzeem were hovering in my mind, like ominous clouds. Why did they all disturb me so much? I had wanted to be friends with them all, and for periods had succeeded. But the friendship inevitably became enmity, and I did not know why. They were all different. Terry exercised deadly control over his employees, wife, and, by telling me not to attack him, me. Jim was a sorry excuse for a man, who had run away from confronting himself. Malcolm had rejected me because I had rejected him; Jamyl had accused me of being lazy; Dr Dory had congratulated me for being industrious. I could find no common link.

I tried to connect these men with my father. In the group I had accused him of being weak and unambitious. 'How would you feel if your son never forgave you?' Stuart had asked me once. He had touched a tender spot. I felt a failure as a father, and had begun, during the first weeks at Shipley, to explain to Ben what I was learning. I admitted to him that I realized that my anger, so often directed at him, had been misplaced. I told him that I had been unfair. I wanted to do to him what my father had never done to me – apologize. I remembered what Terry had said to me, years previously, when Ben was ten years old – 'You're trying to make him a little "you".' Although our relationship improved enormously, Ben continued disrupting the class at school, and withdrawing from the family at home. Men! From my father to my son to the others, all seemed determined to thwart me. Why wouldn't they give me what I wanted? What *did* I want? My thoughts raced in unconnected, contradictory circles.

After Jim left, the only other male in the group was Stuart. As a member of staff, I thought of him as 'authority'. I wanted him to approve of my progress at the unit. On one occasion, I told him that I wished he could give me marks, out of ten, to indicate 'how I was doing'. 'Why?' he asked. 'Because I feel that I'm at school, and need to know if I'm succeeding.' I expected him to respond, but he made no reply, and whereas, when I began the conversation, I had felt relaxed with him, I suddenly felt let down, convinced that I had made a terrible blunder. His silence made me feel angry. We never discussed 'marks' again. On another day he asked me why I always looked at him when I spoke in meetings. 'You disturb me,' I replied. 'I always think you're mocking me. You make me feel that I'm talking rubbish.'

Receiving no help from Stuart, I turned to my diary. I headed the entry 'Men'. 'Why do I find it so difficult to get on with men?' I wrote. Three pages later I came to a conclusion. 'I regard men as "authority figures" who try to dominate me. If I am dominated I feel threatened. When I am threatened, I attack.' But where did Jim fit in?

I discussed this with the group, looking at Stuart. 'You don't like women, either,' he said, apparently paying no attention to my carefully worked-out thesis. I denied his accusation. 'Some women, I don't like,' I agreed, 'but my mother tried to dominate me, so that explains why. I've always got on better with women than with men.' I stopped talking. Again, he had frustrated me. I had devoted hours the previous night, working out why I did not like men; he accused me of not liking women. If he was right, and I did not like men or women, I was running out of people. Always, always, accusations. Never, never, answers.

When we held the inevitable inquest, after Jim's unexpected and angry departure, I told the group that I felt betrayed that he had left. 'Who did he remind you of?' Stuart asked. 'My father,' I replied before I had time to think.

Two's company

Cathy had been with the unit for five weeks before Linda joined. 'I wish I'd had a father like you,' she once said. I did not admit that I saw her as a daughter, because if I did, I had not recognized it. Within hours of our first meeting I believed that I understood many of her difficulties, particularly with her parents and boyfriends. None of the residents spoke easily or freely during formal group meetings; we depended on our sub-groups for support, to make shameful admissions of past behaviour, or admit fears. 'I'm not your father,' I told her sternly several times, wondering what she'd be like in bed.

After four weeks, each resident had an assessment meeting with the whole group, to decide whether he or she should stay. (Mine had led to the shameful confessions about my crimes.) At hers, Cathy was advised by Val that, if she stayed, it was imperative that she stop relying on me. I felt thrilled that my part in her 'coming out' had been recognized, and angry that it had been criticized. Cathy and I ignored the advice. Linda joined the following week.

From the first day, Linda and I were attracted to each other, although neither of us could then have explained why. In the evening, when everyone else was in bed, we sat talking in the living room, sipping hot chocolate drinks, beginning a routine which, with few exceptions, lasted throughout our months at the unit. Many evenings, Cathy was with us, but, usually, she went to bed before midnight, leaving the two of us alone until 2, or 3 or 4 in the morning.

At the end of October we organized a Hallowe'en party.

We made and painted gruesome hats in the art room, planned an extensive menu, obtained permission to bring alcohol into the house, checked that the record-player was still alive, and issued invitations to other members of the staff who had previously worked at the unit. We were ready for a long night's fun. We were also on the edge of panic: I worried about the organization; Jim stormed out of the living room before anyone had arrived, accusing me of staring at him — 'It's not my fault if I can't do anything right,' he said; Barbara was frightened to wear what she wanted, in case we thought she was showing off; Linda hid away in her room trying to put together a complex witch's costume. Cathy and I worked in the kitchen.

By 8 o'clock there was a lot of noise, and most of us seemed to be enjoying ourselves. Val cavorted cheerfully round the room; Stuart danced with all the women. We ate, drank and tried to keep the jollity going. Until the party, Linda and I had talked, but never touched, other than during psychodrama sessions. That evening we danced, and danced, slower and slower, clinging more tightly to each other as the hours passed. I danced with the others, occasionally, because I thought I 'should'. The hours passed, the party ended, and by midnight only a few of us remained chatting. Cathy had gone to bed early with a headache. Linda and I were finally alone, and we cuddled up on the sofa, listening to records until 5 o'clock in the morning.

The following evening Cathy had another bad headache, and went to bed without eating. I was on my own in the kitchen at 11 o'clock when she came down to make herself a drink. She looked unwell. 'What's the matter?' I asked. She bowed her head and remained silent. I tried again, and again. 'Do you need a doctor?' She raised her head, and I saw that she was crying. 'It's you,' she said. She became hysterical: I was confused. When she had calmed down, she explained that I had ruined the party for her. She had expected that we would spend the evening together, and accused me of hating her. 'It's nothing to do with Linda,' she told me, 'we're good friends.'

They were. Most days they shared their unit housework, cooked meals together, spent hours in their bedroom chatting and sharing confidences. They supported each other in group meetings, and were quick to laugh or cry together. Their friendship had become so powerful that it began to disturb the group, and that included me. I joined them sometimes during the day. We'd go for walks, sit together at meals or on the settee, talking; but I was disturbed. Cathy was as friendly towards me as ever. Linda and I had our evenings. I knew that I resented their friendship, but worked hard not to show my feelings.

Cathy's reading was weak. She had to choose books with large type from the library, the sort which youngsters read when learning. I offered to listen to her read and try to teach her to improve. She was delighted. For a week or two during this period she came and sat with me most afternoons for a half-hour or so. One afternoon I was explaining a word to her. 'Do you understand?' I asked. She flared up. 'I wish you'd stop saying that,' she fumed, 'it makes me feel stupid.' I was careful not to repeat my mistake. Our reading kept the two of us together when she could have been running off with Linda.

Linda and I loved walking, particularly through the narrow country lanes and across the nearby farms. We enjoyed this most when the weather was bad – strong autumn winds or sleeting rain. Our time together during the day compensated for the unexpressed feelings I had about her friendship with Cathy. And it kept them apart. However our sub-group was surviving, the other members resented it. We were accused of being a separate family. Cathy and I were the parents, they said, and Linda our child. We were furious. We knew that we belonged together, the others were jealous. I could not admit that I felt jealous of the two women's friendship. When they went off on their own I felt rejected, and angry.

The frustrations inside our 'family' seemed less important than letting the rest of the unit understand that we were a group who wanted each other, and could do without the others. The night the three of us demolished the living room for 'fun' confirmed our unity.

Autumn turned to winter. By mid-December, Linda and I were talking of living together after she had completed her six months at the unit. As far as we knew, it was our secret. We thought that nobody, not even Cathy – especially not Cathy – knew how we felt towards each other.

Meanwhile, Cathy was finding her life unbearable. Week after week she was beginning to understand the dangers in her life, and when she did speak in the group, which was not often, she spoke with the ferocity we had seen at her vetting meeting. Each weekend she roamed between her parents' home and that of a boyfriend. During the week, she began rowing with Linda. Her attacks were savage. She levelled every accusation which only a few weeks earlier she had rebutted from other residents and staff. One evening I lost my temper and angrily accused her of loading her family problems on Linda. 'You feel so rotten that you want to damage anything good you've got,' I said. She calmed down, briefly, for an hour. But their friendship, which had previously disturbed the group, changed into silent and mounting antagonism, and the group wanted to know why.

January. Cathy returned to the unit. She had wanted to speak to me during Christmas, she said, but had not been able to. I felt hurt. We went into the meeting room; for the first time that I could recall, she began speaking immediately. 'I want to say that I hate Linda,' she said. 'I always have. I pretended that we were friends to keep her away from (me!).' She said a lot more, but that was the gist of it. Linda sat staring at her in awful amazement. Our triangular sub-group had turned in on itself. Cathy had finally openly rejected Linda; Linda, one of the quietest members in the group, turned furiously on the friend who had betrayed her. I felt like a 'piggy in the middle', angry with both of them for humiliating our sub-group in front of the others. The two women fought their battle to its conclusion, the only conclusion Cathy could face. She left the group, angry and disillusioned. Her last words to me were 'I'm sorry'. I was, too, and knew that I would miss her. I understood that she had attacked Linda because she felt the stronger of the two, and that she had wanted to retain my support, which I refused to give. For days, I had waited for an attack on me, but nothing happened, except that on the day she left she kept repeating 'I'm sorry'. I asked her not to go.

She launched her attack on me in a way I would not have believed possible. She telephoned my wife and told her that she knew that Linda and I were having an affair.

There were other conflicts, hundreds, perhaps thousands of them, which I experienced at the unit. I had journeyed backwards, to my childhood and grim memories which I had thought long-forgotten. I had revisited years of depression, and acts of destruction. I had learned through my encounters in the group that I was not the person I had pretended to be. I understood that deceit, jealousy, and my behaviour generally, were directed at people, not things. Emotions which I had not been able to identify became clearer to me. I accepted that I was secretive and profoundly distrustful towards other people; that I tried to control others to avoid them controlling me; that I craved attention and approval.

I had gone to Shipley Grange to find answers. I expected that the sympathetic nursing staff would know what was wrong with me, and explain it carefully. All I had to do was remember, and, like my examinations, I would pass with honour. When I realized that no one was going to 'give' me answers, I felt as disillusioned as Cathy, and Jim, and Barbara, and Linda, and the others. Why were we there, if there were no answers? Once I had understood that I was being guided, and had to find my own solutions, I felt angry at the group for making my life more difficult. When I began finding my own answers, my anger remained, but I became excited. Perhaps, after all, there was a way to balance my see-sawing *U*, which persistently raised me high and then dumped me like a sack of refuse: had I, at long last, discovered how to straighten myself out?

I began to understand that the complex emotions I felt

could not be isolated. The effort of accepting each emotion as truth invariably made me wish that I could isolate them. 'That's anger,' I wanted to say. 'That's jealousy.' And so on. It was hard to say that. It was harder to accept that 'that' could be anger and jealousy; or that one twinge of feeling might include anger, jealousy, rejection, and most other feelings which I was beginning to think about — and feel. 'Get in touch with your feelings,' Stuart said. 'Express them.' 'What the hell is he talking about!' a silent voice moaned.

But I *was* beginning, with difficulty, to get in touch with my feelings; and I was having to accept those of the rest of the group, which increased my frustration. I was prepared to exhaust myself on myself. Why should I have to add to the torment by letting their feelings exhaust me as well? These questions and answers developed day by day, slowly and tortuously, relentlessly invading my privacy, and digging deeply into my mind and feelings. I grappled at what was inside and, like an excavator unearthing new land, I dug a huge hole, throwing the rubbish out for examination.

The more I excavated, the more I needed the group. The more I needed the group, the more I realized that the group represented more than its individual members. One by one, they presented individual problems; put them together, and I faced the world. The small group at Shipley Grange was not a small group at all. The Cathys and Billys and Jims were 'outside', too. Through the staff and residents, I was meeting my family, friends and business colleagues. Above all, I was meeting myself. And it hurt. Mixed with the hurt was excitement. I was not an excavator, I was an explorer, discovering a new world, and I wanted to shout with joy and relief. I wanted my family and my friends to discover this world with me. The early discoveries were often inaccurate, my emotional maps faced south when they should have faced north, but it did not matter. I was on the move. Often, despite the turmoil and hate, I loved the group more than I had loved anyone. I loved the group as a symbol of the future, and its individual members for their help. The love seldom lasted, but while it did, I felt brief moments of tranquillity which surpassed any previous experience. I wanted to share the group. I wanted to take it home to Helen and my children. Especially Helen.

I had found some answers. What I could not understand was why, after months of pain and excitement, I felt as bad as ever. Each brief period of pleasure, when I had grasped a new truth, always ended in despair. A voice continuously screamed 'Help me!'

Weekend retreat

'Help me' was what I had wanted to say to Helen, on the evening in 1975 when all my hopes for repaying my partners were dashed, and I was too afraid to tell her. Her last words to me before she went to bed — 'I wish I could go to sleep and never wake up' — were as threatening as a pistol aimed at my head. If she felt as hopeless as I, what future did we have? Hours later, after I had tried to hammer her out of my life, unable to understand why I had done it, the only explanation I could comfort myself with was that 'It wasn't me'. Hadn't the police officer said, 'You're a professional man, well-off. Doesn't make sense, what you did.' The years passed. From prison I returned home. She was there, waiting for me. But being alive, she remained a living accusation. 'I know it wasn't you, not the real you,' she said sometimes. The charge of attempted murder had been real, and the prison sentence which followed. The memories of her screams, when she woke and felt my hammer blows, were real. Why, then, did the attack itself seem so unreal that whenever I remembered it, I cried out 'No! Not me'? I did not understand why I had done it. I wanted someone to tell me. The prison psychiatrist had failed me: nothing he said made me feel better, not even breathing through my nose. My family chose not to discuss it, which made the crime seem worse. I did not want to keep quiet. I wanted to scream, 'If it wasn't me, why does it make me feel so bad?' I felt more ashamed of what I had done after

I left prison than while serving my sentence, and I had felt terrible about it there. In prison the crime had been an unexpected asset. 'Attempted murder' placed me higher in the hierarchy than most prisoners. That was some, not much, but some, consolation. And there had been a few 'cons' I could share the experience with, which helped. But after returning home, and mixing with people who had not smashed a four-pound hammer on to their wife's skull, I felt that I was a victim. I agreed with everybody that 'It wasn't me'. I wanted absolution; but nobody took away my suffering.

I knew in prison that I never wanted to return home. In San Diego, five years later, I knew it too. One of my hopes when I joined the group at Shipley Grange, was that finally, after years of confusion, I would stop feeling the need to escape. Helen disliked the idea of my going there. I resented her anxiety, and initially consoled her by implying that it would only be for one month, even though I promised myself that, if I needed to, I would remain for six.

My feelings towards my wife were ambivalent. We had known each other for more than twenty years. In my teens, before we were married, her love and support had felt like the only true friendship I had known. During our early years of marriage, I often laughed at myself for the doubts which had disturbed me the night before our wedding. She gave me as much of herself as she could, and converted my youthful dreams of a stable family life into what I believed to be reality. At my most difficult emotional periods she had tried to help. When, unable to cope with my family responsibilities, I had run away from her and the children – to Paris and California – she had seemed to understand my distress, and said how much she still needed me. Several of her family and friends, particularly after I attacked her, advised her to end a dangerous relationship, but she ignored their advice and welcomed me back into her life.

I remembered all this, and wanted to feel grateful and appreciative. Nobody else had ever shown me such love and loyalty. But something which I could not identify disturbed me about our relationship. When I thought that I should feel love, I felt instead a desperate loneliness.

I resisted discussing her in group meetings for several weeks, believing that to do so was disloyal; but she became more and more unhappy at my involvement with the group. Her efforts to make me leave the unit actually brought her into it. At first, I used her misery as a reason for my leaving; then, knowing that I had to stay, I wanted the group to understand how difficult it was for me to convince her. Stuart suggested that he and Val meet the two of us privately each week – a form of marriage guidance service the unit sometimes provided. I wanted to feel grateful at the suggestion, but accepting their help made me feel angry – why couldn't I sort it out myself? Would they disclose secrets I had revealed in group meetings? Would they take her side against me? I did not trust any of them.

During my second month at the unit Helen became depressed and visited her doctor, who prescribed tranquillizers. 'I explained what I'd been through, these past years,' she told me, 'and he was astonished that I'd still kept going.' I felt bitter. She needed me with her, but I needed to be with the group. I tried to admit that I had made her suffer; that she had tried to help me as best she could; that I should leave the group and remain with my family seven days a week: but my attempts to indoctrinate myself failed. My worst fears were confirmed. I could understand more about myself, but I could not control my feelings. I knew what I wanted, and anyone who tried to thwart me was an enemy.

When I started at the unit I had telephoned her most evenings. Her telephonic accusations and pleas were worse than the weekend ones not to leave her. I felt that I was being emotionally blackmailed. She was spoiling my group. She wanted to keep away from it; she had said that it frightened her. My absence from home became such a major problem that I reluctantly told her about Stuart's offer. 'If you think it will help', Helen said, 'then I'll come.'

The meetings were disastrous from the start. I wanted to

bring into those sessions what I was beginning to understand and feel, but my feelings got mixed up, and all I could see opposite me was an accusation. I did not want her there and regretted having agreed to Stuart's suggestion. After each meeting I wanted to forget her. Stuart had said to us, 'You don't listen to each other.' I did not want to listen; I wanted to escape. When I had first discussed her in a group meeting, Val had said, 'You make your wife sound like a paragon of virtue.' What must she think now, listening to my contradictions? Emotions were stirring inside me and I could not release them. When Val left I was convinced that I had lost the chance to find an answer. And week by week, my anger, at everyone and everything, increased.

The Monday after Val left Jo, her replacement, joined. She felt like a barrier to my discussing my marriage in the group, and Stuart did not suggest that she join our private meetings. I felt as distrustful towards her as I had initially towards Val. She was an inadequate replacement, I thought.

After lunch on the last Thursday in November we had to vote for the week's social activity. Swimming was agreed by everyone, except me. I refused to vote. I wanted to be free of them. Stuart was not there that day, so Jo was the only staff member present. 'Why won't you join the group?' she wanted to know, while the others sat round, some of them impatient at the delay. 'Just leave me alone,' I said angrily. But she would not. 'We can't go until you explain what's the matter,' she insisted. My anger grew. I sat rigidly at the end of a settee. What I wanted to say was 'Help me', but I could not.

I refused to speak. Linda said, 'Why can't we let him stay here, if he wants to?' She thought that she was helping me, but she made me feel worse, and I silently cursed her. Didn't she know how I felt! My anger increased. Jo was adamant. 'We stay. This is a crisis meeting. Someone take the minutes.' I had to grip my fingers tightly and bite my teeth to avoid crying. The person I thought least likely to help was doing the unexpected.

When everybody had settled down, I began trying to talk about my wife. I told the group that I did not know what to do. Friday was coming, and I had to go home, and that meant seeing Helen, and that made me feel awful. For the first time since I had attacked her, six long years earlier, I heard myself saying that I could never forgive her for the support she refused me when I needed it most. During that meeting I admitted more bad feelings towards her than I had in the twenty-one years since we had met. While I spoke I argued with myself. Why am I saying these terrible things, I wondered, why don't I admit the good things as well as the bad ones? The choking feeling in my stomach made me stop, and in the silence I heard Jo ask, 'Do you need your wife?' I stared at her. 'No,' I replied, 'I don't need her.' One simple question. One spontaneous answer.

'I don't need her,' I repeated to myself, and as Thursday, and Friday, passed, 'I don't need her' had to compete with 'I'll never forgive her' and 'I want to hurt her'. And all the time these angry words flashed inside me I felt guilty. Why do I feel such a desperate need to hurt someone who loves me and wants to be with me?

Helen came to meet me on Friday afternoons, when the group's week ended. Usually, we stopped on the way home for a break, and had tea out, to give us a chance to talk before being besieged by the children. Over tea and pastries, each week I explained what had been happening, what I had learned about myself, how I could relate my behaviour to my feelings. 'Well, darling,' she said during the early weeks, 'if they can make you better, that's wonderful.' She would do anything I wanted, she promised. 'We could buy a small shop in the country. We don't need much. The children are growing up. Soon they'll have left home.' She spoke of a glorious future, a loving partnership. 'No,' I said, 'I don't want to hide away in some distant village.' During my early weeks at the unit I believed that I could share my experiences with her, and if I could do that, we had no need to run away from what we had.

Another time she said, 'If you have to go through this, and it will make you better, then you must. I couldn't. I don't want to examine myself the way you're doing. It frightens me.' As our weekends passed I realized that she was right to be frightened. I was discovering a new world, one which we had never shared. And because it was a new world, one which made the old seem fraudulent, I wanted to escape from it. Helen hoped that I would get better, so that our future life together could settle down. I wanted a new, a completely new, life. I remembered my past worries, after prison, and after she brought me back to England from California. An incipient awareness took root. 'Getting better' began to sound as demanding as 'getting a job' had sounded after I had destroyed my previous careers. If I had to do it again, I wanted to feel different, and at Shipley Grange I did feel different.

But at home, each weekend, I felt that I was entombed in what I had to escape from. As I gradually felt able to discuss my anger, when it surfaced at the unit, I needed to feel the same freedom to do so at home. But it was not possible. Secrets I discussed with the group remained secret at home, and that made me feel more and more distant from Helen. I felt as isolated as I had as a teenager living with my parents. A gap was opening in my marriage which, despite feeling responsible for so much of our misery, I wanted to grow wider. I needed somewhere to dump my anger.

When I ran away from the group, and felt humiliated having to return, we talked about why I had done it, and I felt better. When I returned from prison and, later, from America, and went home to Helen, we resolved nothing. And now, my weekly fear of returning home felt as disturbing as my weekly fear of returning to the unit. I dreaded them both; but of the two, only the unit seemed to open up the new life I wanted. I arranged to return to Shipley Grange on Sunday evenings, and stopped telephoning Helen during the week.

Then Jo simplified my confusion. 'Do you need your wife?'

I felt that an epic movie was slowing down. Instead of a continuous film, I was seeing each frame. Examining minute details, I began viewing the drama of my marriage for what it was: a confused story with a weak script and actors who had never understood their lines. We were acting out parts we had chosen; but we spoke in different languages. She wanted protection: I wanted control. It was not true. We both wanted to control the other, in our own way; and we both wanted protection. Neither of us had achieved either. Jo's question projected the real story, and it terrified me. Twenty-one years, most of them as husband and wife, and I felt that we did not know each other. I wanted to rewrite the past, and although I knew that I had misjudged myself, I needed an outlet for my guilt and anger. Before I could rebuild my life I wanted to destroy everything which made me feel bad. I didn't understand it then, but I was using my marriage as a target for forty years of revenge. I couldn't attack my mother, she was dead, so I attacked my wife. While I was unleashing my hatred I knew that I was being unfair, but I could not control the fury I felt.

Early in December, by which time Linda often contacted me at weekends (many weeks before Cathy made her telephone call), Helen asked me if I was having an affair with her. I said 'No'. One weekend I told her that I needed to be on my own. She went to stay with friends. Linda and I went to Eastbourne. I refused to admit that I intended leaving Helen. At the same time, I began taking a few extra personal possessions to the unit each week, including a rucksack and sleeping bag.

I knew that it was over, but did not know how to end it. My rages at her were harsh. I had wanted her to suffer, and she did. Leaving her meant leaving my children and my home and admitting another failure. I flung at her the foulest accusation I could think of. 'You're worse than my mother.' Christmas was coming.

I acted out as best I could the festive husband and father. I told Linda that I could not buy Helen a present. 'You must,' she said, and came with me to choose it. On Christmas Day I made the strongest champagne cocktail I could. I poured in brandy as though I was drowning Helen, and she drank it, and became tipsy. We laughed when she swayed across the lounge, but my laugh was as false as the demands I had made of her during the previous weeks. Had she acceded to every one, and she tried to, nothing would have changed. I needed my target.

My children stood at the edge of this battle, bewildered. They had never seen such an onslaught, except for the night my son saw me attack Helen with a hammer. My fury and Helen's pleas were unrelenting. The attacks were not physical, but they wounded us as if they had been. I tried to assure the children that what was happening was nothing to do with them. They had suffered over the years, and when I raged and stormed, their presence made me feel guilty and ashamed. But I could not stop. When Helen threatened to take an overdose I felt a surge of delight.

On the last Friday in January we had our final meeting with Stuart. He had tried to explain that it was important that I understood how I felt, and that if Helen and I intended parting, we should 'talk it through'. Talk was the last thing that I wanted, but the meeting was arranged. For the first time I told her that I thought we should separate, perhaps for a trial month. That was another deceit. When I asked her for money she refused. She needed it 'for her and the children'. Stuart said that she obviously felt she 'had given enough'.

We drove off together. No tea that afternoon, only a deathly silence. 'Are you coming home to tell the children?' she wanted to know. I thought about it carefully. If I did that there would certainly be another ghastly scene. 'No,' I replied. 'I'll speak to them on my own in a day or so.' I told her that I had practically no money on me. She had all our cash, a few thousand. 'I want £400. You keep the rest.' She offered me a cheque for fifty, and I told her to keep her precious money. I left her in the middle of the village high street, with our car, and waited at the bus stop, not knowing what to do or where to go.

I travelled to the nearest town and telephoned her. 'I must have some money,' I demanded, 'or you'll regret it.' 'Don't threaten me,' she replied. 'You're not going to break my skull a second time.' I was desperate. The pound or so I had on me symbolized all the failures in my life. I returned to the house, and saw a police car parked outside. My first reaction was one of fear. Then I felt relieved. She did not trust me, and I did not trust myself. The police, like Stuart a few hours earlier, provided protection for us both. I opened the door. Two policemen were sitting in the lounge. I smiled at them and said, 'Good evening.' They explained that my wife was frightened because I had threatened her. 'Are you intending to stay here?' I was asked. 'No, I've come to collect some things.'

I spoke briefly to the children, packed some clothes and books, and again asked for some money. 'I haven't any cash,' Helen said, 'but here's a cheque for £50.' I told her to stuff it. Ben was helping me to pack. 'Come for a drink with me,' I suggested. He carried one of my bags, and walked with me to the village. We talked together for about half an hour, and he agreed that my leaving was probably best. 'I'm not taking sides,' he said. For a moment I wanted him to. I wanted his approval that I was right, and his mother wrong. 'That's best,' I said. I explained that Helen did not want him or Vanessa to see me. 'She can't stop me, can she?'

I went to my dead aunt's husband, Jack, and stayed the night. 'Never knew why you two stayed together,' he said. 'You've both been blind for years.' He was not taking sides, either. I told him about Linda. 'You must be mad. I'd keep away from women for a while, especially anyone from that place.' At 11 o'clock the telephone rang. It was Helen, not to see how I was, but checking that I was not near her. On Saturday I telephoned my father and said that I was coming to see him. Jack gave me all his cash, £20-odd, and wished me luck.

I arrived in London in the evening and travelled to my father's home, the home where I had lived in my teens. I stood opposite the building. How could I ask him for help, I thought? He was less than a hundred feet away, waiting for me. I stood there for many minutes, wanting to go and ring the doorbell, but unable to do so. I left, travelled to Victoria station, and waited for the last train to Bournemouth. It was the only safe place I knew.

Sunday morning was cold. Dawn came, revealing vast

stretches of pink and grey clouds. I sat by the deserted beach watching gentle waves scramble across the soft sand. Memories of my aunt and I trudging along the beautiful chines to Sandbanks flooded my mind, and tears flooded my face. I wondered how it would feel if I walked into the sea until water and the weight of my clothes drowned me. I sat there, shivering in the January dawn, romancing that I had the courage to end my life in the place where I was born. A car passed the bench where I sat and I knew that death was not what I wanted. I wanted to feel as peaceful as the silent sky. I could not believe that my marriage had ended. I had no regrets, not then, or afterwards, that it was over. My only regret, one which took several years to develop, was that I had made the right decision but had been unable to deal with it calmly. Neither of us should have had to endure the final, violent weeks, but, as with every relationship I had ended, I rushed at it in uncontrollable panic.

Then, sitting on the deserted beach and contemplating my future, I thought of Linda. I wanted to speak to her, but she was with her family, and they had no telephone. I needed her, but did I love her? I remembered the doubts I had the night before I married Helen. Was I falling into another trap? Perhaps, but if I was, at least it was one we were both prepared for. Few people, I believed, could know so much about each other, good and bad, who had not examined themselves as closely as we had at Shipley Grange.

I booked into a small hotel, worried that my money was vanishing quickly, and slept until late on Sunday afternoon. I wondered what Helen and the children and Linda and my father were doing. An hour or so later I was on the move again. I knew what I wanted, and I headed north – to the unit. I travelled on hate and hope. Everything in my past – twenty years with my parents and twenty more with Helen – felt wasted; but if the unit had helped me escape from some of that waste, and my marriage in particular, then perhaps it could help me look forward to the future.

Because of a strike by railwaymen, I was late arriving at the unit on Monday morning. Linda rushed to meet me. She had been in a state of panic throughout the weekend. The last thing she had heard was me shouting in Stuart's office, during my meeting with Helen on Friday. Television news had reported that a man had thrown himself into the English Channel from Beachy Head, and she feared that it might be me. She telephoned hospitals, and my father, whom she had never met, and Helen, twice. 'I never thought I'd see you again,' she cried. I thought of soft, rippled sand and lapping waves.

As always throughout those months, too many things were happening too quickly. I needed time to 'get in touch with my feelings'. At the unit I felt protected. I felt that I had embarked on my new journey and the group would help me travel in comfort. Stuart was right. I needed more time there. I needed to escape from the rage which had violently ended my marriage. I needed to decide whether Linda was a clawing trap or a welcoming beacon. I had no home and no wife. The unit and Linda seemed to be my replacements.

And then, the following day, the day before my fortieth birthday, Barbara did at the unit what Cathy was to do a few days later.

Escape

By the last Tuesday in January 1982 Jim, Cathy, Billy, Val and others, had left. The group, the one whose mural I had destroyed months earlier, had disintegrated. Our meeting-room circle was smaller, five chairs almost touching each other; three for the residents, Barbara, Linda and myself; and two for the staff, Stuart and Jo. In her quiet voice Barbara accused Linda and I of having an affair. The walls seemed to collapse, crushing us together in disaster. I thought I heard Stuart ask me, 'Have you had gentle contact?' but immediately realized that he had said 'genital'. Linda and I looked at each other. I answered for both of us. 'Then we'd better close the meeting and all have a chance to think about what to do,' he said. I enjoyed his confusion.

Two weeks previously Stuart had advised me to remain for a further three months. When we reassembled two hours later he asked Linda to agree to end the sexual part of our relationship. She refused. 'Then only one of you can stay,' he said. 'You'll have to decide.' There was no decision to make. We both needed more time to understand ourselves, but we believed that we needed each other more than we needed the group. We told him that we would leave together. He seemed surprised. 'It's not the first time this has happened,' he said, 'but it's never lasted.' He could not hide his anger. Barbara interrupted. 'I'm going too,' she said. 'I can't take any more of this.' Jo looked on impassively, and said nothing.

We tried to be polite to each other. Barbara was crying and I went over to her and tried to apologize, not knowing what I wanted to apologize for. Linda left the room to pack her suitcase. We had discussed our plans during the break between meetings. She decided that she was ready to leave her home as well as the unit, and would go with me to London. We had one immediate practical problem. Money. Annoyed that I had to do it, I asked Stuart to lend me £10 from the cash fund, which he did. I don't think that he expected to see it again.

Barbara left at 5.30. Linda and I followed her ten minutes afterwards. All the residents had left. Behind us, in the large, ugly house, only the staff remained. I felt excited. At last! I had escaped from the chaos at Shipley Grange! I felt an awful sense of responsibility for Linda. I felt elated and terrified. One of my final memories, as we walked arm in arm past the wooden garden gates, was feeling angry that we had had to borrow that £10.

7 Two of me

We are, I know not how, double in ourselves, so that what we believe we disbelieve, and cannot rid ourselves of what we condemn.

Michel Eyquem de Montaigne (1533–92)[1]

'Life begins at forty' had a deeply personal meaning, because the day after Stuart's ultimatum was my fortieth bithday. By then the unit had acquired an anthropomorphous role, as if I had converted the six-month group psychotherapy experience into a new set of parents. I felt that I had been reborn. When, during the days immediately after I left, I sensed that something bad or confusing was happening to me, I could usually relate the circumstances to some event, large or small, which had occurred while I lived with the group. My anxieties and fears remained as disturbing as they had always been, but, feeling better equipped to recognize them, I believed that I was better able to avoid some of the conflicts which previously I had not understood, affecting both my own behaviour and my relationships with other people. 'Mummy says I mustn't take sweets from strangers' was altered to 'Shipley Grange says I don't trust people'. This lack of trust seemed to be a critical starting point in my new life, because I believed that if I could use what I had learned about myself, by examining how I felt from day to day, then I would stop feeling so distrustful of my own actions. In particular, I wanted to accept that life was not a series of distinctly black or white experiences, but a varied mixture of feelings and reactions which were ordinary, everyday experiences. Instead of classifying each confrontation as specifically bad or good, I expected that I would be able to shrug my emotional shoulders philosophically — 'that's the way it is, don't fight it.' I felt that I had what I had not had before — ground rules for living with myself and other people.

But the rules, though sometimes useful, often proved of little value because many of my feelings were too raw and overwhelming for me to think clearly. I still had to face the most difficult conflict of all — the two *mes* perpetually fighting with each other. One *me* — the one who worked hard to remember what I had learned from my new parents — found life easier and refreshing. Gone were the confusions of the past, and some of the fears of the future. The other *me* — the one who still lived in the past, refusing to understand anything about a rebirth — floundered regularly, as it always had. When I realized that I could not stop battling with myself I understood that my months at Shipley Grange had not ended my journey into self-understanding — at best, I was merely going in the right direction. I thought of myself as reborn because I wanted to believe that I was capable of changing.

Because I felt so much more able to understand who I was, I needed to test myself with other people, particularly those who had, and still did, disturb me. ('Mummy and Daddy say that I must understand my expectations.') I wanted members of my family, and the few friends with whom I was in contact, to accept that I had experienced a momentous adventure. Before I could feel relaxed with any of them I needed to explain what had happened at the unit. Most of them were interested, fascinated even, and very quick to agree that, yes, I had been a difficult person to accept in the past, and that, yes, they could see how much calmer and happier I seemed. But I quickly became aware of an unexpected problem. The knowledge which I had gained about myself extended to other people. Facets of their personalities which I had not previously thought about or understood now appeared clearly and unavoidably. I didn't just want them to understand what I had learned about myself: I wanted them to understand how they, with their own particular self-misconceptions, had contributed to problems which had arisen between us. I felt like an evangelist, thumping out a new message – 'Come to me, step up and see the light.'

Family and friends, willing to agree with my self-confessions about my past confusions, rapidly retreated when I extended my opinions to themselves. I had to accept that, however much more I understood them, huge gaps – which I now called conflicts – remained between us. One or two admitted, as Helen had, that they were frightened to examine themselves too closely. Several simply changed whatever subject we were talking about to something safer. Whatever they did, I felt cheated, as if I was being ignored. I thought about this carefully. If I could not control my family or friends, as I had unknowingly expected to in the past, could I, now that I understood my behaviour, accept them?

The most important past relationships I wanted to understand were with my children, Ben, fifteen when I left Shipley Grange, and Vanessa, three years younger. They were in the middle, not only of my needs and theirs, but also of a family disintegration which involved them with divorce. At first, when I separated from Helen, I worried that I would lose them. Perhaps they would reject me because I had rejected them, by vanishing from home on several occasions, and then to the unit for six months. Then I needed to work through my feelings towards my father and sister. Would it be possible to share part of my life with them, or were old feelings too bitter and tainted to change?

And what about Helen? Within a week or two of leaving the unit we were sharing a new experience – divorce proceedings. How could I cope with that? It was too early to understand the similarity between divorce and death. Just as I had expected, when my mother died, to feel relieved of a heavy burden, but had not, so divorce provided no escape from years of mixed feelings.

As well as having to relate these relationships, and a few less important ones, to my new expectations, I had to deal with new people and new groups. One of the most worrying was the small office group I joined when I accepted a job, a month or so after I left the unit. ('Mummy and Daddy say I use hard work to escape from my feelings, that I'm excessively ambitious and over-competitive.') How could I, after a working life-time of craving success and status, learn how to work comfortably in a less demanding career; one in which, for the first time since I had been an articled clerk, I was an employee and not my own 'boss'?

And possessions – what about possessions? I had no home, no car, only the few personal items which I had collected at Shipley Grange, and practically no money. But, happily, I had no debts or unwanted financial commitments.

I knew that my rebirth – whether it would be a grotesque deformity or a welcome chance to live comfortably with myself – depended upon how I would reconcile the *me* who had been unable to live with people and who had been desperate to create emotional escapes, with the *me* whose recent memories included 'get in touch with your feelings', 'don't be too hard on yourself', 'express your needs' and 'you don't trust yourself'. I understood that to reconcile the past with the present I had to remember another lesson which had emerged at Shipley Grange: that it was not the big, obvious confrontations which created my greatest difficulties, but the seemingly minor conflicts which I either ignored or did not recognize.

Whenever I felt that I was losing control of myself – if I could recognize that that was what was happening – I read extracts from my Shipley diary. Often, I updated it with recent experiences, describing how I had gone awry, or, occasionally, how I had foreseen a conflict, and dealt with it in such a way as to avoid unnecessary problems.

Three years flashed by.

Depression as I had once known it – periods of frightening fogginess which had ended with my nervous breakdown eighteen years earlier – never returned. Triggers – when I felt a sudden SNAP – never returned either. I made no silent pleas to be dead, and did not fantasize about suicide. I believed that psychotherapy had enabled me to take evasive action, to avoid the uncontrollable panics which had led to so many disasters.

My divorce had been finalized. I saw my children regularly, and my father and sister, with all of whom, in different ways, I could communicate more easily. I had a 'nine-to-five' job, which involved less responsibility than any work I had done previously. My old need for possessions seemed laughable and ridiculous. But, towering above all these changes for the better, I had one asset without which I knew my life would have been unbearable – my second wife, Linda.

No other person had ever known so much about me. With her, I felt that I had nothing to hide. She had seen me, and heard me, at Shipley Grange. As far as I knew who I was, so did she. For the first time in my life, when I wanted to, I could share myself with someone without a furious *alter ego* shrieking emotional obscenities inside me. Often, I struggled and fought with myself for hours, or days, before I managed to express verbally some deep hurt or anxiety, but when eventually I succeeded in admitting how disturbed I felt, and we talked about it, I felt refreshed and more secure in our relationship, and with myself.

But despite having found one great need in my life – someone I could trust – hardly a day passed during those three years when I did not feel overtaken by old, bad feelings which continued to disturb my attempts to live with myself. I frequently felt crushed by the effort of accepting how miserable I felt, and tempering that with the joy of sharing my days with a woman I needed. I felt frightened, too. If I felt so bad, and – trusting Linda – I admitted it, would I disturb her so much that one day she would leave me, having had enough of my anxieties? We discussed that, too, and, although I wanted to believe her when she assured me that I was not as impossible to live with as I thought, I found it hard to trust what she said.

Trust, both in myself and her, advanced and retreated in slow, rolling waves of talking. Talking, more than any other change in my behaviour, was what I had learned from psychotherapy. If you feel it, talk about it, I told myself. Talk. Don't keep quiet. Remember the art therapy painting *silence*, and how it showed that if I stay silent I stay furious. Remember *secrets*, with its padlock, chains and ugly, black cage. Remember that if I keep quiet I am withholding secrets. Remember *time bomb*, remember that inside me, if I stay silent and secretive, a great explosion will one day erupt. So I – we – talked, more than I had ever talked before.

But I still felt bad, most of the time. Headaches and insomnia disrupted several days each week. Suddenly, for no apparent reason, my mood would swing wildly from enthusiasm and hopeful expectation about the future, to hateful fears inherited from the past. Why couldn't I come to terms with the past? Why, when I felt miserable, did I retreat into my teens and early childhood? Talk about how you're feeling, I kept repeating to myself. I did, and felt better, for a short period.

The most difficult feeling was my fear of loss. As my career became more secure; and we bought our home, and my need – I still found it difficult to define love – for Linda grew, I had an awful dread that I would lose her, and my new security, as I had lost so much in the past. I could not believe that when I had what I wanted I could keep it. I felt that there remained a part of me which would always destroy what I most wanted. My rebirth, which had felt so glorious, began to feel like one more fraudulent attempt to pretend that I could cope with my life. I comforted myself with the knowledge that, however bad I felt, it was less bad than it had once been. It was the closest I could come to balancing my fear of loss with a 'gain'.

For three years I fought to accept the new life which I thought I had discovered at Shipley Grange. But most of the time I distrusted what I was doing. Every day I did, thought or said things which contradicted how I was feeling. I acted as if old relationships had improved, when I knew that the improvements, if any, were merely superficial. I worked energetically in my new job, at the same time despising much of what I did. For a year or so I overcame this particular problem by escaping into career challenges created by my involvement with computers, and that enabled me to hope that my career was not as 'lost' as I dreaded. Socially, I withdrew into a tight circle of limited friendships, unable to arouse any interest in mixing with new groups. Social groups had been lost in the past; if I minimized my involvement with people, I had less to lose in the future.

Gradually, during a period of about three months, I became aware of destructive, uncontrollable feelings re-emerging from my past. The first signs that something particularly bad was happening were furious feelings of *not having enough*; of not having a new car, or a larger home, or more money. I could not understand it. Why, after three years of being satisfied, did I feel so angrily dissatisfied? Then I began to feel abused. People were taking advantage of me, I thought. They expected me to cope with their problems, without being interested in mine; or, as far as my employers were concerned, they expected me to work unreasonable hours. I could feel myself withdrawing from everybody, and tried to remind myself that this was dangerous, but it did not work; of the two *mes* fighting each other, the old, familiar one whom I had lived with since a child easily outman-oeuvred the more recent, hopeful one. Fantasies about death and suicide returned. Talk. Talk! I said to myself. But I could not.

In the early hours of a Friday morning, after a period of hectic daytime work and several sleepless nights, it happened again, SNAP. CLICK. I had to die. A week or two later I left a brief note for Linda, and drove away towards Wales, dreaming of high mountains and precipitous, deathly drops into suicidal finality.

But unlike my previous vanishing acts, that one lasted only a few hours. I wanted to survive, somehow: uppermost in my thoughts and feelings was the need to be with Linda. By midnight I had returned home.

The following day I visited my GP, telling him that I felt depressed, but unable to explain the intensity of my feelings. While talking to him I could not breathe easily, and was embarrassed that I felt tearful. How can he, how can anyone, understand the chaos raging inside me, I thought bitterly. 'Take a holiday and three of these each day,' he said, and I cursed him for not realizing that I had been unable to admit my wretchedness.

I could not work, nor think clearly, nor understand why all my hopes had disappeared. I knew only one thing — I had to talk, not in a haphazard, uncertain way, but in a professional environment, where my worst fears could be admitted and examined. Linda agreed. We both understood that however much we wanted to, we were unable to resolve the confusions which felt so destructive. I wanted more psychotherapy treatment, to return, as it were, to my parents.

It wasn't easy. My GP sounded unenthusiastic. 'Change your job. Stop worrying so much. Psychotherapy won't solve your problems,' he said. When I eventually managed to describe my tumultuous emotions and suicidal thoughts he arranged an appointment at St Mary's hospital. (Perhaps I've always been unfair to general practitioners, expecting from them the one thing they cannot provide — time, as much time as I wanted to discuss how I felt.) The frustration of having to wait four weeks for an appointment to see a psychiatrist made me consider other means of survival. I contacted MIND and discovered a helpful, understanding organization which, through weekly counselling meetings, confirmed what I knew, that I had to talk. With their assistance I was introduced to a psychotherapy unit.

I assumed that I would once again join a group. The counsellor who interviewed me, and to whom I willingly recounted all my recognizable feelings, said: 'I don't think joining a group will help you. You need something more personal. Can you come along twice a week and see me?'

I'm still going, many months later.

It takes time to understand what happens when my feelings erupt and my behaviour becomes uncontrollable. Individual therapy — one-to-one — is very different to group therapy. In the unit at Shipley Grange, as with my childhood family group, my adolescent social groups and all my career groups,

I was always aware of fighting many people at once, desperate to defend myself, becoming more disheartened each time I felt betrayed, neglected, thwarted or 'beaten'. Control and dominance seemed the only forces which could protect me from others, and I exerted what I thought was power to attain these dubious achievements – the group mural symbolized the futility of that type of behaviour. Individual therapy introduces the same forces (I often stumble into attempts to control my counsellor), but it provides something which no larger group can – enough time to examine my most minute acts, and the feelings which precipitated them. Recently, I said to the man I now visit regularly: 'If I had a diary for the rest of my life, I'd arrange to come and see you every week.' My old, childhood voice is still crying out 'Help me!'

As I wrote at the beginning of this book, this is a personal history. 'Personal' is a huge word. It includes every person who has been part of my life, those who have left indelible marks of misery and those who have brought happiness and hope. At times I have wished that most of them had never appeared, but I am not one of those people who can say, 'I prefer being on my own.' Quite the reverse, I hate being alone. I need people, not many, perhaps only one, with whom to share my feelings and aspirations. Depression, or whatever else it may be called – emotional disturbance, personality problems, or any other label – is a lonely business. But occasionally, because of the isolation, I enjoy a wondrous experience – a day when after a good night's sleep I wake up refreshed, my head clear of worrying thoughts, my body supple and relaxed. There are not many of them – perhaps one in two months – but when they arrive, unexpectedly, I want to shout out with joy that there aren't two of me at all, just one person who sometimes believes that he can come to terms with himself.

And then I begin worrying – it can't last, something's going to go wrong.

Notes

1 'Are you angry?'

1 The San Francisco General hospital is a large, multi-storey building
located close to the city centre. I was in a mixed closed ward, on the
fifteenth floor, secured by locked doors, through which could be seen
the entrance to the high-security area set aside for prisoners. Attempted
suicide patients were initially kept under close supervision, on beds in
the communal area, immediately next to the staff desk. Once
'unstrapped', private rooms were available, or larger ones, if a patient
preferred not to be alone at night. During the day, time could be spent
in the large communal area, which contained a television and library,
and which also served as the visiting centre; or in a recreation room,
equipped with games and a piano. Meals, which were excellent, and
attractively presented, were eaten in a canteen.
   Each morning, at 9.30, a meeting was held at which all ward patients
and staff had an opportunity to discuss their problems or plans for the
day.
   I presented an administrative problem. I had no money, no medical
insurance and was an alien. Throughout my two-week stay I was
regularly approached by a gentleman who became increasingly anxious
as to how he could account for the cost of my hospitalization, and, in
particular, the surgical operations required. A few minutes before the
operations he told me that he had no authority to permit them to take
place and only after a heated argument between himself and the ward
staff was I wheeled into the theatre.

2 Part IV (sections 25 to 32) of the Mental Health Act, 1959, provides for
compulsory admission to hospital. Applications may be made by
relatives, medical practitioners or a mental welfare officer, and the
purpose of the application may be for observation or treatment, or
both. Grounds for an application include mental disorders, the health
and safety of the patient, or to protect other persons. Various time

269

limits for detention are imposed (e.g. 72 hours, subject to rights of extension, for emergency observation, section 29; and 28 days for applications for observation supported by two medical practitioners, section 25).

3 The National Association for Mental Health − MIND − has its headquarters at 22 Harley Street, London, W1N 2ED. Information and general assistance is available, but if specific help is required they direct you to one of their affiliated associations − autonomous organizations which provide counselling services, day centres and a wide variety of supportive facilities for the recovering mentally ill.

   Factsheet 4, Manic Depression is published by MIND Publications.

4 Because this 'history' is not necessarily related in chronological sequence, a summary of main events is given below:

Event	Year(s)	Author's age
First period of diagnosed depression	1955	13
Left school	1958	16
Marriage and professional qualification	1964	22
Partner in accountancy practice	1965/74	23/32
Son's birth	1967	25
Nervous breakdown	1968/9	26/27
Daughter's birth	1970	28
First suicide attempt	1974	32
Prison sentence, bankruptcy and loss of professional qualification	1975/6	33/34
Financial consultancy practice	1976/80	34/38
Mother's suicide (15 March)	1977	35
Aunt's death (15 March)	1980	38
Second suicide attempt	1981	39
Group psychotherapy at Shipley Grange	1981/2	39
Grandfather's death; divorce and second marriage	1982	40
One-to-one psychotherapy	1985/	43/

5 Among the books which I have read − and mostly forgotten − the following contained informative, interesting and, occasionally, helpful, words:

Berne, E., *Games People Play*, London, Penguin Books, 1967.

Harris, A.T., *I'm OK − You're OK*, London, Pan Books, 1973.

Lambley, P., *Insomnia and Other Sleeping Problems*, London, Sphere Books, 1982.

Rowe, D., *Depression, the Way out of Your Prison*, London, Routledge & Kegan Paul, 1983.

Wood, C., *Living in Overdrive*, London, Fontana Paperbacks, 1984.

2 *Neurotics at war*

1 'Resident' is not my euphemism: it was the unit's word. There seems to be a tendency among psychotherapists, unlike psychiatrists or GPs, to avoid the word 'patient'. When I have not been a 'resident' I have been a 'client'.

2 All my therapy has been provided through the National Health Service, for which I have been grateful, because, on each occasion that I have received help, I have been very short of money. However, one unit to which I was recently referred advised me that there was no point in their seeing me, due to a waiting list of up to a year. I obtained a directory of private psychotherapy units — from MIND — and was surprised at how many of them there were in London. Fees for individual therapy varied from £8 to £25 for a one-hour session (1986 rates).

3 The closed wards at the hospital were depressing places, which I only entered once, on an errand. Unlike the one in San Francisco, the wards I saw in England were crowded and lacked recreational facilities. There were different categories of closed wards, depending upon the nature of patients' illnesses. Some of them were only 'closed' (i.e. locked) at night. Patients in those wards were free to roam around the hospital grounds during the day, which I found a frightening experience. They were harmless, we the 'residents' were told, but many of them appeared to be permanently disorientated, and if one of them approached me, usually with a friendly smile, I hurriedly walked away. Occasionally, a patient innocently wandered into 'our' territory, and I was interested to see that the staff seemed as anxious as the rest of us to tell them to go away. Open wards, also locked at night, accommodated patients who were often 'regulars', driven, or forced there, by acute periods of stress. They lived in a ward which, while depressing, mainly due to the old-fashioned buildings, was similar to the one I was in in San Francisco. The closest building, geographically and administratively, to Shipley Grange was the nearby alcoholic unit.

4 We had several unit catch phrases (e.g. 'get in touch with your feelings'). One, usually shovelled into an angry confrontation, stoked many unexpected fires. 'Who does he (she) remind you of?' often made us aware of the extent to which we used each other as outlets for our feelings towards parents, children, brothers and sisters. At different times I was someone's father, mother, brother and sister. Anything could spark off this transfer of roles: a voice tone, how we sat, words we used, etc. Frequently, weeks of antagonism between residents would pass before the first recognition of a role was understood. Jealousy and anxieties about authority were two of the most common reasons expressed for this important part of the unit's function. (Julie, very large and ungainly, obviously detested the smallest woman in the group. When they were in the middle of a furious confrontation someone

asked Julie, 'Who does she remind you of?' Julie became silent, but quickly admitted that she was shouting at her mother. It had not occurred to any of us that such a big woman might have a diminutive mother.)

4 *Sinking not soaring*

1 Bach, R., *Jonathan Livingston Seagull*, London, Pan Books, 1973.
2 I have restricted my description of psychodrama games to those I remember well and which left the strongest impressions. There were two other types of games which I have not illustrated: trust games, when we took responsibility for another member, or they did for us (for example, by standing behind them as they fell backwards, to see how far each of us could trust the other to protect them); and word games (for example, one of us would leave the room while the others wrote down the first three words spoken by them to describe the absent member.)

7 *Two of me*

1 I first felt an empathy with Montaigne when I discovered that he gave up one way of life for another when he was almost forty years old. Then, when I read a selection of his *Essays*, I felt admiration and envy for a man who had so many wise things to say about his sixteenth-century world, many of which could have been written today. My (abbreviated) copy of his autobiographical work is the Penguin Classics edition translated by J.M. Cohen, first published in 1958.